MAGIC,

MYSTICISM,

AND THE

MOLECULE

MAGIC,

MYSTICISM,

AND THE

MOLECULE

ALTERED STATES AND THE SEARCH FOR SENTIENT INTELLIGENCE FROM OTHER WORLDS

MICAH HANKS

ROCKETEER PRESS • ASHEVILLE, NORTH CAROLINA

MAGIC, MYSTICISM AND THE MOLECULE, 2nd EDITION

Edited by Vance Pollock

Cover photo by Juskteez Vu on Unsplash

Layout and Design by Micah Hanks

Rocketeer Press, Asheville, North Carolina. Published by the author. Printed in the United States of America.

For more information about this title, you may visit the author's website at www.micahhanks.com, or by emailing the Publisher at info@micahhanks.com.

DEDICATION

For my parents, who continue to encourage me to keep a
sense of wonder for the small things in our universe.

ACKNOWLEDGEMENTS

So many individuals were instrumental in helping bring this book together that naming them all might produce a short book-length manuscript itself. Thus, to name a few, I wish to thank Vance Pollock for his patience with the editing process, and Christopher McCollum for helping with interviews and research; also Caleb Hanks for the surreal imagery that helped inspire the works herein; to my friend Mobius for always fueling interesting discussions and providing new resources; to Brad Steiger for the inspiration; Tim Beckley for the knowledge (and the occasional humor), and to Joshua P. Warren for the timeless adventures we have shared over the years. Also, my thanks to Patrick Huyghe for lending advice and experience, and Greg Bishop for being a "space brother," as well as lending his knowledge on the subjects of DMT and the eerie "fractal-mantis" of the DMT experience; to Rick Strassman, M.D. for his insight and advice, as well as the wise and engaging Slawek Wojtowicz, M.D. for his enlightening knowledge on mysticism and entheogens. Special thanks goes to Nick Redfern for writing the foreword, and his encouragement. And finally, my sincere thanks goes to Tiffany Mac, for all the deep conversations, the unparalleled friendship, and for sharing my passion for the mystique of starry nights. For all here mentioned, I am so very thankful; may fortune shine its light on each of you, as it so graciously has done for me.

CONTENTS

FOREWORD

If the late, lamented and sorely-missed Jim Morrison—singer with the legendary band, *The Doors*—had not been cruelly taken by that most grimmest of all reapers back in 1971; but, instead, decided to give his firm endorsement to a book on the strange and twilight world of Forteana, that book would surely be Micah Hanks' *Magic, Mysticism and the Molecule*.

Let me explain.

When, as a young child, I first became interested in all things of a ufological, cryptozoological and paranormal nature, everything was pretty much black-and-white to me: Bigfoot was a giant ape of a type that science had yet to classify; UFOs were piloted by little black-eyed men (or possibly by long-haired men and blisteringly-hot, curvy space-babes) from far-off worlds; and the creatures of Loch Ness represented a still-surviving, and thriving, colony of plesiosaurs.

But, as time progressed, and my early-teens became my twenties, I began to realize that the many and various entities of unknown origin that were said to inhabit our world were not just strange: they were actually *too* strange.

They didn't act in a fashion that we might expect of them. Rather than operating like flesh-and-blood life-forms, they were more akin to being phantasms of the night: appearing and vanishing at will; manifesting in locations that they had no business intruding upon; stalling car-engines; destroying camera-film; putting on what were obviously stage-managed appearances; and generally wreaking havoc, mayhem and high-strangeness whenever and wherever they pleased.

Clearly, the conventional "Bigfoot is an ape;" and "UFOs are piloted by aliens" scenarios were—and still are—in drastic need of a very big overhaul.

Enter Micah Hanks.

As I have noted myself in countless blog-posts, the conventional image that many of the veteran (i.e. the bloody old and the wrinkled) players within Forteana precariously hang-on to, is that the beasts, the entities and the aliens they seek are really not that different to us: yes, they may lurk in darkened woods, or on far-off worlds, but there's nothing too radical about them.

Right? No: wrong, actually. Very wrong.

The dinosaurs of Ufology, Cryptozoology and Forteana will one day all be gone, and in their place will be the likes of Micah Hanks and others who astutely realize that collecting and collating (*ad infinitum*) reports of lights in the sky, or making casts of alleged Bigfoot prints will never, ever solve the riddles at issue.

We need to—both metaphorically and literally—open the doors (yes, I *do* mean those doors of perception) that will finally allow us access to the answers that we seek, and to the entities we seek, too.

Many of those aforementioned wrinkly-veterans who have studied the world of the unknown for decades have been very careful to steer clear of the undeniable links that exist between (A) the manifestation of Fortean phenomena and (B) the ingestion of certain mind-altering substances that may provoke radically-transformed states of mind, and/or open doorways to those shadowy regions in which the entities that we strive to find really inhabit.

Those same veterans don't want to be associated with psychedelics, with shaken-up states of perception, or with scenarios that they perceive as being politically, or more likely morally, incorrect.

Too bad: let the old men and their worn-out morals go back to their bulging filing cabinets filled with countless reports carefully prepared over countless years, yet that have provided absolutely no answers whatsoever—at all.

Clearly, something is going on that cannot be reconciled in down-to-earth fashion. And, thankfully, Micah Hanks realizes this; even if many of those who came before him stubbornly fail to do so.

Within the pages of Micah's book, you will learn much about visionaries like Terence McKenna; of the pioneering research of Dr. Rick Strassman; and of the way in which such historical characters as John Dee, Aleister Crowley, and Jack Parsons played key and integral roles in the search for the truth that Micah Hanks has uncovered.

DMT; Ayahuasca; Tulpa-style thought-forms; and minds that are open to being reorganized, elevated, transformed, and illuminated, are the absolute keys to the puzzle. In the pages of his book, Micah Hanks travels a long-and-winding road that covers territory that some will see as fascinating, others might view as disturbing, and a few might even interpret as downright terrifying.

At the end of the day Hanks is, in my view, firmly on the right track. A new, fresh approach to the world of Forteana is sorely needed if we are to actually get some answers, instead of merely collecting more and more reports. Micah Hanks is one of those individuals at the absolute forefront of skillfully negotiating the dark waters that will ultimately provide us with the answers that we seek.

Enjoy his book, digest its contents carefully, and above all else: learn. And before I forget: throw out your bulging, aged and yellowing files and reports. They are now as extinct and redundant as a T-Rex.

-NICK REDFERN

Nick Redfern is the author of more than a dozen books on the unexplained, including *Contactees*, *There's Something in the Woods*, and *Secret History: Conspiracies from Ancient Aliens to the New World Order*.

INTRODUCTION

Were early humans visited by intelligent beings from other worlds? This question has been proposed many times throughout history, typically under the pretence that alien visitors with advanced spacecraft might have travelled to Earth at some point, to commune with our ancient ancestors. Many in the modern era maintain this idea, and advocate belief in an ongoing interaction with alien beings from other worlds that continues to this day.

Seldom is equal credence given to the idea that humans in ancient times may have sought wisdom from other worlds—or if not other worlds, at least *altered states*—by traveling to these places themselves. Without aeronautical knowledge, physical travel through space would have been impossible for our early ancestors; and despite the advances we can expect in the coming decades, distant space travel will likely still remain impossible for some time. If only there were other ways to contact intelligent life "out there," we might gain detailed knowledge about space travel from them. Or, we might learn that other methods of relocation exist, and that the concept of physically piloting aircraft to a distant star system is as outmoded as lifting the melted, feathery wings of Icarus to glide away toward the heavens.

What if exotic methods of engaging other parts of the universe, as alluded to here, not only existed, but also had been used for thousands of years? Since ancient times, humans have claimed to harness abilities that allowed the passage beyond time and space, enabling travel toward galactic boundaries within realms belonging to what mystics throughout history have called sentient "others." To better understand how this could be possible, this book presents an examination of various processes used to evoke *altered states of consciousness*, which, defined roughly, refers to any condition that differs significantly from our normal state of mind while awake and aware. Here, we will divulge how shamans, practitioners of arcane magic, and mystics over the ages have managed to achieve such variant states of mind; but in order to truly understand the mysteries of the cosmos as they have, we must examine what brought us here, together, at this very moment in time, where you are reading this book with intent of gaining such knowledge for yourself.

There are many aspects of the human experience that remain strange to us; these include sleep paralysis, premonitions, astral projection, and out-of-body experiences, to name a few. Such anomalies persist among a diverse range of cultures, enough so that their presence can hardly be ignored. And yet, to be ignored might do them more justice than the prejudices they receive instead; those claiming to wake from a vivid dream, only to find themselves paralyzed, were once told they had likely suffered a variety of psychotic episode. Some were even prescribed medications after having experiences that seemed far too strange to be natural. Similar to sleep paralysis are episodes referred to as "out-of-body experiences"; these may occasionally involve descriptions of buzzing and other loud noises, sensing "presences" nearby, and again, physical paralysis. Experts in sleep disorders suggest things like inner-ear issues, sensory deprivation, or even the body's tendency to instigate sleep through "blacking out" in reaction to extreme stress or hyper-arousal, may be at the root of these phenomena. But do such explanations rule out the possibility that the mind is able to operate in unusual ways under special circumstances, which may even result in separation between consciousness and the physical body?

Among the more bizarre elements of our culture are the stories recounted by alleged UFO abductees. Many claim to have been taken from their homes at night, and subjected to frightening experiences that involve such things as medical experimentation (often predominantly sexual in nature), among other things. Interestingly, parallels seem to exist between stories related by abductees, and psychedelic visions recounted during experiments with drugs the likes of dimethyltryptamine (DMT). In each scenario, people have described awakening to medical environments, where they are surrounded by anthropomorphic "aliens" that resemble a variety of archetypal figures, ranging from angels, to mantises and spindly insects. Colored lights, strange sexual sensations, psychic phenomena, unusual coincidences, and a number of other similarities have reported in relation to each of these experiences.

This need not be taken as an implication that *all* experiences that appear to be otherworldly in nature are mere hallucinations. It is, however, fair to consider whether having a better knowledge of hallucinatory experiences, and what conditions may allow them to occur, could help us understand the true mechanics behind a number of encounters with seemingly "alien" environments and intelligences.

Or, there could be a stranger possibility: what if there are processes that actually *do* allow the human mind to interact with other states, and perhaps even the intelligences that inhabit them?

At some point in the lineage of all things capable of being observed, those experiences once labeled "strange" existed among the ranks of what we call the supernatural. On the other end of the spectrum, the word *science* conjures images of scholarly-looking fellows wearing lab coats, carrying beakers and vials around machines that perform any number of imaginable functions; all hopefully capable of providing one thing: *answers*. But in reality, "science" simply refers to the method or system we use to acquire knowledge. Even more simply, the Merriam-

Webster dictionary defines science as *knowledge distinguished from ignorance or misunderstanding.*

Long ago, humans wondered how birds were able to fly. No doubt, there have been cultures over the centuries that assigned mystical reasons to why our feathered kindred seemed to defy gravity. Today, the knowledge we have gained about flight over time—and through observation—allows us to harness mechanical wings of our own, granting humans similar abilities. Though we now understand the mechanics of flight much better, at one time this method of travel must have seemed more like strange magic, rather than something explainable through the forces of nature alone.

This may also be the case with a number of the unexplained things that riddle our existence today; they appear so far-removed from our ability to observe and understand them objectively, that they may seem to exist outside of what we deem normal. Hence, they become "paranormal." This taken into consideration, perhaps one of the biggest problems the scientific community faces today deals with how, at some point along the road to discovery, attempts at rational observation of those things deemed "unexplained" seems to have become almost taboo. Rather than to try and use science to explain what we don't understand, today the strangest aspects of our existence—things not unlike flight, or other mysteries that captivated us long ago—are labeled "pseudoscience" and tossed aside, with hopes they will just be forgotten.

This is not always an unfair assessment. Plenty of genuine pseudoscience does exist, whether it involves the illogical reshaping of our past, in order to account for mysterious ancient things by inclusion of "alien" intervention, to the absurd beliefs and practices of modern cults and their leaders (one, at least, has even proven remarkably successful at gaining traction among the rich and famous). We would all do well to pay attention to the things we believe, and ask whether we believe them based on good evidence, or simply for belief's sake alone.

With the application of true science, a researcher develops a theory for how a specific portion of the observable world works. This theory is tested by performing an experiment, the results of which can then be used to determine whether the theory fits the given "setting", as defined by the accumulation of other phenomena observed and catalogued through science. If the experiment is successful, it can result in the creation of a scientific rule.

However, this set of circumstances doesn't always have to occur in this same order. In the realm of speculative physics, for instance, just because a rule fails testing does not make it invalid. What if we could guess that speculative rules do fit *some* setting, even if it is one that hasn't been conceived of yet? What this discussion outlines for us is the difference between *natural* and *speculative* physics; in the universe viewed through the eyes of a speculative physicist, rules can still be useful, even when they don't appear to fit the setting accurately.

The same logic might be applied to certain taboo subjects we call "paranormal" as well. With this book, I have taken three staples of early cultures from around the world—magical rituals, mystical practices, and the use of entheogenic substances to induce psychedelic hallucinations—and considered their possible function as "tools." These tools, therefore, would be of further use in the study of hypothetical interactions that occur during altered states, which may represent certain things existent beyond the five senses, or even beyond the stretches of space and time as we know it.

Astronomers tell us it is virtually impossible to use our present understanding of space travel to get to distant galaxies. Still, many of them also agree that such places, if only they could be reached, may be home to life like ours. Even if conventional science won't allow us to access such places, perhaps there are what could be likened to "spiritual sciences" that have existed much longer, which might be capable of getting us there. If they exist, they would have such profound implications on our understanding of the universe—and ourselves—that they might render aircraft and rockets to being mere playthings, no more capable of serious exploration of the cosmos than a child's bicycle or wagon.

Prior to writing this book, I'd never had any interest in things like magic or rituals, let alone the scientific study of psychedelic drugs. Mysticism, particularly in relation to things like yoga and eastern meditation, is perhaps one of the most recognized and widely practiced of the three elements that became the focus of this book; it is something that has always fascinated me, but it had nonetheless alluded me in actual practice and application.

Many of us probably feel this way. Addiction to our jobs, and the general speed of living has grown into a nasty habit for many of us here in the West. Thus, we must consider that maybe this sense of separation from the mystical has something to do with the frenzied preoccupation most of us have with simply making ends meet. On the other hand, it could be just the opposite; instead of a dire yearning for materialism as a result of necessity, maybe the gross availability of modern convenience that the technological age has provided has caused us to distance ourselves from the unseen wonders of this world; or for that matter, other worlds of which we remain unaware.

True, we exist in an age of convenience, where our "rituals" deal in the sacred art of *escapism*. They take place on a nightly basis, helped by things like the excessive consumption of alcohol; a social lubricant without which most people would flounder should they be faced with the monumental task of conversing with a friendly stranger of the opposite sex. Prescription drugs are ingested to aid simple processes like focus and attention, or more often, simply to get us to sleep at night. Thus, looking back at the masterful prose of Wolfe, Wilde, Shelley, Hemingway, Austen, or countless others, to expect that most people today would absorb the intricacies of their writing would be like expecting a house cat to relish a weekend spent deciphering Latin. Indeed, as humankind progresses, we seem to lose more and more of ourselves, and the things we once cherished, to the convenience handed to us by the modern age.

Nonetheless, I've always felt the underlying sense of "something more" that so many have described throughout the ages must be more than mere wishful thinking, or some deeply-rooted survival instinct that manifests in a desire for companionship. On a fundamental level, it's as though we already know this proverbial "something more" *does* exist, but only in places we can't seem to access directly.

The implications of studying parallel worlds and "alien" intelligences in this manner—that is, from a mystical perspective—might seem fruitless, if not absurd to some. Until fairly recently, it seems to have been difficult for most to imagine contact with alien life occurring without advanced technologies, capable of propelling intelligent beings—or messages from them—across the expanses of our universe. However, unlike our classic depictions of this sort of contact—Arthur C. Clark's monoliths bestowed upon ancient humans, or even Buck Rogers' travel to distant star systems to find "space brothers" and other sci-fi weirdness—it seems that the true keys to discovering whether we are alone in the universe might be far simpler.

Some time ago, I began to wonder if we, as humans, aren't merely receptacles to constant streams of information, and perhaps our strangely sublime little magical tools, meditative practices, and sacred mushrooms are merely instruments that allow us to tune our minds to the wider spectrum of cosmic stimuli. While Western scientists are essentially just beginning to branch out and explore these poss- ibilities, cultures elsewhere in the world claim to have known these things all along, having accepted them long ago as universal truths to their way of existence.

I am fascinated with the idea of discovering more about why we have this deeply rooted perception of distant, spiritual, or even *alien* places, having been passed along by cultures worldwide for ages. If such "places" are accessible to humans, also of great importance is how to locate them, and how to understand the nature of any consciousness that may inhabit these strange realms of the altered state. Cultures since time immemorial have described entities they called angels, demons, gods, faeries, aliens, inter-dimensional entities, hallucinations, archetypes, and Transcendent Others in mystical practices and studies of the mind spanning the ages. Indeed, if there are worlds parallel to our own, it seems we've known about them for a long time, to the extent that some of us find brushing elbows with their inhabitants to be commonplace.

What truly does lie beyond Huxley's "doors of perception"? What inner realities might linger all around us, cut off at times by a nearly *suffocating* requirement for objective proof of their existence? Whatever the circumstances, these mysteries have existed longer than our known history, and perhaps even helped instigate our earliest inner reflections, which led to the awakening of consciousness itself. Hidden alongside us for far too long already, they can no longer be ignored. What follows is my own pursuit of the mysteries of consciousness, and whether it can exist or travel beyond the physical realm of our daily lives. Together, we will seek to understand if a deeper knowledge of ourselves can be learned through the altered states afforded us by magic, mysticism, and the molecule.

PART ONE

MAGIC

CHAPTER ONE

A History of Magical Contact with Other Realms

There exists an as yet unidentified form of energy that is the source of all so-called magical or supernatural powers, and I believe that the human psyche serves as a conduit for this force. Throughout history, certain gifted shamans, seers, and prophets have channeled this energy, this 'supernatural force', to create apparent miracles of healing, levitation, mind-over-matter, prophecy, and communication with spiritual intelligences on other levels of being.

—Brad Steiger, *Beyond Shadow World*

Cultural traditions the world over have long shared tales of their interaction with nonhuman, supernatural beings. "Contact" of this sort may date back to the earliest remembrances of our prehistoric ancestors, remembered today only in such forms as ancient cave art and petroglyphs, depicting strange humanoid "gods" and other entities with magical powers. Whether they were merely depictions of dreams or nightmares, or were in fact representations of things once seen by the ancients, these entities appeared to possess abilities that surpassed the imagination, and their apparent presence among humans in ancient times suggests what may have been man's earliest attempts at contacting sentient intelligences from other worlds.

These beings our ancestors first came to know would eventually take their places as gods, angels and demons, revered and feared alike throughout the ages among the world religions. Arguably, the principles upon which most religions are traditionally built have involved encounters between founders of the religion and some clandestine source of ultimate wisdom. Regardless of the nature of the contact, whether it occurs through some divine revelation, telepathic communication, or access through the use of mind-altering substances, it is hard to deny the seemingly magical nature of the contact experience.

Today, the term *contactee* is often associated with UFO subcultures, particularly the so-called "Golden Age" of flying saucers that was underway by the 1950s. The summer of 1947 marked the advent of the term "flying saucer," based on descriptions given by pilot Kenneth Arnold regarding the behavior of a group of objects he observed while flying over Mount Ranier, Washington; this was followed by an alleged UFO crash at Roswell, New Mexico only weeks later, which became cemented in history as one of the most widely recognized incidents in the history of UFO phenomena.

This pivotal year in early Ufology also provides a point where the contactee idea began to converge with notions of visitation from outer space via alien spacecraft. Christopher Partridge, a Professor of Religious Studies at Lancaster University, UK, and author of *UFO Religions,* notes that contactees before 1947 almost never included UFOs among the ways they interacted with otherworldly beings, opting instead for use of magic and the occult through "an existing tradition of extraterrestrial contact via séances and psychic means." [1] In essence, the concept of communication with beings from other worlds was hardly anything new by the time flying saucers arrived on the scene.

UFOs and spaceships were only adopted into the "contactee" mythos once they became an item of public interest, and by the 1960s, spiritualist and mediumistic methods of contact would begin to resurface to some extent. Viewed in this manner, the predominant associations made between UFOs and contact with beings from distant places can be seen as a relatively recent development in the history of alleged contact with other worlds; in at least some cases, they were also a new way for clever charlatans to attempt to cash in on movements associated with New Age philosophies.

MEDIEVAL CONTACTEES AND OCCULT PRACTICES

The use of magic and the occult in contacting nonhuman intelligences not only predates the arrival of UFOs as a cultural phenomenon; it represents a medium that has a much broader history, in relation to humanity's search for answers to things perceived as being "from beyond." A focal point in the lineage of magical attempts to glean knowledge from other realms began in the mid-to-late 1500s, under the work of English mathematician and occult scholar John Dee, who employed the magical arts in attempts at contacting angelic beings. Though he was not the first to do so, it is without question that Dee is recognized for being one of the most significant figures in the history of Western thought, both in relation to the development of the sciences, and for his interest in magic.

Well-known and recognized as one of the most capable intellects in all of Europe during his lifetime, many over the centuries have continued to promote Dee as being a sort of wizard or "magus" of his era. However, despite his occult preoccupations, Dee, a pious Christian, viewed the culmination of his interests as only smaller parts of a greater, more enduring mission he had created for himself. During the last three decades of his life, Dee's goal was to try and learn a "universal language of creation" from angelic entities he contacted by means of magical practices; primarily, this involved the art of *scrying*, which entails using a reflective surface to glean certain knowledge, such as a foretelling of future events, by looking into a reflective surface and allowing the eyes—or at least the mind—to perceive any resulting "visions." Dee hoped to eventually use this divine universal language to help bring unity to humankind prior to the coming of the apocalypse. Thus, the use of magical tools and occult practices were, to Dee, only for the purpose of learning about these "pure verities," as he called them; divine beings or angels that exist beyond the normal perception of those in the physical world. [2]

Among the magical artifacts employed by Dee had been a *speculum* crafted from obsidian, which the explorer Hernán Cortés brought back to Europe after the Conquest of Mexico. [3] Dee acquired this unique item, which was similar in appearance to a hand-mirror, in the late 16th century. However, perhaps the most important tool in all Dee's collection was a *shew stone*, essentially a "crystal ball" of the same sort wizards are stereotypically seen using to peer into the past, present, future, or alternate realities. Dee learned of this item, and its magical potential, after it was allegedly "shown" to him, during one of only a handful of events he ever claimed to experience personally that were deemed supernatural in nature during his lifetime. On this occasion, an angel Dee believed to exist named "Madimi" was said to have appeared, levitating outside his window, clutching the object. Dee, with the help of his associate Edward Kelley (the medium who actually perceived and related the visions back to the scholar) used this item for the next several years to relay further information from Dee's "angels." The problem with this arrangement, at least with regard to Dee's judgment, can only be faulted to him on account of the trust he had for his companion; most accounts of Edward Kelley, the medium with whom Dee had worked so closely, suggest an opportunist who took advantage of Dee's intellect, as well as his personal property in a variety of ways.

A medieval charlatan and convicted criminal, Kelley had likely used a variety of pseudonyms throughout his life, first introducing himself to Dee as "Edward Talbot", a name he also used while attending college at Oxford (though his education is uncertain and remains unproven, it is believed that Kelley had at least some education in languages that include Latin and Greek). [4] Kelley, having had both ears removed as punishment under law for accusations of forgery, shared John Dee's interest in alchemy, preferring this pursuit to the laborious "spiritual conferences" which Dee considered to be of such great importance. The "conferences" practiced by the duo consisted mostly of meditative scrying sessions, in which Kelley provided a physical medium for communication with angelic entities. Thus, the two began to collect knowledge of the arcane forms of communication sought by Dee, which he believed to be an antediluvian "first language" used by God while speaking to Adam. The two worked together in documenting this "Enochian Language," as it came to be known, from 1582 until 1588, a period in which the medium's patience for Dee's obsessions grew increasingly thin. Kelley, after all, was far more attracted to the monetary incentives being offered him by the Bohemian count Vilem Rožmberk, who would later fund Kelley's pursuit of alchemic research. Hence, by 1587, Kelley seemed to have begun fabricating various "messages," which he alleged had come directly from Dee's trusted angelic contact Madimi, commanding the two occultists to share all they owned—even their wives—in an attempt to rid him of Dee's laborious methods of research. Dee, though in anguish, foolishly agreed to this, and allowed Kelley to share his wife, but shortly thereafter withdrew from the agreement, parting ways forever with Edward Kelley in anguish. [5]

Of this so-called "Enochian Language," it is generally argued that Kelley might have fabricated the entire thing, or perhaps that he plagiarized it using elements he borrowed from existing languages. However, at least some scholars have argued that there are no known languages today bearing any conclusive resemblance to the scripts Dee recorded through Kelley's mediumship. Some scholars have also argued that Kelley's limitations as a writer were not evidential in the Enochian scripts, which, based on analysis of Kelley's known writings, seem to share little similarity with other documents penned by the medium. [6] Whatever depth may have lay hidden in Kelley's interpretations of the language Dee sought, they were soon overshadowed by misfortune; not long after Dee's departure, Kelley was imprisoned by Emperor Rudolph II of Prague, after proving unable to meet the emperor's demands for producing alchemical gold, as well as for having killed a man in a duel. In a treatise written to the Emperor during his imprisonment titled *The Stone of the Philosophers*, Kelley seems to refer to his former associate John Dee:

> A familiar acquaintance with the different branches of knowledge has taught me this one thing: that nothing is more ancient, excellent, or more desirable than truth, and whoever neglects it must pass his whole life in the shade. Nevertheless, it always was, and always will be, the way of mankind to release Barabbas and to crucify Christ. This I have—for my good, no doubt—experienced in my own case. I venture to hope, however, that my life and character will so become known to posterity that I may be counted among those who have suffered much for the sake of truth. [7]

Could it be that this statement indicates remorse expressed by Kelley, or even sorrow at the disunion that resulted after the years he and John Dee worked so closely together? Whether or not this is the case, John Dee's legacy has been preserved to some degree at least, regardless of the damaging elements of his association with Kelley. It is worthy at this junction to note that, contrary to views held by many regarding Kelley's shadier aspects, centuries later English occultist Aleister Crowley would hold an entirely different view of the duo; while maintaining profound reverence for Kelley's work, Crowley referred to Dee as "a humorless old man." [8]

After centuries of doubt and shadow cast on the practices and intentions of these men, a newfound respect for Dee's work seems to have emerged in the modern era, as evidenced by such endeavors as *The John Dee Memorial Theater of the Mind*, founded by Raymond Moody (a man whose own work with mirrored surfaces we will examine in a subsequent chapter). The institute continues Dee and Kelley's practices of *crystallomancy* in modern ways, involving various forms of mirror gazing—especially Moody's adoption of the ancient Greek *psychomanteum*—with the aim of inducing altered states of consciousness.

Interestingly, some of Moody's patients over the years were reported to have described seeing visions of deceased loved ones in reflective surfaces during their counseling sessions. [9] Perhaps it is worth noting certain parallels here, in relation to Dee and Kelley's studies, which likely possessed elements that were psychological in nature as well. For instance, was the childlike angel Madimi, who both Dee and Kelley claimed to see on separate occasions, a variety of shared archetypical manifestation, stemming from their like-minded fascination with the occult?

PSYCHIC TRAVEL TO DISTANT PLANETS

Nearly a century after Dee and Kelley parted ways, Christian mystic Emanuel Swedenborg would claim to learn the language of "angels" as well, in addition to visiting other planets by means of out-of-body experiences. This, he said, was made possible after a spiritual "awakening," during which Swedenborg claimed that God opened his eyes, allowing him to see the spirit-world around him, as well as its various inhabitants. In his popular 1758 work, *Heaven and its Wonders and Hell From Things Heard and Seen*, Swedenborg claimed to have witnessed firsthand the vastness of the afterlife, and spoke of the manner in which angels communicated both to him and to one another:

> Angels talk together just as men do in the world, and also on various subjects, as on domestic affairs, on civil affairs, on the affairs of moral life, and on those of spiritual life; nor is there any other difference than that they converse more intelligently than men, because more interiorly from thought. It has been given me often to be in company with them, and to speak with them as friend with friend, and sometimes as stranger with stranger; and then, because I was in a similar state with them, I knew no otherwise than that I was speaking with men on earth. [10]

In addition to being made privy to angelic languages the likes of Dee and Kelley's "Enochian," Swedenborg took things further by claiming to have visited other planets in his out-of-body travels, a practice similar to traditions in Hinduism that refer to "planets" or *Vaikuntha* in relation to out-of-body journeys. [11] Claims like these would place limits on Swedenborg's credibility in the minds of many scholars and theologians, prompting arguments that questioned the mystic's sanity, particularly in his later years. Swedish co-founder of the Royal Academy of Sciences Count von Höpken once posed the question whether it "would not be best for him to keep (these angelic accounts) to himself, and not publish them to the world?" However, von Höpken also provides rationale for Swedenborg's actions:

> He answered that he had orders from the Lord to publish them; and that those who might ridicule him on that account would do him injustice; for, said he, why should I, who am a man in years, render myself ridiculous for fantasies and falsehoods." [12]

Similarly, the Swedenborg Scientific Association dedicated an entire issue of its publication *The New Philosophy* to the question of whether Swedenborg might have suffered from failing mental health in his lifetime. Editor Kurt Simmons Ph.D. notes that, "Swedenborg presents a particularly, indeed perhaps uniquely, daunting challenge to any observer attempting to evaluate the applicability of the madness hypothesis to his claims of revelation." [13] When taking into consideration the sheer volume of scholarly study Swedenborg undertook in his time, ranging from interest in biology, physics, philosophy, engineering and, finally, his theological works, it is difficult to leave with any notion that Swedenborg's "esoteric interests" were purely the ramblings of an unsound mind.

Of particular interest, however, may be another book Swedenborg published in 1758, titled *Concerning Earths in the Solar System*. In it, Swedenborg describes his bodiless travels to nearby inhabited planets, the furthest from Earth being Saturn. This is peculiar, as noted by J. Gordon Melton in his essay *Contactees*, especially due to the fact that Saturn was indeed the furthest planet from Earth... of those *known* to exist at the time Swedenborg wrote the book. [14] Had he been aware of the existence of planets further out in our solar system, would he have known to visit those, also? Could it be that Swedenborg wasn't insane at all, but instead that he had such a fertile mind that he began to create associations between his theological interests and the budding astronomy of his day, producing "visions" akin to science fiction, set on a stage elsewhere in our planetary neighborhood?

Aside from his alleged contact with angels and other planets, there is one other unique element regarding Swedenborg's psyche that may be worthy of consideration; in many instances, the man was said to have displayed incredible instances of psychic prowess. Namely, a 1768 letter written by German philosopher Immanuel Kant described how, at a dinner in Gothenburg, Sweden on July 29, 1759, Swedenborg began to relate to his company at six o' clock that a fire in Stockholm had consumed his neighbor's home, and was now threatening his own. Two hours passed before Swedenborg reported that the fire had been halted, and just three doors from his residence! Within two days, reports arrived which confirmed his visions, with every statement matching to the precise hour, just as Swedenborg had dictated to his company a few days earlier. Kant later resolved that Swedenborg's alleged psychic abilities were probably illusions, though while downplaying such incidents, the philosopher admitted he could find no scientific explanation for Swedenborg's knowledge of the fire that nearly consumed his home in 1759. Nonetheless, Kant appeared to ridicule Swedenborg in his published writings, while his private letters often expressed an apparent reverence, and even fascination for the man and his unusual "gifts." [15] Kant, it seems, was rather conflicted on the enigma that was Emmanuel Swedenborg.

Throughout the late 1800s and the majority of the nineteenth century, methods attributed to contact with otherworldly beings were primarily psychical in nature, specifically pertaining to the nineteenth century spiritualist movement where magical and occult practices were considered fashionable, to put it one way. Another century would lapse between Swedenborg's psychic travels and the founding of the Theosophical Society in September 1875, though it marked the beginning of what is perhaps the next most-notable marker along the winding road of contactee involvement throughout history. One of the Society's founders, Helena Blavatsky, who was living in New York City at the time, would go on to describe her own psychic communications with what she called "Ascended Masters." These intelligent, supernatural entities bear a number of similarities to the Christian concept of angelic deities, although by definition Ascended Masters represented those who have existed in the past on Earth with physical bodies, having "ascended" beyond the realm of the physical to exist in an enlightened spiritual state. [16] These "masters", which included notable historical figures such as Jesus Christ, Serapis, Morya, and other religious figures from various cultures, were first discussed in the 1870s by Blavatsky, and later adopted by Guy and Edna Ballard in the 1930s during what became a sort of religious movement called the "I AM Activity." [17] The Ballards and their movement may represent one of the earliest shifts in perspective from contactees and their focus on "angelic" beings, to an interest in physical encounters with benign alien visitors from space. Specifically, the Ballards believed their alien contacts hailed from the planet Venus, which parallels Swedenborg's earlier belief in life on planets elsewhere in our solar system. A few years prior to his death, Guy Ballard claimed that on one occasion he and more than one hundred others witnessed the appearance of twelve Venusians in a cavern beneath Mt. Shasta, California. These friendly Venusians, upon manifesting before the enlightened assembly, proceeded to perform a musical concert before showing them a device resembling a large mirror, which conveyed images of their lifestyle on Venus. Before they departed, the friendly aliens reported to Ballard and his company that the earth was destined to suffer through a period of warfare, from which humanity would eventually prevail, spreading worldwide peace and goodwill. [18] This theme of impending doom would become a common message imparted by friendly "Space Brothers" to a multitude of alien contactees for years to come.

However, even prior to the Ballards and their religious movement, authors like Théodore Flournoy were publishing books that examined the concept of travel to alien planets and visits with entities living there. In Flournoy's 1900 book, *From India To The Planet Mars*, he presents a critical review of the claims of medium Helen Smith, who described bodiless travels again reminiscent of that described by Swedenborg, which she achieved while in a trance-like state.[19]

One decade later, a renowned physician, skeptic and debunker named William S. Sadler began to relate to a small study group consisting of his friends and colleagues a similar case, which involved trance communications he claimed to have witnessed. Sadler perceived these to be evidence of valid psychic communication from someplace other than planet Earth, eventually indicating that he and his group would be allowed to ask questions about the nature of the contact, with answers provided directly from "celestial beings." This series of communications resulted in *The Urantia Book*, a text that again seemed to bridge the gap between what would later become alien contact with the already popular notion of angelic communications. [20]

ALEISTER CROWLEY, "LAM" AND THE
AMALANTRAH WORKING

During the early twentieth century, reports of contact with "Ascended Masters", angels, Venusians and other sentient intelligences lent themselves to what was likely the greatest marriage between the angelic and extraterrestrial (or inter-dimensional, a term which researcher Daniel V. Boudillion notes was also used at the time to describe extraterrestrial beings). [21] However, no one is said to have achieved this, particularly in ways that utilized traditional magical processes, more effectively than occultist Aleister Crowley.

One of the most notorious historical figures of his era, Crowley's mystique preceded him in life, and has continued into the present day. Highly regarded as one of the most influential occultists ever to have lived even in modern times, he adopted the rather dark moniker "The Beast 666," a reputation that helped solidify his title as "the wickedest man in England" during his lifetime. [22] Crowley seemed to counter-balance his devout studies of the occult with sensationalist ideals that lived up to this self-prescribed "beastly" image. No less, the significance of his influence on occult circles and other fields of interest exists without question, as Crowley authored books and papers that dealt with everything from ceremonial magic ("magick" as he spelled it) to early records of the effects of hallucinogenic drugs on human behavior. [23]

Though it is well known that Crowley spent much of his life attempting to summon entities from dimensions beyond, even utilizing the various Enochian scripts gathered by John Dee during his spirit conferences with Edward Kelley, perhaps what is lesser known of his "magickal" workings dealt with a particular summoning Crowley began in 1918 called "The Amalantrah Working." Crowley, living in New York City at the time, performed these rituals in his apartment near Central Park West over a period of several months, along with his medium (and mistress) at the time, Roddie Minor. Much like Crowley, Minor had maintained a penchant for opium use, of which Crowley had expressed that "bad results" were rare. Known for having a very sophisticated view relative to his era regarding the use of such drugs, of his own opium use he once wrote, "I indulge very mildly when the company is attractive; I have tried long and vainly to acquire the habit." [24]

Apparently, the aim of the Amalantrah Working had been to invoke certain "intelligences" to manifest physically, although similar to Edward Kelley's role with John Dee's research, most of the noted results were merely visions and communications Minor conveyed to Crowley. Nonetheless, the duo claimed to have succeeded in manifesting something unusual by way of ceremonial Magick; accompanied by symbolic imagery involving depictions of an egg, the entity itself bore small, piercing eyes and infantile physical features mounted upon a large, bulbous head, as indicated in a drawing of the being made by Crowley himself. Crowley dubbed this being "Lam", the meaning of which he summarized in a caption below the drawing, which was first published as a frontispiece to Helena Blavatsky's book *The Voice of the Silence*:

> LAM is the Tibetan word for Way or Path, and LAMA is He who Goeth, the specific title of the Gods of Egypt, the Treader of the Path, in Buddhistic phraseology. [25]

Crowley's drawing alone provides one of the more interesting elements regarding the summoning of the "Lam" entity, as it was Crowley's assertion that the image had not been produced from memory, but was instead a *portrait*; the creature that manifested before him had allegedly remained long enough for Crowley to produce the detailed sketch of it while perceptible before him.

Strangely, Crowley would have little to say of Lam after its appearance in 1918, though later in 1945 he noted in his personal diaries that one of his protégés, Kenneth Grant, had shown interest in the drawing. Crowley eventually gave the drawing to Grant, who later formalized elements of what occurred during Crowley's Amalantrah Workings into a "Cult of Lam" structured around the strange being. In 1987, Grant stated the following pertaining to the image, the symbolism involving the "egg" around Lam, and the bearing these elements would have on the formation of a cult:

The Cult [of Lam] has been founded because... It is Our aim to obtain some insight not only into the nature of Lam, but also into the possibilities of using the Egg as an astral space-capsule for travelling to Lam's domain, or for exploring extra-terrestrial spaces. [26]

Michael Staley, a prominent member of Crowley's Typhonian OTO who once also was allowed to view Crowley's original drawing of Lam, says that the entity is actually a glyph or symbol representative of "a gateway to wider and deeper ranges of consciousness". [27] Staley goes on to say that "the absence of Crowley's exegesis on Lam gives us a great deal of freedom and creativity to discover the implications for ourselves, and to use them as magical and mystical tools in our initiation." [28] He notes that a wealth of material orienting Lam with Crowley's magick and the mythos surrounding it has been published, though "a definitive interpretation has yet to emerge. This is because we are dealing with something that is living and growing, rather than a matter simply of academic study."
Staley continues:

Nevertheless, a broad outline is emerging, enough to make clear the primary function of Lam as the Gateway to wider and deeper ranges of consciousness—our extraterrestrial, pan-dimensional Reality. [29]

Though Staley makes it very clear that various interpretations could be made regarding Lam, what he describes does seem evocative of Lam acting as an interdimensional conduit—an ambassador, of sorts— to an alien realm.

ROCKET-SCIENCE, ALIENS AND OCCULTISTS

It is obvious, by now, that some followers of Crowley do make use of the term "extraterrestrial" in reference to Lam. Though it seems this may be in reference to otherworldly intelligence of a *spiritual* variety, rather than nuts-and-bolts extraterrestrials flying around in UFOs, the distinction between Lam and alien visitors isn't always so clear. This is evidenced by a sub-cultural interpretation that has emerged regarding Lam's possible connection to extraterrestrials popularly reported by UFO witnesses over the last several decades. Indeed, Lam's infantile frame and large, egg-like head do bear some similarities to "gray aliens," the most widely recognized of all UFO occupants as reported by alien abductees, reports of which date back as far as the 1950s. Daniel Boudillion points out the following in his essay *Aleister Crowley's Lam & the Little Grey Men: A Striking Resemblance*, which deals with similar parallels between Lam, Crowley's spiritual practices and the modern concept of alien visitors:

The Great work for Crowley, "...involved precisely the establishment of contact with non-human intelligences." Intelligences such as Lam. Using the language of Crowley's time, certain non-human intelligences such as Lam were what we today would term "extraterrestrial." [30]

Boudillion's interpretation seems to help solidify precisely what is meant by use of the word "extraterrestrial." He also asserts that, based on the assumptions of those in occult circles, Crowley had intentionally created a magical gateway "through which Lam and other extra-cosmic influences could enter the known universe, and most particularly, our earth-world. According to occultists involved in such things, the Portal has since widened." [31]

According to occult literature, what exactly caused the "widening" of such a portal—no doubt similar to the one which produced Lam—may have had to do with the continuation of Crowley's rituals by aspiring magicians in later years. Jet Propulsion Laboratory founder and rocket propulsion scientist Jack Parsons was chosen by Aleister Crowley in 1942 to be leader of the Agape Lodge, one of Crowley's Thelemic Ordo Templi Orientis outposts in California. In spite of his professional dedication to science and rocketry, Parsons made no bones about his occult interests, and was even known to perform rituals aimed at invoking the Greek god Pan in conjunction with each of his rocket test-launches. [32] In 1946, Parsons, along with science fiction author and, later, Church of Scientology figurehead L. Ron Hubbard, began a series of rituals similar in nature to Crowley's Amalantrah Working, referring to theirs as "the

Babalon Working." Much like Crowley's work, the ceremonies drew heavily from John Dee and Edward Kelley's Enochian magical systems, in addition to Crowley's very taboo "sex magick." The ceremony aimed to summon the essence of the Thelemic goddess Babalon, "The Mother of Abominations" or the "Whore of Babalon," and cause her to manifest physically in the womb of a surrogate human mother. Based on a similar concept expressed by Crowley years earlier in his fiction novel *Moonchild*, Parsons had hoped Crowley would find his experiment favorable; Crowley on the other hand, in a personal correspondence from around the same time, seemed to indicate conflicting opinions:

> Apparently Parsons and Hubbard or somebody is producing a moonchild. I get fairly frantic when I contemplate the idiocy of these louts. [33]

Despite Crowley's feelings toward the matter, here again the separate schools of magic and UFOs seem to converge, this time over the alleged outcome of Parsons and Hubbard's ritual. Proponents of this idea say that the "Magickal portal" Crowley opened, which originally brought knowledge of Lam into our reality, "was reestablished with considerable intensity by Parsons and Hubbard." [34] Incidentally, the dawn of the modern UFO mystery, beginning with Kenneth Arnold's sighting in June of 1947, began roughly one year after Parsons and Hubbard's Babylon Working.

As for Parsons, though he never succeeded in creating a Moonchild, his longing to immerse himself in the dark arts would remain a familiar presence in his life, right up until his untimely demise:

> He remained deeply enamoured of Babalon—some might say obsessed. The expected Daughter of Babalon did not, though, manifest. He had been told that she would come to him bearing a sign that he alone would recognise. On the other hand, he had also been told that he would become "living flame" before Babalon incarnated. [35]

In a display of chilling irony, this prophecy that Parsons would become "living flame" appears to have been deadly accurate. On June 17th, 1952, while working in his laboratory Parsons dropped a highly unstable explosive substance; he died of injuries from the resulting explosion within hours.

CONTACT: "SPACE BROTHERS" AND THE RETURN OF SÉANCES

Thus ended the life of Jack Parsons, as well as perhaps the darkest period of occult-oriented contact with sentient interdimensional intelligences during the twentieth century. However, the end of one era brought about the dawn of a new one; within months of Parson's death, George Adamski would declare his initial encounters in the Colorado Desert with a Venusian he called "Orthon." Some of those who still practiced the bygone arts of mediumship and séances leapt on the bandwagon soon afterward, and before long various methods of magical conjuring had again become popular methods of communicating with alien beings. Mediums used trance channeling, automatic writing and, in a handful of curious cases, spirit-materialization to summon and manifest what were being called "Space Brothers".

Bertie Lillie Candler was a popular spiritualist during the 1950s, described frequently as "the greatest physical medium of the world." [36] Candler is credited with allegedly summoning an entity called "Diane," a very beautiful, eight-foot tall Venusian woman first encountered by contactee Dana Howard beginning in 1939. Sixteen years later, Howard and several friends had gathered together in the presence of the Reverend Candler, where she was conducting a séance at the Church of Divine Light on South Parkview Street in Los Angeles, California. During the climax of the session, Howard described seeing "a rising glow of phosphorescence. It was very tall at first, but out of this phosphorescent substance a form began to manifest itself. She was definitely different from the other 'spirit' manifestations, a solid, fleshly being, delicate in charm and manner." [37] Soon, the entity introduced herself as Diane, the same entity Howard had met in 1939, in addition to revealing that she had been responsible for imparting telepathic messages to her during their sixteen-year hiatus:

She called for DANA. Overwhelmed with emotion
I could not choke back, I went up to her, standing

only inches away from the manifestation. While I did not recognize her instantly, I knew there was something quaintly familiar about her. Standing like a sylph-like goddess, and bowing low in greeting to the twenty-seven persons present, the rich tones of her voice vibrated through the little church. *"I AM DIANE. I COME FROM VENUS."* [38]

"My daughter," Diane purportedly told Howard, "always remember, without inner perfection there can be no outer perfection. There must be perfect balance between the realm of spirit and the realm of materiality." It is interesting to note how the motherly overtones of love, fellowship, and "inner perfection," followed by Diane's promise that Venus would ultimately be the future home for humankind, share rather interesting religious parallels. Blogger Regan Lee commented on the religious nature of the symbolism in Dana Howard's otherworldly reunion with the Venusian Diane:

> The symbolism in these encounters is interesting. Was it a true encounter with an alien? Or the same presence that is manifest in appearances of the Virgin Mary? It is interesting the experience took place during a séance; a perfect setting for manifestations of all kinds of spirits and entities; including some part of Dana Howard herself that was Diane. [37]

Could it be, like Regan points out, that if not some perceived incarnation of the Virgin Mother,

"Diane" might have stemmed from some inner connection within Howard herself? Also noteworthy is the fact that alleged alien contactees in some abduction scenarios discuss similar feelings of union or familiarity, where they frequently describe sharing a particular, almost motherly connection with one of their alien captors (Whitley Streiber's *Communion* might be considered one example of this motif).

Political activist William Dudley Pelley was among those who claimed to have witnessed a similar manifestation created by the Reverend Candler. A popular spiritualist in the 1930s and 40s, Pelley was notorious for his associations with fascist organizations, having founded and served as head of a pro-Nazi group called Silver Legion of America. Pelley also claimed to have been present during the manifestation of a young Indian girl calling herself "Silverleaf" during one of Candler's séances; in his book *Why I Believe the Dead Are Alive*, he described with great excitement the odd circumstances of her departure back to the spirit realm, which included the discussion of a very sci-fi sounding "ray" used in the manifestation of such spirits:

> Finally she said that she had to go back into the cabinet and help "build up the ray" for others.
> I asked "What ray?"
> "The materializing ray," she answered.
> What she alluded to was, that to obtain such results in actuality, this was what took place: As the medium sank into deeper and deeper trance, her body began to release its ectoplasmic content, which poured out through its orifices into a sort of

pool in the cabinet before her. This is one of the chief reasons for the cabinet at all, that such exhibition does not frighten or disgust the spectator. Into this flood of released ectoplasm, the more tenuous Light Body of the materializing entity steps and concentrates—with the help of "guides" like Silverleaf who are in the cabinet discarnate—on what his or her physical appearance was in mortality. This concentration acts as a sort of magnetic ray that begins to draw up the ectoplasm around the discarnate Light-Body like mercury filling up the glass stem of a thermometer. When the Light-Body, or pattern-self, is completely substantialized, the materialization is accomplished and the discarnate entity can leave the cabinet, to all intents a normal human being. [38]

Pelley then argues the validity of the experience, comparing the manifestation capabilities he believed mediums like Candler to possess to that of an infant being formed in the womb:

Don't say, "It can't be done!" It can be done, and is done in a thousand bona fide séance rooms on five continents year after year. It is the operating of a law just as natural as the growth of a blood clot in a woman's womb into a perfectly formed human being, within the first twenty-five days after conception, though too minute to be recognized for what it is. One is no more a mystery than the other. [39]

Incidentally, "Spacemen" were also said to have appeared during séances at which Pelley was present. In spite of his reprehensible political views, Pelley was reputed for possessing an astute sense of rationale; yet he wholeheartedly professed belief in manifestations like "Silverleaf", as well as confidence in the abilities of mediums like Candler. Had she indeed possessed an innate ability to summon entities, some having been formerly human, while others manifested from distant worlds beyond? Or was Candler, like so many of her era, a medium who was equally skilled in the arts of misdirection?

Perhaps one of the most unique elements regarding the appearance of physical manifestations of this sort has to do with the fact that the circumstances surrounding the manifestations are often similar, and bearing emotional intensity and ritual-like elements. Though the "ritual" aspects are more obvious in the conjuring of those like Aleister Crowley and John Dee, the séances of mediums like Bertie Lilly Candler also bore ritual elements steeped in spiritualism. For instance, prior to the séances themselves, those present at Candler's sessions often gathered together beforehand to sing hymns before a psychic session. We might assume that building spiritual energies in this way among the participants helped to stimulate their minds, prepping them for the "manifestations" that would later occur. Then, at just the right moment, an entity would step from the closet, cabinet, or other medium, revealing universal knowledge, or perhaps merely closure to loved ones still among the living, who were present during the session.

In retrospect, this isn't completely different from the ways the ancient Greeks were believed to have used variations of the mirror-gazing techniques described earlier to manifest the dead. At locations like the temple of the Oracle of the Dead, which, in accordance with tradition, was located on the banks of the Acheron river near the ancient city of Ephyra, priests were once believed to have used a large cauldron filled with water as a reflective surface in a fairly low-light setting, creating a uniform field of vision capable of inducing a trance-like state. Once this state was reached, apparitions of the dead and other visions were supposed to appear within the subject's field of view. Modern applications, including the Ganzfeld Technique, involving the placement of ping pong ball halves over the eyes, can create a similar effect. However, one modern psychologist, Dr. Raymond Moody, M.D., went so far as to attempt to replicate the conditions used by the ancient Greeks in an effort to recreate their methods inducing altered states. Surprising, if not groundbreaking results were allegedly achieved, as recounted in his book *Reunions*, which resulted in what Moody believed to be a veritable conduit to the spiritual world. Borrowing terminology from the ancient Greeks, Moody dubbed this mirror-gazing apparatus the *psychomanteum*.

This "psychomanteum," a form of mirror gazing, seemed to represent one of the most vivid, and yet accessible means by which one may attempt to induce an altered state of consciousness. Thus, in the winter of 2008, I decided I would learn as much about this practice as I could; how better to go about doing so, I thought, than to head directly to its source? As I would later learn, seeking to unravel the mysteries of the psychomanteum would bring me face-to-face with something else unforeseen: an evening spent with the progenitor of what we know today as *the near death experience*.

CHAPTER TWO

LABYRINTHS OF THE MIND: THE ANCIENT GREEK ORACLE OF THE DEAD, REVISITED

Psychics and others who travel in other nonphysical realms like the astral world report that polarities are switched. Left becomes right. Future becomes past... Mirrors represent these shifts. Labyrinths help the individual make them.

-SIG LONEGREN, *Labyrinths: Ancient Myths and Modern Uses*

In February 2008, I had the pleasure of spending a snowy evening with Dr. Raymond Moody M.D. at a small conference in Ridgecrest, North Carolina. Moody is a leading authority on the *near death experience*, a term he is credited with coining in the late 1970s, as well as being a respected therapist and grief counselor. His preferred methods over the years involved one particular meditative technique, first developed by the ancient Greeks, and later adopted and refined by Moody for use as a variety of therapeutic tool.

I entered the small lodge where the event was being held, where an intimate crowd of fewer than thirty attendees waited, all gathered with hope of learning Moody's techniques. Small groups were seated around fancy tables, and as I stood in the doorway to the room that held our seminar, called "the library" by the owners due to its scholarly décor, a short, whiskered man with an earring stepped through and politely greeted me. It struck me then that, to my surprise, I recognized him.

"Pardon me," I said, "but you're Ray Buckland."

"Why yes," he responded, grinning. "Yes, I am!"

Buckland is a name that remains well known in relation to the occult, having been the first to introduce Gardnerian Wicca in the United States in 1964. [1] Standing here talking with Buckland, our attention shifted to the various old rare books and other trinkets that lined the walls; the library seemed quite appropriate for such a gathering, and proved to be a stimulating environment for the knowledge that would be passed along to us throughout the course of the evening.

Raymond Moody sat across the room at a table where several had gathered, shaking hands and chatting with people eager to discuss their personal experiences. To his right sat Rosemary Ellen Guiley, author of *The Encyclopedia of Magic and Alchemy* and several other volumes on witchcraft and the occult (some of which I would enlist as resources for this book). Also, before the two of them stood Joshua P. Warren, a paranormal enthusiast and friend of mine of several years, who glanced our way and, with an excited gesture, motioned for Buckland and I to come over for an introduction.

Moody was sincere and approachable, and received the two latest arrivals warmly. We shook hands, and his pronounced grip matched well with his smooth southern dialect.

"Micah, it's great to meet you, and I've heard so many wonderful things from Joshua," he said as we greeted each another.

"Well Dr. Moody, don't believe everything you've heard," I joked with him. The character that radiated through his words made it easy to see why people loved him so much. Following some casual conversation among the attendees, waitresses began to enter the dining area, rolling bottles of red wine and expensive Belgian beers into the room on metal carts. As beverages were selected and poured, Moody began to speak with our group, explaining how some of his classical leanings and early education led to an interest in mirror gazing, the eventual discovery of the psychomanteum, and how he used it in his own unique brand of grief counseling.

CLASSICAL MUSINGS: A LIFE IN THE PRACTICE

As a young student studying philosophy at the University of Virginia, Moody had been fascinated with the works of the Classical Greek philosophers, and felt right at home absorbed in the musings of Socrates, Plato and others. It was during his time in Virginia that he first learned of people's encounters with what Moody would later call "near-death experiences." He had learned about a psychiatry professor at the University named George Ritchie who, during a life-threatening experience several years earlier, had been pronounced clinically dead. Ritchie was revived in nothing short of a miraculous medical recovery, and to Moody's great interest, had described having "an astonishing experience" while lingering between death and the afterlife. [2]

"I had heard about experiences of this sort, and was interested in it from the perspective of consciousness," Moody said. Later, once he became a philosophy teacher himself, one of Moody's students approached him with a similar story, where the student had been in a near-fatal car accident, and remembered having a remarkable experience. Moody was stunned by his student's description of the incident, which related an experience nearly identical in every way to that of Professor George Ritchie.

Over the years, experiences like this began to change Moody's feelings about the possibility of life after death. "What people who have near-death experiences tell me is that what they experienced wasn't even temporal or spatial in the sense that you and I appreciate it. So, what I'm interested in is altered states of consciousness and I think that the old questions of whether there is a life after death or the beyond... have to be revised." [3]

It was through his study of Greek philosophy and ancient history that Moody first discovered the concept of the *psychomanteum*, which entails a room or area that utilizes a mirror and dim lighting, believed to serve as a conduit for communications with the spirit realm. Since the 1960s, Moody had been brainstorming ways near-death experiences could be reproduced or "triggered" in a clinical setting. This would allow researchers the benefit of studying these experiences in real-time as they occurred, without having "to fall back on anecdotes told after the fact." [4] Moody, always the optimist, had also hoped to be able to harness some of the positive effects described by those who had these experiences.

One evening in 1990, he had been pondering how one might separate the common elements reported during near-death experiences, when he came to a realization: if perceived experiences with apparitions of the deceased are as common as they appeared to be in demographic studies he had conducted, then humans must be highly predisposed to having them. "Why not rearrange circumstances in such a way as to heighten the likelihood that (encounters with apparitions) would occur under a given circumstance so that we could be there to monitor the person with electroencephalograms, and get a fresh account before the mind might have had time subconsciously to distort or elaborate it?" [5] It was then that Moody says he recalled a moment in 1962 at the University of Virginia, during a session in his liberal arts seminar class. It involved the ancient historian Herodotus, who wrote of a place where the ancient Greeks were said to go visit their departed relatives. Whatever the circumstances were that allowed it to happen, Herodotus described that people who went to this place somehow had first-hand experiences with the spirit realm.

Legends involving similar circumstances, namely the Oracle at Delphi, described the *Pythia*—a sort of medium acting as a seer and interpreter—being lowered into a pit to converse with spirits rather than those individuals who actually sought to make contact. Emerging from the pit, which, according to some anthropologists may have contained gases that caused hallucinations, the Pythia would then bring messages back for those meant to receive them. [6]

Moody was fascinated by Herodotus' descriptions of direct spirit communications, and found similar references to such things in Homer's *Odyssey*. Here, the hero Odysseus actually travels to the same location described by Herodotus: the Oracle of the Dead, or the *Nekyomanteion* at Thesprotia, in a region to the Northwest of Greece called Epirus.

"What in the name of God were they doing there?" Moody asked, while other scholars had long assumed that the writings of Herodotus and Homer, as well as similar references to the Oracle of the Dead made by the Greek geographer Strabo, were all based on mere legends.

However, in 1958 at least one other scholar appeared to have found people's dismissal of esoteric things in Classical Greek literature to be in bad taste. Greek archaeologist Sotirios Dakaris decided that he would, much like Schliemann in his search for Troy, try and find the location described by both Homer and Herodotus, and see if any evidence of a temple existed there. If he succeeded, he hoped to see, once and for all, if any remnant of the "Halls of Hades and Dread Persephone" truly existed, where Odysseus consulted the prophet Tiresias about how to find his way home to Ithaca. [7]

Incidentally, in Homer's Odyssey, the location was described as being "near the city of the Cimmerian people wrapped in mist and cloud." Moody argues that scholars have misread this for generations, and that Herodotus meant *Cheimerians*, a group of people who lived near Thesprotia, exactly the location of Herodotus' *Nekyomanteion*. [8] Upon going to the area and following clues in the landscape as related in Homer's *Odyssey*, Dakaris discovered a remarkable complex on the hill of St. John the Baptist, overlooking the Acheron River. Beneath this building, Dakaris also discovered an enormous subterranean chamber, complete with a vast corridor, and what he believed were dormitory rooms where people would stay while waiting their turn to visit what must have been the Oracle of the Dead. Dakaris found that one end of the long corridor emptied into a complex maze, which ultimately lead to a fifty-foot long "apparition hallway." [9] Here rested an enormous bronze cauldron surrounded by a banister, which Dakaris believed was evidence that people who came to see the apparitions had been staring in the direction of the cauldron.

Though Dakaris had discovered what he believed to be a real-life counterpart to an enduring Greek legend, his interpretation of the role of the cauldron was rather simplistic; he guessed that the Oracle would merely hide within, and emerge at a later time, play-acting the role of an "apparition" before those who visited. However, whether Dakaris's site was indeed the classical Nekyomanteion remains disputed among a number of scholars. In 1979, a German researcher named Dietwulf Baatz pointed out that a number of bronze attachments discovered during Dakaris's survey, which included ratchet wheels and a series of bronze rings, "all belonged to third-century B.C. catapults." [9] These items, it has been suggested, might have fallen into the lower chamber in 167 B.C. during Roman acquisition of the site. Then in 1980, another German archaeologist, L. Haselberger, argued that the entire complex, rather than resembling a labyrinthine chamber, was likely the base of a tower similar to other structures found along the Greek countryside nearby. [10]

James Wiseman, a professor of Archaeology at Boston University, notes that further studies at the site may help determine if Dakaris was indeed correct about the location, and its historical significance:

Despite growing skepticism, the matter remains unresolved in the minds of many scholars, and several of Dakaris' interpretations remain plausible. Subsurface exploration of the slopes might reveal some conclusive feature (part of an earlier sanctuary? a collapsed cave?) to confirm Dakaris' identification of the Nekyomanteion. The Nikopolis Project did not have time for geophysical prospection in the area, but that technique would be worth employing in the future. Whatever the resolution, we are indebted to the late Sotirios Dakaris for his discovery and excavation of such a fascinating site, and for seeing to its preservation so that others might continue to explore it and debate its significance. [11]

Whether Dakaris was correct in his assessment of the identity of the site is of little concern, at least in terms of the inspiration it provided Raymond Moody. Relying on ancient Greco-Egyptian sources, Moody came to believe that the cauldron—had it indeed been used for mystic rituals—would instead have been filled with liquid, providing a reflective surface and used in a fashion similar to mirror gazing. "I decided that this must have been what they were doing at Epirus, the Oracle of the Dead on the Acheron. I set up a situation in my own research facility; I built a chamber, not using a cauldron but a mirror surrounded by a black velvet curtain and arranged in such a way so that a person sitting in the booth does not see their own reflection, but a clear optical depth." [12] Then, Moody began allowing people to enter the room and gaze into the mirror, dimly lit with indirect lighting, to see if indeed any strange experiences might occur. What he found surprised him more than he could have imagined.

"I thought it was going to be at least ten percent," he guessed, hoping at least some of his participants might report odd experiences. "It ended up being closer to fifty!" Even more astonishing, a portion of the test subjects that were having experiences described full-body apparitions appearing in the mirror, some of which slowly emerged from it to interact with them in the room. According to Moody, thirty percent of the subjects even described hearing the voices of deceased loved ones appearing before them, some even describing elaborate conversations they had with the apparitions. [13]

"And very nicely," Moody adds, "the subjects who have been going through this have reported that it helped them with the grief. It helped them tidy up the unfinished business." Comparing his experiments with themes appearing elsewhere in occult literature, some of it dating as far back as antiquity, Moody further determined that his experiments using the psychomanteum environment seemed to parallel modern reports dating back more than a century, which involve apparitional forms witnessed in mirrors or reflective surfaces.

"The accounts that subjects give in the psychomanteum," Moody says, "are identical to the accounts we hear from people who have (witnessed) spontaneous apparitions.

"So, I think we've done it!"

"I'm Looking at the Man in the Mirror"

The concept of using reflective surfaces as a medium for observing apparition is nothing new. As far back as 1863, English novelist and playwright Wilkie Collins wrote of his experiences with mirror gazing, inspired by John Dee's experiments, which sound remarkably similar to what Moody describes during a fruitful psychomanteum session:

> I retire to my private sitting-room, take up my black mirror, mention what I want—and behold! On the surface of the cannel coal the image of my former travels passes before me, in a succession of dream-scenes. I revive my past experiences, and I make my present choice out of them, by the evidence of my own eyes; and, I may add, by that of my own ears also—for the figures in my magic landscape move and speak! 13

More recently, the late "King of Pop" Michael Jackson once described a room in his home at Neverland Ranch, the walls of which were covered with mirrors. Within this room, Jackson said that on many occasions he had spoken with the ghost of the famous flamboyant pianist Liberace, who died in 1987. "I have my own secret room, with a moving wall and mirrors," Jackson once said. "That's where I talk to Lee. His is the voice I hear in there. I feel his presence so very close to me. (Liberace) is like my guardian angel. He's even given me permission to record his theme song 'I'll Be Seeing You'." [14]

As the examples here make evident, it seems commonly accepted in occult traditions that mirrors bear some kind of potential that is conducive to the appearances of ghosts. Similarly, there are various methods of "spirit photography" that involve aiming the lens of a camera into a mirror to capture its field of vision, which some believe will reveal the presence of ghosts in a location alleged to be haunted.

During our retreat in Ridgecrest, many of the participants described strange things that occurred while staring into Raymond Moody's mirror. For instance, Ray Buckland described feeling a dark, disturbing presence in the room with him at one point; another time, he also described sensing a presence that reminded him, quite distinctly, of his deceased father. Others would describe shadowy silhouettes and cloudy "forms" that would drift in and out of their field of view while staring into the mirror. Several of those in attendance returned from the weekend in possession of "psychomanteum grief counseling" certification, complete with Raymond Moody's seal of approval.

One of these individuals was Joshua Warren, my friend who had been the organizer of the event with Moody. A self-taught researcher, filmmaker and author, Warren's interests over the years have ranged from the study of natural luminous phenomena, to selling books and devices based on the "Law of Attraction," a concept with roots in the New Thought movement of the 19th century. Although Warren's philosophies have often differed from mine, we have remained good friends over the years.

Several days after the event in Ridgecrest, I found myself sitting in Joshua's home in Asheville, where he described, with great excitement, the process said by Moody to open pathways to these profound interactions with the spirit realm. "Moody told us that, ideally, you need to combine elements within the sessions," Josh explained one evening at his home. "One part is speaking with the person who has lost a loved one, the other involves a session within the psychomanteum. Each successive visit gets a little longer... and a little longer."

Josh's voice began to fade to a whisper as he said this. "Finally, after several discussions, and visits to the psychomanteum, you leave the individual in there for two, maybe even three hours. The idea is to not tell them how long they're staying, but let them know that you're just going right down the hall, and that they should take all the time they need.

"That's when they really start to see shit," Josh confided bluntly.

Josh began to backtrack, although touching on something of particular interest to me; the precise moment when the councilor would know the grieving person is ready to enter the psychomanteum.

"It happens very quickly. You begin the first session by asking a series of questions like, 'who do you want to contact? Tell me your fondest memory of them. What is your least pleasant memory of this person? Did this person ever make you feel uncomfortable? What, if you could speak to the deceased person one last time, would you ask them?' After a while, there is an exact instant, and you'll know it when you see it, that the energy just *shifts*." Josh made a gesture with his arms and upper body as he described this, dropping his hands and allowing his shoulders to droop as though he were tired or exasperated. "This is the moment where, sometimes along with a brief pause, they will tell you, or maybe express to you without words that 'this is it, that's all.' It's as though there's nothing more to say, and they are completely overcome with emotion, or have maybe reached some sort of mental or emotional barrier. At that moment, they are ready to enter the psychomanteum."

Ever since leaving the seminar, Josh had planned to convert his guest bedroom into a fully operational psychomanteum, complete with a few additions that he felt would make it more conducive to people having experiences. Along with a black light he placed behind the comfortable armchair that faced the mirror he purchased for his setup, he also included a small radio that he kept tuned to the white noise between stations. The mild hissing it provided would help create a wall of ambient sound, which both calmed the senses, and blanketed one's ears from any noise that might come from outside the psychomanteum.

However, with time, I also learned that Josh would sometimes introduce other variables—odd, subtle things of his own choosing—which he hoped to use to amplify the effects of the psychomanteum experience.

FINDERS KEEPERS

There was one final twist to this story, and a remarkable one, to say the least. As Dr. Moody and his wife had been leaving Ridgecrest in February, they asked Josh for a favor: The Moodys had planned to leave early on Sunday morning, although many of those attending the seminar wished to stay through lunch time, hoping to be able to experiment within the psychomanteum a little longer. Josh began to inquire about acquiring a different mirror for the guests to use, since Moody brought his personal mirror from his home in Georgia—the same that hundreds of individuals had used during sessions with him over the last several decades. To Josh's surprise, Mrs. Moody told him, "Don't worry about it. Just keep that one for now and ship it back to us." On that note, Moody and his wife departed, and several of the attendees were able to continue with their experiences. Once things finally drew to a close, Josh gathered the mirror and, after being wrapped carefully in cloth and bubble wrap, it was placed in the trunk of his car.

That's when the strangeness began to occur.

Ridgecrest, where the event was held, sits on the lower slopes of Old Fort Mountain, which lay on the outermost edges of the small town of Black Mountain. Josh and his wife, Lauren, stopped to have brunch there in town before heading back into Asheville. As they locked their car and headed into the restaurant, the Warrens both heard a distinct knocking sound, which appeared to be coming from their car.

"I think Lauren actually noticed it first," Josh recalled. "We began walking back in the direction of my car, and as we got closer to where we were parked, it sounded like the knocking was coming from inside the trunk." Perplexed, they unlocked the vehicle and threw open the trunk, thinking a small animal might have been trapped inside at some point during their weekend in Ridgecrest. Instead, once they opened the trunk, there were no further signs of knocking, nor any evidence of what might have caused the noise; only Dr Moody's mirror, still wrapped in cloth as Josh had left it.

"When we got back to Asheville, I was dreading having to go to the hassle of sending the mirror back in the mail," Josh admitted. "That's when it occurred to me that maybe he'd allow me to take it off his hands." After a brief email exchange and a bit of bargaining, Moody agreed to allow Josh to purchase the mirror from him.

Imagine my surprise when I arrived at Josh's house for what would end up being my own first experience in the psychomanteum, and there on the wall hung Raymond Moody's personal mirror—the very same used by the likes of television journalist Diane Sawyer, and other famous guests who visited Moody's "Theater of the Mind." However, Josh had decided that, upon obtaining the mirror, it was time to retire it. Thus, instead of acting as a portal that would carry my mind toward another dimension later that evening, it seemed destined to remain on the wall in his living room as a centerpiece instead. Perhaps this was for the better anyway; Josh believed the mirror to possess a healthy bit of "juju," to borrow the term I once heard Moody's wife use while referencing it.

My initial experiences with the psychomanteum were uneventful at best, though I remember feeling an urge I likened to "holding back" during my early sessions. I envisioned entering the psychomanteum and placing myself before a formidable "gateway" of sorts; perhaps, if not a *literal* portal to alien realms, at very least it could open paths to whatever horrors might exist, hidden deep within my own psyche. As entertaining an idea as that of "spiritual dimensions" had been, where good and evil fought it out amidst bodiless specters, these weren't things I particularly cared to have leaping out of a mirror at me. Whether the psychomanteum merely produced "specters of the mind," as I liked to call them, or *truly* something else, as others had speculated, I knew that if my mind was the limit, I could expect just about *anything*.

As I sat down in the darkened room for the first time, my eyes just beginning to adjust to the light (or lack thereof), Josh remained with me for several minutes and described the setting, what I might expect to see, and finally, how to get to the state of mind where a visionary experience might occur. During those few minutes, I was far more relaxed, having Josh only a few feet away, and found myself instantly able to perceive strange visual distortions. As he spoke, and as my eyes became slowly capable of distinguishing shadows and other features in the room around me, I noticed that gazing into the mirror for long enough created a strange effect, like a reversal or "negative" version of the room. Not in the sense of a negative energy, but literally an exchange between light and dark attributes. Watching the mirror intently, the lightened walls, illuminated only by the black light behind me, seemed to darken. This strange effect was accompanied by a glow, which began to cast about the surface of the mirror, as though it insisted on being the only visible presence in the room. By this time, Josh was announcing that he would be back soon, reminding me that I would only remain alone in the psychomanteum for ten minutes this first time, after which he would come retrieve me. I closed my eyes, so that the light from the hallway wouldn't compromise my vision after getting accustomed to the dark, and once I heard the door close, I opened my eyes again, and kept them fixed on the mirror.

Again, I began to see this negative-space effect take place, something I would later hear another describe as the point where "the mirror exits." This would come and go, and I found it frustrating that blinking seemed to cause the effect to regress somewhat. Beyond the coming and going of the light and dark areas surrounding the mirror in this way, what I've described thus far comprises all I saw during my first session. I was fully aware that all this had been nothing more than a bizarre, but interesting sort of optical illusion. Still, I gathered that perhaps the strange sensations that occurred from stimulating one's vision—and mind—in this way *could* possibly induce an altered state of consciousness. Further, the series of questions that Moody described asking a patient prior to entering the psychomanteum, which often resulted a degree of emotional arousal, appeared to serve as a sort of catalyst for the later experience to come. Did the key to the appearance of "apparitions" actually lay in the series of questions Moody instructed us that the counselor was to ask of the grieving, prior to the actual experience?

I recalled being a bit disappointed after my third uneventful experience inside the psychomanteum (during which I further recall actually falling asleep for a short period). Perhaps, I reckoned, I was part of the "other fifty-percent" of Moody's demographic, representing those individual who didn't perceive *any* apparitions, visions, voices, or the like. Thus, I decided I would shift the focus of my studies toward what experiences others said they were having.

Only a few weeks later, an opportunity soon presented itself, during a visit Josh had with a few of friends from out of town. Among the group of visitors had been a young lady with the peculiar nickname of "Tigger", who, conveniently, had never heard of a psychomanteum. Rising to the occasion, Josh suggested that Tigger enter for a short session, which ended up lasting maybe thirty minutes. Prior to entering, she was given no information as to what a psychomanteum was, or what might occur within.

At the end of her session, she emerged in tears, saying that she had seen her deceased grandmother first appear in the mirror, and then *emerge* and enter the room, where she spoke to her! Much of the remainder of the visit was spent consoling the young lady, and explaining the strange nature of what she experienced.

Around this same time, during a telephone discussion with my friend Vance Pollock, he revealed that Josh had scheduled a session for him too, which would occur on the evening of Wednesday, July 2, 2008. I was interested in hearing what kind of an experience he would have, especially after hearing about Tigger's unusual "encounter." Vance always had been, and remains, one of the most intelligent, discerning, and reasoning people I know. Hence, I felt I could rely on his judgment, as far as being able to accurately relate the details and circumstances of any experiences he might have.

I was introduced to Vance at a small event we both attended at a restaurant in the Asheville area a few years ago. During the 1930s, it turns out that this spot had been the temporary domicile and headquarters of none other than William Dudley Pelley. A Nazi sympathizer and World War II political activist, it was Pelley who wrote about the striking manifestations produced by spirit medium Bertie Lilly Candler on a number of occasions (as described in Chapter one). Pelley had lived at various locations in and around the Asheville area prior to the war, and had published a variety of strange propaganda and occult material, including a book titled *Why I Believe the Dead Are Alive*. Also of particular interest was a pamphlet Pelley wrote called *Seven Minutes in Eternity*, detailing an out-of-body experience he claimed to have had around 1928.

For several years, Vance had been contacting Josh, urging him to "investigate" a few of the old haunts that Pelley had been associated with in his lifetime. Once we finally met and talked with Vance about Pelley's notorious activities and around the Asheville area, Vance became an instant friend, and regular associate of ours.

"Yeah, if you're not doing anything that evening, you should definitely come out with us," Vance said over the phone. "I'll be bringing Lee along as well." This also inspired me, since Lee Brooks, a high school friend of Vance's from Florida who had also relocated to Asheville, shared our bizarre interests in mysticism and the esoteric.

"Count me in," I told him. "I'll be there with bells on, scribbling notes about all this." Though I fully expected Vance's experience would be more or less similar to my own, I secretly hoped something weird, or even *extraordinary*, would take place the following Wednesday. While there were to be many similarities between our experiences, to my surprise, what Vance would recall from his experience ended up being far stranger. In fact, I doubt I could never have prepared myself for just how *dark* things would end up getting.

CHAPTER THREE

THE MIRROR EXITS: A TERRIFYING "TRIP" WITHIN THE PSYCHOMANTEUM

One moment everything seems normal, and the next moment a vision occurs. A surprising number of spontaneous apparitions of the deceased are seen in mirrors or other reflective surfaces.

-DR. RAYMOND MOODY, *Reunions:* Visionary Encounters
with Departed Loved Ones

I arrived at Josh's home on the evening of July 2 at about 7:30 PM. I was running late, and after a narrow brush with danger that involved his young (and very protective) Rottweiler, I made my entrance. Vance, Lee, and our charismatic host had been sitting around together in the living room, discussing one of Josh's latest adventures. It involved a project he had hoped to put together in Puerto Rico, after a cruise he recently attended and helped orchestrate with A&E television network. Josh was clearly very excited about this, as the better part of the next hour was spent discussing it. I accepted a cold beverage to bide my time; in the spirit of all this talk of Puerto Rico and the tropics, I asked for straight rum on ice, which I noticed Vance was also drinking.

Once the sun had gone down, presenting a dim environment more suitable for the psychomanteum experience, Josh turned out all the lights in the living room and lit candles in select places to create an eerie, ambient atmosphere. I imagined this being similar to what the ancient Greeks might have experienced when they would go and speak with the oracle of the dead. Our oracle however, instead of being some elderly, Mediterranean mystic, was the host of a popular Saturday night radio program, and with his broadcast-friendly voice, he asked everyone to make themselves comfortable on the couches in his living room. Everyone settled in, and Josh began a very calm, simple discussion with Vance.

Before long, I recognized a subtle shift into the same sorts of questions Josh had described several weeks earlier, intended to draw out emotion and, perhaps, a psychic semblance of the individual Vance would attempt to communicate with; a man named Guy Harwood, who whilst among the living, had known William Dudley Pelly during his time living in Asheville.

At this point in the narrative, as opposed to detailing each individual question Josh asked Vance,

I will opt to include the "raw" notes I scribbled in the dim candlelight that evening, as they seem to better express Vance's stream of consciousness as this was all taking place. To my surprise, in several instances the conversation seemed to draw a very emotional response from him, quite in contrast to Vance's normally very calm and subdued demeanor:

> Vance hopes to contact Guy Harwood, a contemporary of William Dudley Pelley.
>
> He feels that Harwood died "leaving himself open" to the possibility of communication with the dead. Vance hopes that, in the afterlife, Harwood may still "be willing to cross the barrier separating the life and afterlife realms."
>
> Vance's fondest memory of Guy Harwood: Vance described driving him through Biltmore, where Harwood would show Vance the old Galahad College. Guy had hopped a trolley and rode out to Galahad College as a young man, after reading an article about Pelley and his essay "Seven Minutes in Eternity." Harwood also described to Vance a pamphlet that he had received decades ago during the visit about "contacting the dead." Guy produced the same pamphlet, and handed it to Vance as they drove together.
>
> "Sixty years fell away," Vance said of Guy handing him the pamphlet during this visit, in March of 1995. It was the same Harwood had received from a young woman he met on the trolley so long ago, as he went seeking Galahad College and, ultimately, W. D. Pelley.

The young woman had worked there at the College in the 1930s, and upon meeting there on the trolley, she and Harwood returned to Galahad College together.

Again, Vance describes, "sixty years falling away," as he first shook Harwood's hand and received the pamphlet from him.

Vance's "prize moment" with Harwood: Vance describes standing outside the Grove Park Inn with a light snow falling. He describes this moment as being very surreal, and travelling around Asheville with the elderly Guy Harwood almost feeling as though he had travelled back in time with the man.

Vance's negative memories of Harwood: Vance's negative recollections are nonetheless endearing: "Folks said he was a smelly old guy with birdseed in his pockets." Vance considered him an "archetypal" man to whom pigeons flocked.

Vance felt "pathetic" that he could relate to Harwood, and also confessed of reading the old man's writings that "they weren't very good."

Guy described going to Mills River and meeting Bertha Allar, a popular medium who had told him "God has handed you a golden pen. You will write the textbooks of the Aquarian age." This occurred at an early age, and Harwood's sense of being and belonging seemed to stem from this event (also tells why and what he felt compelled to write, as described above).

Josh asks Vance what color Harwood's eyes were: Guy had "pale gray or blue" eyes. Josh asks what his teeth looked like: Vance asks him "which one?" Vance describes that Harwood "smelled like coffee and bananas." Vance says he once met a guy who claimed to have taken a bath at Harwood's apartment; having been homeless at the time, Harwood allowed him to bathe there.

This instance led Vance to believe that Harwood may have been "slightly pedophilic", and may have taken a "fancy to young boys." Harwood had once told Vance that a psychologist had instructed him that "surrounding himself with youth would maintain youth," as an explanation of his affinity for cutting out pictures of Macaulay Culkin, Fred Savage, and what Vance describes as "Norman Rockwell-type photos of young boys in various stages of undress," and pasting them on the walls around his apartment.

So far, the impression the rest of us were getting of the late Guy Harwood wasn't particularly endearing, although Vance emphasized that the man, in his advanced years, was a strange, often-confused, and altogether harmless collection of the weirdness he had accumulated throughout his life. Vance continued to share his unusual (and at times unsavory) recollections of Harwood:

He apparently would openly discuss masturbation and other "lewd subject matter", making him a "social leper." Vance describes overhearing a conversation Harwood struck up with a woman one day, where he began to describe, "knowing a man who had invented spirit television".

Vance felt like his "mission" of sorts was to care about him genuinely, and he describes visiting him many times after Harwood could no longer remember much of his life, shortly after suffering a stroke. As Harwood had lived most of the last years of his life alone, Vance seems to struggle slightly with this.

What did Guy Harwood feel like to the touch: "Guy Harwood to the touch was like a marshmallow; clammy, but electric." Vance describes Harwood as "having an electricity." Vance discusses feeling as though he wanted to "give something back" to Harwood when he visited him after the stroke, and mentioning certain names of people he had known would occasionally bring a "little sparkle" back into his eyes.

(Vance begins to break up slightly at this point, as he describes his last visits with Harwood, and again described feeling that he had "just needed to give.")

Vance describes having taken Guy Harwood to a meeting or a sort of "homecoming" where others related to Pelley had gathered together. Harwood was the "guest of honor", and Vance likened it to "going to someone's 80th birthday."

Vance feels like it was important to bring Lee along tonight because he was able to "share in the madness" with him, naming several books dealing with the "hollow earth", a subject that fascinated Harwood, who had been the personal assistant of Raymond Bernard.

Josh asks, "If you could speak to him now, for a couple of minutes, what would you say to the man?" Vance pauses for a long while... then replies, "For all the times that you felt that you were alone, I just want you to know that there are people who will keep looking to uncover these eternal truths." Vance says he appreciates that

Harwood was there in that period in history, and thanks him for sharing it with him.

"If not for guys like Guy Harwood, we'd all be ants on an ant hill," he says.

Vance describes his last meeting with Guy Harwood. He took his mom and his aunt along. He discusses squeezing his hand, and the ladies described him as a "sweet old man". "What a sweet spirit, what a kind man."

At this point, the "shift" Raymond Moody described, and which Josh subsequently discussed with me, became apparent; a total change in the atmosphere of the room became palpable, and Josh recognized it too:

> I didn't see it, but I heard it; Vance's arm slapping against his lap as he gave "the signal". Josh had described this to me before, and the instant at which it occurred, where "all had been said," was quite clear.
>
> Josh asks for a moment of silence after this. Vance remains silent for several moments longer, even after Josh asks "are you ready to see him again tonight?" Vance says, "We'll give it a try." Vance takes a book given to him by Harwood, a copy of Pelley's *The Golden Scripts*, with him into the psychomanteum.

After Vance entered the psychomanteum, we stepped outside with Josh while he smoked a cigarette, the rest of us reflecting briefly on the session and, particularly, Vance's recollections. Most conversation was casual at this point, and after a few minutes, Josh proposed a better way to pass the time rather than merely waiting for Vance's session to end.

"Let's try an experiment," he said, motioning for us to follow him indoors.

As we gathered again in the living room, trying to keep our voices down for Vance's benefit, Josh brought out a collection of small black ceramic bowls and plates, each of which he filled with water. These were meant to be used for scrying, functioning very similar to the way Edward Kelley had been able to visualize John Dee's Enochian angels. One begins by peering into the reflection on the surface of the water in the bowl—the dark color of the ceramic prevents one from actually seeing the bottom of the bowl at all, thus allowing the subject to gaze into "clear optical depth" as Moody had described of the mirror in the psychomanteum. After a brief period of meditative breathing exercises intended to "tune our minds," Josh dimmed the lights again, and had us begin peering into our scrying bowls. Similar to my earlier experiences in the psychomanteum, I found that our scrying bowls produced a few minor optical illusions as well. However, somehow the curvature around the bottom of the bowl I was using managed to capture enough ambient light in its reflection to create a pale, glowing half-moon form; this seemed to make it difficult to focus on the surface of the water. Sitting across from me, Lee was using a large deep plate instead of the rounded bowl I had been given, and seemed to be having more success at shifting his visual perception. Though our session provided only a few interesting optical occurrences, by now Vance was due to come out of his first session in the psychomanteum. Josh moved quietly down the hallway as we continued peering into our scrying apparatus, and eventually returned with Vance, who blinked furiously as Josh raised the lights again.

"So how was it?" Lee asked anxiously.

"Definitely plays with the senses," Vance replied. "Didn't see any apparitions, but the way that it plays on your vision is fascinating. You see the frame of the mirror quite clearly, but further on, say ten or fifteen minutes later, it would just drop out. It's as though the mirror exits."

I liked Vance's description of this process, familiar to me from my own sessions in the psychomanteum. "Something definitely gets *triggered* while you're sitting there looking," he continued. "I've been around a few mind altering substances in my day, and various aspects of all that definitely come to mind here also."

"Was there any sense that Harwood was there?" Josh asked hopefully.

"With him in mind," Vance said with a healthy pause, "there were certain similarities."

Josh was already preparing another experiment. Since Vance's first session had been uneventful (at least so far as seeing any apparition), Josh asked if any of us had ever experienced what is called the "Ganzfeld technique". Lee was familiar with it, and Vance had also heard of it, though neither he nor I had ever tried it. Josh removed small ping pong ball halves from a zip lock bag, and from looking at his props, we recognized the experiment was indeed familiar. Most of us could recall seeing images (like in Psychology text books, in my case) depicting a person with small white ping pong balls over their eyes, sometimes paired with headphones or other apparatus intended to provide enough sensory deprivation that the brain would be allowed to drift into a "theta state".

"I've tried this dozens of times," Josh explained. "The technique is designed to shift your mind into a theta state. See, right now, we're all in the beta state. The next state from here would be the alpha state, and going from here to there could be compared to..." As his voice trailed off, he seemed to really concentrate for a few moments on finding the right analogy. Then, with an irreverent grin, he said, "its like going to the john, and getting a bit reflective."

We laughed at his choice in analogies, though everyone seemed to know what he meant. "The theta state," he continued, "is the most fascinating state. Many mystics, like the Tibetan monks for instance, go into this state when they meditate. But the crazy thing about the Ganzfeld technique is that while monks in Tibet spent decades, maybe *centuries* learning to focus their meditations and achieve this, this takes you instantly—well, within three minutes or so—into a theta state. This is why some people refer to it instead as the 'Tibetan Technique'."

Later I would learn that the enigmatic, trance-like theta state also occurs just before we fall asleep, and when going into or emerging from a deep sleep. Similar to what Josh described, the human brain will enter the theta state during various forms of deep meditation, and several cultures have found that constant rhythmic tones, like the chanting of Tibetan monks or the beating of drums in many shamanic practices, seem to compliment these meditations. The fact that 4.5 "beats" or cycles per second corresponds to theta activity in the brain may have something to do with this, and many researchers believe that such meditative techniques, paired with specific rhythms, can be used to "tune" the mind to various brain states; much like tuning a radio to different stations. [1]

"The way we're going to do this tonight is particularly special," Josh continued. "Because to my knowledge, nobody has ever induced a theta state in someone before they entered a psychomanteum." Josh instructed us all to lie back in our seats and relax as he handed out the ping-pong shells. Placing these over our eyes, we began by staring straight upward, the shells illuminated from the front only by the lighting overhead in Josh's living room, which created a strange sense of "nothingness" before our eyes. We all remained silent as Josh dimmed the lights, instructing us as to what colors and other features he would introduce, and one at a time he would bring around different colored lights and pass them before our faces, each color producing different kaleidoscopic effects. I found quickly that I had a particular affinity for red, and recalled briefly seeing what appeared to be long, glowing slabs of "checkered" surfaces extending into the infinite, as well as occasional swirling patterns and geometric images. Blue light produced similar patterns, though not as pronounced as the effects produced by the red filter.

The relaxation that accompanied the meditative state of mind we were attempting to reach seemed to make me very drowsy; the fact that it was well after one o'clock in the morning by now surely didn't help my drooping eyelids. After several more minutes of the swirling colored light show, Josh turned the lights back on and told us we could remove the shells from our eyes. Indeed, this time *everyone* had experienced the colorful illusions he had promised, but by now I was of no mind to stick around and discuss it; I had been awake since six o'clock the previous morning, and thus, ended up parting ways with my company before Vance ever entered the psychomanteum for his second session.

I made it home by a quarter of two, but even at this hour I felt compelled to call Joshua the minute I walked in the door. Something had seemed terribly *off* as the evening tumbled into the early-morning hours, though I hadn't been able to unravel what exactly I had been feeling; was it foreboding? Somehow, what had begun as a session in the psychomanteum for Vance had evolved over the course of the night into a bizarre chef's salad of insightful experiments, paired with parlor tricks. Josh had obviously intended both to educate *and* entertain us with his experiments, and in spite of the occasion being planned for Vance, in a way I felt almost like Josh had catered to me the entire evening, as though concerned that I had begun to grow skeptical after so many uneventful sessions in the psychomanteum myself. I had experienced this before: Josh's tendency to "watch over me" at times, in an almost brotherly fashion. Before we left, he had urged each of us to take a pair of the ping-pong shells home with us and to continue experimenting with the Ganzfeld technique on our own time. Indeed, I couldn't argue that all Josh's experiments had been aimed at "altering consciousness," and after all, that had been the sole purpose of the visit. If this were the case—that he had hoped to give us our own unique "experiences"—then it had been a tremendous success. I left his home that night, feeling more interested and intrigued by all this than ever before, especially in lieu of our theta state experiments.

Still, none of this overpowered the sense that there had been an underlying *weird* sensation, and I began to wonder how the second session with Vance in the psychomanteum would go. Though tempted, and perhaps against my better judgment, I decided not to call Josh out of fear it may disturb Vance. I fired off a quick email instead, opting to wait until the next day to see what might have transpired in my absence, and fell asleep shortly thereafter.

Thursday was calm, more or less. I thought little of what might have happened after I left the night before, knowing that even in the wee hours of the morning, I could have expected a call if anything astounding had occurred. That phone call I secretly hoped for never came, though I assumed this was for the better, since by now I was long-due for a good night's sleep.

I eventually did receive an email from Vance the next afternoon. The subject line read "Bad Craziness," a term he had no doubt chosen with intent of evoking the unstable moods of the great gonzo poet, Dr. Hunter S. Thompson, as well as to hint at the foreboding content that would follow. I was eager to hear what Vance had to relate about his final session in the psychomanteum; little had I known it might be his last session ever.

Micah,

Thought I should recap for you, while trying to make sense of it myself, my second session in the psychomanteum. Creepy shit, my friend.

After the Theta experiment, I was completely disoriented and having trouble keeping my balance. When I re-entered the room and sat down the "mirror's exit" was immediate; phase-shift, screening out of my actual surroundings... I remember having to swallow rapidly for a minute to fight back the urge to vomit.

The next thing I remember I was staring into blankness and the mirror frame became visible again. I don't remember feeling so much like I had woken up as simply snapped out of some state of altered consciousness, kind of like coming down from a deep meditation session, which I've done probably a dozen times in a group setting at Science of Spirituality meetings in Winter Haven. This SoS group was hosted by the founder, Bill Achor, who died a few years ago while I was in Iceland. Had my old friend Bill Achor come through instead of Harwood?

I was trembling and uncomfortable. Joshua and Lee might be better witnesses of my state when I emerged from the chamber, but I was shaken up and feeling pretty down. Joshua offered a drink or a cigarette. I declined. I think I had a glass of water and then realized it was 5 o'clock in the morning! I had been in there for quite a while.

I told Lee and Joshua about what I could remember, or more notably couldn't remember, and they said they heard talking in the room. I swear I don't remember talking or making any noise whatsoever. I had moved the page marker in the Golden Scripts and I haven't read where it is, but that could prove interesting. I must say I'm a bit intimidated and not overly excited about going back in there. I have a feeling some very unwholesome things plagued my

mind during the blackout. Not related to
Guy Harwood I think, but more demonic;
maybe closer to the Crowley and Lovecraft
darkness that is obviously imbedded in my
psyche by now.

I think I had a "bad trip."

I was surprised that Vance described having one
of the most frightening and negative experiences to-
date in Josh's psychomanteum, perhaps within an
hour of my departure the night before. What else had
I missed?

Sensing the urgency of the situation, I contacted
Vance as quickly as possible by phone. He mentioned
that Josh and Lee, in the relative silence outside the
room in which he sat, had said they heard Vance
mumbling and even shouting during his final session.
After detailing various other aspects of his
experience, he finally told me, "Honestly, I'm a bit
intimidated about returning for a second round." I
listened intently, but glancing at the clock I suddenly
realized that in less than two hours Joshua and I went
live on his Saturday night radio show, *Speaking of
Strange* (of which I was producer at the time). I
stretched the conversation out as long as I could, but
already running late at this point, I had to cut our
phone call short, well before I felt like either of us
had gotten into the "meat" of the discussion.

At the radio station, Josh and his wife Lauren
arrived only fifteen minutes before we went on the
air. I was busy preparing all the equipment for
broadcast as they walked in the studio, leaving little

time to pick Josh's brain about this psychomanteum fiasco. Lauren told us on her way back out the door that she was headed to a nearby convenience store, offering to get us beverages or snacks if we needed them. Josh asked for an energy drink; I on the other hand was concerned that my extra-strong Sumatran coffee ("black gold" as I have often called it) might be a little more than I needed this late in the day anyhow. Once we were alone together in the control room, I had planned to leap on Josh with a number of questions, but to my surprise, before I could say anything Josh was asking if I had spoken to Vance since our gathering the previous Wednesday night.

"Well, he emailed me, and we spoke for just a few minutes earlier this afternoon right before I came up here" I said. "Seems he didn't have the best experience."

"To say the least," Josh added. "Did he tell you that Lee and I heard him talking from all the way over in the kitchen?" I acknowledged that, in his email, he had mentioned this. "We were standing there together, Lee and I, fixing a drink. Vance had been in there for a while at least, and all of a sudden we heard him talking. It sounded so strange that we even asked each other, 'is he talking to himself?' I had expected that sort of thing, of course, since many people have those kinds of subjective experiences in the psychomanteum. Not long afterward though, we began to hear his voice get louder and louder, and he seemed to be almost shouting at times—nothing coherent that we could make out."

Something humorous flashed through my mind; I asked Josh if this had been in any way reminiscent of the scene in Stanley Kubrick's film, *The Shining*, where Shelley Duval enters the room to find Jack Nicholson, asleep with his head lying on the desk in front of him as he suffers from a vivid nightmare, shouting incoherently. Josh agreed, somewhat amused, and continued.

"Finally, after a while we hadn't heard anything else, and Lee and I decided it might be best to go and get him. We were a little worried. Right that instant, as we approached the room where he sat, the door open, and he stumbled out."

"How did he act?" I wondered aloud.

"He wasn't in the best shape. He said he felt cold, disoriented, and seemed shaken. I offered him a drink, but he refused and poured himself a glass of water instead. We went outside after this, and Lee and I had a smoke. Vance literally almost fell down when he got outside, and told us his sense of balance seemed out of whack."

I listened intently to all this, never breaking eye contact with Josh. What he asked me next surprised me a little. "You don't think he's upset, or that he feels like I may have intended for his experience in the psychomanteum to turn out this way, do you?" I told him I didn't know for sure, but doubted it. I decided at this point that I would find out what Josh might have known about Vance's potential mindset beforehand, and asked him especially about what had occurred between the time I left and the beginning of Vance's second psychomanteum session.

"Well, the Ganzfeld technique wasn't the only experiment we tried. I also hooked up the Van de Graaff."

I had forgotten about this; Josh, Lee, and Vance had mentioned that they also planned to experiment with one of Josh's Van de Graaff generators right before Vance had his "bad trip." Essentially, a Van de Graaff is an electrostatic machine that features a moving belt within, which is capable of accumulating very high electrostatically stable voltages, which disperse around a hollow metal globe. Modern designs using these high voltage generators are capable of reaching potential differences of five megavolts, making them ideal for tasks such as driving X-ray tubes and accelerating protons for nuclear physics experiments. Josh's own experiments that evening had been much smaller-scale, and included such things as placing small, pyramid-shaped quartz "antennas" on top of the Van de Graaff's metal globe, then having Lee, Vance and himself lean over the unit together, allowing the static discharges to radiate directly upwards at their faces. It was becoming increasingly evident that Josh's experiments might have resulted in a consciousness-altering cocktail the likes of which no one, to our knowledge, had ever seen. True to form, Josh served it to Vance according to his own personal preference: hard and on the rocks.

"So Josh," I asked. "You never tried the Ganzfeld experiment to induce a theta state prior to entering the Psychomanteum with anyone else? What about *you*, had you ever tried it yourself?"

"No," he replied, "Vance was, to my knowledge, the first. And, as we've seen, his experience was clearly the most bizarre and disruptive that I've personally witnessed." Since the fact that they had also used the Van de Graaff was now coming to light, I asked him if anything else might have "stimulated" the environment for Vance.

I watched Josh's eyelids narrow around his pupils as he thought for a moment. "Oh wait, there was one more thing, and I forgot all about it until right when you asked me this. Do you remember that skull I used in the scene in my movie where I built that 'mock altar' and pretended to try and conjure Satan?"

Josh was referencing a 2008 documentary he produced, called *Inside the Church of Satan*. As the name implies, this film follows Josh as he travels to various locales to interview high-ranking members of the international organization known as Church of Satan, formed on April 30, 1966 in California by Anton Szandor LaVey. Upon completing the travel and interview segments of the documentary, Josh returned home and filmed several tongue-in-cheek segments involving mock-rituals and slayings, which he used to "lighten the mood" in various portions of the film. In one of these segments, he created an "altar" by draping a large portion of black cloth over a fixture, and then topped it off with a nude actress, our mutual friend Angella Adelle Blanton, stretched out across the top to form a "table". As a final garnish, he placed a large, horned yak's skull at one end.

I worked to stifle the smirk forming at the corners of my lips, as I acknowledged that I knew exactly which skull he was referring to.

"Yeah, just as a sort of afterthought I put it in the room, more for atmosphere than anything, facing the chair that Vance was sitting in, before any of you guys arrived. In fact, I had forgotten completely about it even being there." At this point, none of this seemed capable of getting any stranger. Poor Vance had entered Josh's homemade psychomanteum to try and contact a deceased old man who he had met by chance, and instead had some kind of episode as a result of mixing electrostatics experiments and a satanic yak's skull, among other things.

"Josh," I finally asked him, "and let me just say, I don't mean to sound at all as though I'm *accusing* when I ask this; but do you feel at all *responsible* for Vance's condition when he came out of there?"

After a brief silence, he finally answered. "Well, I certainly feel like I may have contributed to it."

That evening after an excellent radio show and an energetic interview with our guest, Timothy Green Beckley, Josh, Lauren and I went out together to a favorite local pub of ours for a late dinner and some drinks. Incidentally, Vance called, wanting to see what we were getting into. Josh and I were both eager to link up with him and discuss his experience, so once he arrived, we talked casually about it.

In spite of the "bad trip" he'd described earlier, the general consensus among us seemed to be that, whatever the circumstances, the result of the evening at Josh's had been fun, and thought provoking, to say the least. Though looking back, while the eager yearning for exploration might have been in our hearts and minds at the time, this series of "experiments" had been anything but controlled, or scientific. Looking back, I would liken them to being the intellectual equivalent to roughhousing, although they still served as an introduction—albeit a strange one—to different varieties of meditation techniques and mind-altering practices. I would return to many of these processes in later years, exploring them in greater depth, and under more controlled conditions.

Still, at that time, I was eager to ask Vance in private about particular things he may have seen, or at least what perspectives he had gained during his second session. We made arrangements to do an interview the following week.

PHANTOM DACHSHUNDS AND DEMONS FROM THE NETHER REALMS

On the afternoon we set aside for the interview, Vance and I, along with his son Sylvan, who was three-years-old at the time, stopped in at a little coffee house in the historic River Arts District of Asheville, where we mused on everything from the weird yak's skull, to the writings of H.P. Lovecraft as possible sources of the "negativity" he encountered in the psychomanteum. "I got to thinking about it, trying to recall whatever I could of that second session, and I don't know how long I was in there," Vance mentioned at one point. "I didn't consciously check a clock before I went in, but I know it was pushing five when I got out!" Vance believed the final session might have lasted close to two hours. Strangely, he asked if I knew whether "the dog" was ever back there in the psychomanteum room with him.

"Which dog?" I asked.

"You know, Lolly, the wiener dog?"

Josh's miniature dachshund, Lollie, was always kept in the back bedroom, where Josh's wife would be resting soundly during late-night romps such as these. "No, she doesn't go back in there," I assured him. "In fact, unless they kept the door open, I don't know how she could have gotten out of their bedroom." As odd as it seemed, Vance was convinced that some small animal had been in the room with him, sitting by his foot as he watched for the mirror to exit again, begging for attention.

"I remember an animal coming up to my leg. I even reached down to pet it, and I thought it was Lolly." Irked by the notion he was supposed to have been in there alone, Vance shifted his attention to the descriptions of hearing speech coming from the room during his second session. "Lee and Joshua said they thought they heard voices back there. Josh described it to me for the first time the other night like I was moaning, like some kind of reaction to something." Again, Vance began to relate this to the friendly little phantom that had been rubbing his leg. "Distinctly, I remember an animal being there, and I think it was the dog trying to get up in my lap. I remember thinking that it was interrupting me; kinda messing things up! But, it might turn out that that was actually part of the experience."

During our interview, I hadn't given this aspect of Vance's recollection much attention, since I knew that Lolly had been in the bedroom with Josh's wife at the time. Later, I would compare notes with Josh, who also agreed that there was no way Lolly could have been in the psychomanteum that evening. Vance, on the other hand, maintains emphatically that there had been some creature in the floor beside his chair.

Only in retrospect did the mystery of the "phantom wiener" become worthy of further consideration. I began to recall how in the introduction to his book *Pet Ghosts,* Josh briefly mentions thinking that the ghost of another miniature dachshund he and Lauren had owned years earlier might have been haunting their house. [2] The particular passage that came to mind details how Josh, known for his use of "ghost hunting" instruments like electromagnetic field detectors to measure subtle changes in energy present in a given environment, had used such tools in an attempt to determine whether the small dog's spirit had lingered around the property. Rather than the spectral formation of Guy Harwood, could Josh's deceased pet have been Vance's phantom? The notion seems bizarre in hindsight—*absurd,* even—but Vance and I acknowledged it as a humorous interpretation of what might have happened to him while in the psychomanteum that evening.

Changing gears, I decided to ask Vance about his state of mind right after the final session. "At the end," I asked him, "did Josh come get you or did you come out on your own?"

"Oh, I eventually walked out on my own," he said. "I became conscious again and knew exactly where I was, at whatever point, and I knew that there was nothing else going on." At this point, I asked him to elaborate on the "experiments" that he, Josh and Lee had done before entering again. He described "breathing electricity for a while" using the Van de Graff generator, with a crystal pyramid placed on top so it irradiated static charges and "spouts electricity." "We actually got on a stool and hovered above this and stared down into the funnel it created out of the top of this pyramid, and I remember breathing electricity, feeling the electric current running up my nostrils and straight into my head. So yeah, there were a lot of things that went on in between the sessions; it was a couple of hours before I went back in there and sat down. But when I did get back in there, the room was almost spinning, and the mirror "dropped out" like I was looking at this wall of static, and I got the sensation."

Probing further, I asked, "Do you think that it was Josh's intention to maybe try and amplify your experience in the psychomanteum?

"Well I don't know; I think probably in the end that it worked, but I think that Joshua was just showing off his 'toys' as much as anything. You know, we were kinda having a little down time between sessions socializing. It didn't seem like a very serious part of the session or like he had any particular intent."

In addition to the strange canine "apparition," as well as what factors might have had any negative effect while gazing into the mirror, I became curious about the darker elements of the experience. "What about the 'bad craziness' you described," I asked. "What was so dark about that second visit?"

"I got the sense of something very negative," Vance continued. "Josh said there was a skull on the mattress in front of us. And I may have been conscious of that. I may have discerned the outline of this skull on the mattress, here in front of me, and not made anything much of it." Regardless, Vance did seem to think some of the negative imagery might have influenced him. "Generally, if I'd walked out after sitting in there a couple of hours, the first thing I'd want to do is, you know, maybe have a smoke and have something to say about it. But I didn't 'bounce back' like that when I came out."

"What did you do?"

"I was a wreck," he said, a twinge of edginess leaking into his voice. "Josh asked me, 'would you like a cigarette?' No, no, don't believe so. 'Would you like a drink?' No, no... I believe all I did was go over to the sink and have a glass of water, and I had Lee drive me home shortly after that. I had a very ominous feeling. It was almost like... like a demonic presence, and I described it to Lee on the way back. That was the first time I had actually collected my thoughts." As we sat talking over our coffee, Vance's three-year-old son sat across the table from us, oblivious to our conversation, playing with a toy of some sort that had squeaky-voiced Muppet characters popping up as he pressed various buttons.

"Speaking of demonic, there's Elmo," Vance joked. At this point, it seemed that a bit of levity was necessary, and we laughed at the odd little noises Sylvan was creating with his toy. "Anyway," Vance continued, "I talked with Lee on the way back, and he told me about the 'voices' at that time, so there was no game to it; just that I had gone back in there that second time, and came out with a bad vibe. A really bad vibe... that's what I was thinking, that it was dark and ominous."

I asked him if he'd ever felt that way at Josh's during previous visits. He said no, and that he almost associated this "feeling" coming out of the psychomanteum the second time with an entity or "being" of some sort, though he was careful about insinuating anything that might seem like an exaggeration.

"It was sort of a dark personality. Not so much human, but almost a 'Lovecraft' thing, because you know I had read a lot of that stuff. That stuff's in my head, and hell, maybe Lovecraft was tapping into that subconscious element with his stories.

"I certainly think that's what it 'drew out' for me. If I had to explain that feeling, it's that it tapped into a very dark layer in my own subconscious."

TRIPPED UP: ENDOGENOUS PSYCHEDELICS?

Certain elements of Vance's experience were causing the candle of recognition to flicker in the back of my mind, as there were more than just a few things that seemed familiar. Though my general impression was that Vance had simply passed out and gone to sleep for a brief period during his second session, his description of various elements—particularly his perceived experience with the strange little dog-like "phantom"—led me to entertain another idea; if nothing else, for the sake of trying to understand ways that the mind could be "opened" to contact with other states of reality.

In his book *DMT: The Spirit Molecule*, Dr. Rick Strassman wrote of the groundbreaking research he conducted during a series of clinical DEA-approved tests involving dimethyltryptamine (DMT). The tests were carried out among sixty volunteers at the University of New Mexico between 1990 and 1995. [3] The powerful psychedelic properties of the DMT in these studies resulted in a number of visionary experiences, described by the various subjects, which bore striking similarity to each other. Among the descriptions were participants that reported seeing clowns, insect-like humanoids, reptilian entities, and "cactus-like" beings. Strangely, these beings would often appear to "examine" the subjects in what resembled clinical environments, already calling into question similarities between strange altered states of consciousness, and alleged UFO abductions.

Strassman supposed that DMT, being a naturally occurring tryptamine found in the human body, might be produced within the brain by the pineal gland. Under the right circumstances, an unusually large, "psychedelic" amount of DMT released into the body could account for various mystic, paranormal, and near-death experiences people in various cultures have described having for centuries. [4]

The problem is that we don't know what those "right circumstances" may be; not only to allow the pineal gland to produce a massive amount of DMT and release it into the bloodstream, but also to remove our body's natural constraints against this kind of thing happening frequently, and at random intervals. In past studies, certain proteins found within the pineal gland have actually been observed interfering with the activity of DMT-forming enzymes. For instance, during research with schizophrenic patients in the 1960s, it was reported that injecting these patients with "pineal extracts," presumably rich with these anti-DMT proteins, showed significant improvement to their condition. The introduction of these doses of the protein-rich extracts suggested that DMT imbalances might indeed be associated with the hallucinations that afflicted the schizophrenia patients. [5]

Thus, one might assume that the presence of these proteins, along with *monoamine oxidase* enzymes in the body that are capable of breaking down DMT molecules, would be prime acting agents which, if manipulated correctly, could alter the way naturally occurring DMT affects us.

Another interesting aspect of Strassman's research had to do with memory loss that occurred when large amounts of DMT were introduced into the body. When administering doses of 0.6 mg/kg or more, patients seemed to be less capable of remembering what they had experienced. [6] I was instantly reminded of this data when Vance described the lapse in memory that occurred right after the appearance of the phantom dog during his second session. Had he emerged from an altered state, with a strange prevailing sense of surrounding negativity? Thinking along the lines of Strassman's research, and ways that a psychedelic release of DMT by the pineal gland could be stimulated, I began to wonder if some of Josh's experiments that night could have affected Vance's mind in ways we hadn't yet considered.

The common ground between Moody and Strassman's work is clear; both wanted to isolate various aspects of the near-death or mystical experience in a laboratory setting. By breaking apart the elements in this way, they hoped the experiences might be more easily examined, and therefore better understood. With the fundamental similarities that exist between each of these areas of research, it stood to reason that drawing parallels between what Vance was describing in the psychomanteum, and what some of Strassman's volunteers had experienced, didn't seem completely far-fetched (though they could hardly be considered correlative, scientifically speaking). Shortly after interviewing Vance, I visited Josh again at his home, where we discussed several of these apparent parallels between various experiences.

"Whenever you take a chemical into your body," Josh said, "whether it is alcohol, or a cigarette, marijuana, LSD, a cup of coffee, or a bar of chocolate for that matter, all these chemicals do is change the pattern of electrical signals that are firing off in your brain. When Vance came here, we were doing a lot of experiments trying to directly change the pattern of electrical signals without needing a chemical, and that included using the Ganzfeld technique. Every time your eyes send light to the brain, it creates a certain structure of electric signals. The Ganzfeld technique can *change* that structure; but add to that the idea of exposing your brain *directly* to hundreds of thousands of volts of electrostatic energy! Altogether, that night Vance's brain went through such a wide range of different stimuli that it could have triggered an unusual response. I mean, there are so many variables that it's impossible to say at this point.

"So, once his brain had sort of been 'opened,' in a way, to all these different patterns, it probably put him in an unfamiliar state, because this is not the kind of thing you do normally. Then, when he went into the psychomanteum, which provides a setting of light-sensory deprivation combined with a lot of introspection, some of these areas of the brain that had been stimulated earlier were probably still sort of 'exposed,' and uncertain about all of these new experiences."

I asked Josh what he thought about the idea of an "endogenous" release of DMT, and whether he thought it could be a factor here. "It's possible with that combination of events that *anything* could have been released in terms of a natural chemical produced by the body," Josh said. "Therefore, as far as I'm concerned, if DMT can be naturally produced, given some unusual circumstances, I don't see any reason to discount that as a possibility for what happened to Vance; that he was undergoing what could be reproduced if you had just taken DMT or some other drug directly."

Some time after our discussion, I had an opportunity to ask Dr. Strassman about this also. I mentioned to him that many individuals who have described alien abduction experiences have also recounted severe electrical accidents that occurred early in their life, sometimes resulting in a form of "electrical hypersensitivity" that is known to cause hallucinations. I then asked Strassman if there had ever been studies or research that he knew of which might support the theory that one possible stimulus for a spontaneous release of DMT from the pineal gland might include exposure to electrical phenomena.

"Well first, the spontaneous DMT release ideas, and the pineal-DMT ideas, are only theoretical,"

Strassman told me. "We do not have data concerning either issue. We do know DMT is made in the body—lungs, brain, red blood cells; but we don't know its dynamics (that is, when it goes up and down, and under what circumstances), and we don't know if it's made in the pineal. That's one of the functions of the assay that we are developing at LSU in Steve Barker's lab, as described on our website (www.cottonwoodresearch.org). There are some electromagnetic field data studies on the pineal, but I am out of the loop when it comes to current pineal research, having left the field in the late 1980's when I began pursuing the DMT research. At that time anyway, it seems as if the data were suggesting the EMFs reduce pineal melatonin production." [7]

This was interesting, since I was already aware that melatonin is considered a "close cousin" to DMT among the other tryptamines. "This being the case, it's possible to *speculate* that other pineal metabolic pathways that are latent become more active," Strassman said, "and the *hypothetical* formation of DMT by the pineal could be one of these latent pathways."

The perspectives Josh and Dr. Strassman had each provided were fascinating, in that the culmination of ideas presented a unique interpretation of what, at least, *might* be at the heart of the psychomanteum experience. Shortly after discussing this prospect with Joshua, I decided there was only one way to find out for certain: we would recreate the circumstances Vance had undergone prior to his second session.

However, for it to be conclusive this time, I realized there would have to be one fundamental difference: this time, I would have to be the test subject.

Josh was accommodating so far as making plans for our final "experiment," and within a few days I returned to his home. Once I arrived, we talked for a while about what we planned to do, and hoped to achieve, then promptly went to work at helping me relax, and begin to shift my brain activity using the Ganzfeld technique. For this, Josh allowed me to experiment in the room where his psychomanteum was set up. I relaxed, stretched out on the bed (as this was also his guest bedroom) and placed the ping-pong ball halves over my eyes, staring straight upward in the direction of a light fixture in the middle of the ceiling. This lasted close to half an hour before I emerged—considerably calmed—and began helping Josh assemble the next experiment, which involved the Van de Graff generator. Within a few minutes, a decent static charge had built up on the surface of the metal globe that capped the machine, and Josh had me lean over the device, peering right into the steady streams of electricity rising off the tiny quartz pyramids he placed on top. I felt the funny prickling of static electricity leaping at my face, and could smell the metallic twang of ionized air as it entered my nostrils. Finally, after several minutes of this, I felt I was ready to enter the psychomanteum.

On my way into the room, I had to admit feeling the slightest sensation of dizziness, which was accompanied by a mild sense of dread. Sensing this himself, Josh asked me if I was certain I still wanted to do this.

"Of course," I told him, forcing a smile.

"So be it," he replied, flipping the lights off in the room as he closed the door. Again, I was bathed in the familiar darkness, and from where I sat the first thing I noticed was the ridiculous-looking satanic yak's skull on the bed. I grinned, trying to use it as a vehicle to help me relax, and shifted my focus back to the mirror.

"The mirror's exit" came quickly. However, as promising as this session had seemed, several minutes, then a half hour or more passed, and I saw very little in the way of the "apparitions" I hoped might appear. There were no spirits of the dead, no phantom wiener-dogs, and not so much as a glimpse of Cthulhu's dark, writhing tentacles. There was, however, one interesting thing that occurred during this session which may be worthy of mention: it involved a bizarre pattern of shapes and images I witnessed—though vaguely—where in a few fleeting moments I do recall seeing what could be likened to anthropomorphic shapes with enlarged heads. Even as I stared at these shapes, I found their silhouettes to be similar to that of stereotypical alien "grays." I freely admit that these images, rather than visions or hallucinations, had merely been the culmination of my hopeful expectations. I also wondered if strange, human-like shapes of this sort—aliens, "Lam", or otherwise—might represent archetypical elements that reside within every person's subconscious?

In my opinion, although the effects I witnessed certainly couldn't be likened to the intense phantoms said to emerge during some people's psychomanteum sessions, I was still very intrigued by the idea. I took described my impressions to Josh, and wondered if the sorts of things some people experience could be purely a result of what already exists within a person's psyche, as Vance had considered of his own experiences. Perhaps I had subconsciously thought of Crowley's "Lam," or maybe my general fascination with aliens and UFO subcultures had somehow bled through, presenting the faintest of echo of something *almost human* during my experience. In conclusion, as intrigued as I was—and regardless of the way Vance's mind had reacted in the same circumstances—my experience had altogether been a calm one.

I accepted, again, that I must be part of Moody's *other* fifty percent.

People's bizarre recollections, like those which Vance and countless others had described after their psychomanteum experiments, did provide evidence of what might be considered "pathways" to other realms, of sorts; even if these "places" were merely unique venues at the remote corners of human consciousness itself. The key to triggering such experiences seemed to lie hidden within the mysterious altered states of consciousness that our minds occasionally enter. Here, all the hidden inner-workings of the mind—as well as the possibility of external realities less often seen—must lay waiting.

All of these possibilities had quite effectively begun to steal my imagination. Many people in ages past, and perhaps many more today include scrying, mirror gazing, and other implements of magic in their attempts at establishing contact with other realms. The profound implications I had already begun to find myself aware of regarding the workings of the human mind only added to my growing interest. But what about other methods of contact, or more specifically, other *instruments* used for purposes of achieving altered states of consciousness? Over the years, Moody's psychomanteum had obviously been successful in linking some individuals with places that exist beyond the everyday living experience; a handful of them were now people I knew personally. Might there be other ways to do it?

I couldn't deny that there were other avenues worthy of consideration; tools used by modern mystics, the likes of Ouija boards, that could elicit even greater results than what I had experienced thus far. Considering the possibilities seemed frightening, though exactly *why* this was the case escaped me; could it have been, for instance, the idea that a device so simple as a planchette darting around on a board covered in letters might actually bring forth demonic personages from the depths of hell? Was it fear of a genuine possibility, or do such things stem purely from ideas made accessible to us through Hollywood, and a film industry that uses otherwise mundane things to produce frightening stories, the likes of William Peter Blatty's *The Exorcist?*

I found it interesting that, returning again to John Dee and Edward Kelley's "spirit conferences," Kelley alleged that while peering into their shew stone, the "Enochian angels" would often communicate their messages—one letter at a time—by pointing at huge boards covered in symbols. What if some hidden aspect of the mind governs the "magic" we witness when employing letters and pointing devices as magical tools, much the same as Moody said would occur in the psychomanteum? If an item such as the popular Ouija board could present access to such potential knowledge, were there legitimate concerns that should be considered first, and how might people protect themselves from harm, mental or otherwise?

After the experiences with the psychomanteum, my mind was riddled already with such questions. I couldn't resist the notion of exploring other potential tools of divination, and accepted that stranger things lay in the immediate future; but I get ahead of myself.

CHAPTER FOUR

CONVERSATIONS WITH GHOSTS: OUIJA BOARDS, AUTOMATISM AND OTHER ODDITIES

During the last 20-25 years I have had considerable personal experience with persons who have complicated their lives through dabbling with the Ouija board. Out of every hundred such cases, at least 95 are worse off for the experience."

-MANLY P. HALL, *Horizon Magazine, 1944*

In 2007 while guest hosting the afternoon radio program *Take a Stand* in Asheville, North Carolina, Josh and I had the privilege of interviewing Ellis Paul, one of America's most talented "Boston-style" singer-songwriters. Ellis will tell you his unique style of songwriting grew out of Boston's thriving folk scene, seasoned with the influence of its colleges, as well as the inevitable radio stations and listening rooms that surround them. With due respect to his hometown, I'd also wager that a healthy dose of the humble troubadour's talent is God-given, which nonetheless speaks of the heart found in his poetic appeal and melodic genius. However, I can also say with certainty that at least one of the many memorable songs in his repertoire actually draws inspiration from some place other than divinity, and if anything, stands as testament to the stranger aspects of this world.

"I have a song called 'Conversation with a Ghost' that's about my one weird paranormal experience," Ellis told us. "I was out for a run with a buddy of mine named Vance in Boston, and he said 'why don't you come over for dinner?' I said sure, and before we left we sat and had a glass of eggnog, since it was around Christmas time.

"Once we got over to his place, his girlfriend, Margaret, was working on dinner in the kitchen, and I said 'Well what have you been up to?' She said, 'I just bought this Ouija board for a dollar at a garage sale.' She said she'd kinda been addicted to it, talking to some 'spirit' with a friend of hers named Beth. She'd been on it like most people get on the Internet, just going haywire. I told her, 'You know, I'm kind of a doubter on that kind of thing, so why don't we get it out as part of the dinner party?' I thought we'd take it for a spin, and see what happens.

"There were about fifteen of us there, and we went into the living room. I was the one asking

questions to the ghost, whose name was 'Pug'—
Margaret Putnam was her real name, but 'Pug' was
sort of a handle she apparently used communicating
through the Ouija board. I asked Pug, with Beth and
Margaret on either side of the board handling the
little wooden triangle, 'what song did I play last
night?' It spelled out R-A-I-N. Sure enough, the night
before I had played a song called 'Let it Rain'." The
singer laughed this off, saying half in jest that "if
you're gonna pick a title for a song, 'rain' might be in
a good percentage of them." This first coincidence
was, perhaps, easiest to write-off, but from this point
things continued getting stranger.

"Then, I asked 'what's the name of my booking
agent', which was something I knew neither of the
women operating the Ouija board new. It spelled out
G-E-R-M-A-N-E, or *Germaine*," Ellis remembered.
Indeed, this was the name of his booking agent,
although he points out that Pug "misspelled it by one
letter." In spite of being correct, Ellis joked that there
must not be a spell check feature on Ouija boards,
and admitted that he "kinda let that one go, too.

Then I asked it, 'What did Vance and I have to
drink before we came over here?' It spelled out N-O-
G, and I got up and I locked myself in the bathroom
for a while, freaked out. I ended up writing a song
about it, based on someone who had passed away,
using a Ouija board to communicate." [1]

"Wow," I remember saying, right before we had
to go to a commercial break. Already a fascinating
story, I couldn't imagine it getting any weirder, but it

certainly did. During the commercial, Ellis went on to explain off-air how he managed to satisfy his own curiosity about the experience, and in doing so, became convinced he had communicated with a form of spirit-intelligence.

"What's even weirder about that story is that, after I calmed down a bit, I decided to go down to the Courthouse and dig through records to see if I could find "Pug" anywhere in Boston's history, since she had told Beth and Margaret a few things about herself. For instance, she had been married to a doctor, and also described roughly the time and circumstances of her death. Sure enough, looking around I found that a Margaret Putnam had not only existed, but had lived there in Boston, and even married a prominent doctor operating in town at the time. I was floored."

Fortunately for Ellis, his experience seemed to have been a pleasant one, with what is perhaps the most infamous of all items used in the practice of divination. However, there are countless stories of people's experiences, where the choices in using Ouija boards as the medium between realms were anything but pleasant. In addition to stories recounting frightening experiences with the devices, traditionally there have been many that look to biblical passages as evidence of their wicked nature, such as this passage from Deuteronomy 18:10-11, which reads:

> There shall not be found among you anyone... that useth divination, or an observer of times, or an

enchanter or a witch, or a charmer, or a consulter
with familiar spirits, or a wizard or a necromancer.[2]

Similarly, many interpret the Quran to be con-
demning of such activity, calling it "an abomination":

> O ye who believe! Intoxicants and gambling,
> (dedication of) stones, and (divination by) arrows,
> are an abomination; of Satan's handwork: eschew
> such (abomination), that ye may prosper. [3]

Regardless, the use of such implements for
seeking advice from the spirit realm has existed for
centuries. Early historical mention of Ouija-like
devices appear in China beginning around 1100 BC,
although the rise of the Ming Dynasty saw the more
frequent use of the *fuji* method of divination, which
involved the use of a stick or stylus crafted from the
branch of a willow or peach tree, roughly resembling
a dowsing-rod. [4] Similar practices were beginning to
emerge in ancient Greece and Rome by around 540
BC, as Pythagoras and his students are widely
believed to have used some sort of table mounted on
wheels (resembling a modern planchette, the heart-
shaped pointing device used on the surface of Ouija
boards) to communicate with the netherworld. [5]
Many historians dispute the "Pythagorean
scenario", although it is far more difficult to question
the obvious prevalence of planchette writing, thanks
to the creation of the Ouija board in America during
the nineteenth century. By the 1890s, planchettes

had become a novelty item, largely due to the Modern Spiritualism Movement. Two businessmen, Elijah Bond and Charles Kennard, leapt on the idea to combine the planchette with a board featuring the alphabet, and together on May 28, 1890 filed for patent protection of their new idea. This was the first official Ouija board to be marketed and sold, with production duties being given to an employee of Kennard named William Fuld in 1901. It was Fuld who first produced the famous talking boards under the name "Ouija," which of course became synonymous with the modern Ouija board. However, Fuld also took liberties with the product's design, even going so far as to reinvent the history of its creation, claiming that he had actually invented the device, and that his employers had stolen its design.

Eventually, several companies began to produce the Ouija boards; Fuld sued as many of them over the "Ouija" name as he could, fighting to stamp out any similar products up until his death in 1927. With the items having grown in popularity, in 1966 Fuld's estate sold the business to the famous maker of children's games Parker Brothers, who today holds all trademarks and patents for the item, although other brands and names do still exist. [6]

As Ellis Paul suggested, recounting his own initial perception of Ouija boards, it is widely understood by the scientific community that the "magic" behind the Ouija board is far less than spiritual in nature. Instead, *ideomotor action* or *automatism* is believed to lie at the heart of the mystery; this entails tiny, subliminal movements made by those whose fingers rest against the board, and though unaware of the movement themselves, participants nonetheless may be amazed to watch the planchette as it drifts with apparent meaning from one letter to the next. [7] The trouble, of course, seemingly arises when attempting to explain the occasional surprising circumstances that emerge with Ouija boards. Someone, or perhaps *something*, seemed capable of answering Ellis Paul's questions, in spite of the fact that he had no direct contact with the board, and at least as far as we know, those operating the planchette had no knowledge of the answers themselves. Whatever force may have allowed the correct answers to be given remains elusive, unless we consider the troubling idea that the deceased Margaret Putnam *did* somehow communicate them from the afterlife.

If you ask around, you'll quickly find that everyone seems to know *somebody* that has had a "Ouija board experience." Some of the individuals I've queried describe downright frightening things, while others are mundane, or even humorous. Several years ago, I had at one point been tasked with answering emails from people around the world who would write to a group I was part of, with questions pertaining to the unexplained. One of the earliest stories I received was sent by a young man in Australia named Artemis, who had recently acquired an antique Ouija board, found by his mother in a thrift shop. The device had been given to Artemis around the same time his grandfather, with whom he was very close, had passed away. Thus, in an effort to make contact with his deceased spirit, Artemis began to use the Ouija board regularly.

In his initial emails, Artemis had merely been asking if Ouija boards were safe to play around with. In subsequent messages, however, he began to reveal more of the circumstances that led to his inquiry. Apparently, during an early attempt to establish contact with his grandfather, Artemis began receiving messages almost instantly. Asking the spirit to identify itself, he was surprised when it claimed to actually *be* his grandfather; even stranger, his deceased patriarch had these words of wisdom to share: *Don't use Ouija boards!*

Fortunate for Artemis, there was obvious humor (and a strong dose of irony) in his experience. Whether or not the message did actually come from his deceased grandfather, I advised that he proceed with caution, at very least.

Too many times to count, I've been told horrific tales of people's encounters with what appeared to be "evil entities" while using Ouija boards. While taking these stories with a grain of salt, arguably, it is not the device itself that is evil; instead, it is presumed to be the "open conduit" these devices can provide—whether to places in our minds, or someplace else—that appears to be the real trouble.

The Little Girl from "H-E-L" and Other Terrors

One of the most disturbing stories of a "demonic" presence supposedly manifesting during the use of Ouija boards was shared with me years ago, while I was still in high school. A good friend of mine named Chris had gone through a period where he and his girlfriend at the time had dabbled with Ouija boards. From a position of general wariness at the outset, he progressed to curiosity, and finally, came to be fascinated with the idea that "spirits" might manifest and communicate through these devices. Every other night, he and his girlfriend would wrap up their dates by heading back to her house, and using the Ouija board to ask various questions.

One evening, the board began to relay messages to them, which produced a rather strange story. Claiming to be the deceased spirit of a young girl who had lived during the early 1800s, she asked the couple if she could be "reborn" into the body of the first child they would have together years later.

"I wasn't particularly thrilled to hear this," Chris told me, so he began asking questions of his proposed spirit-donor. "How did you die?" he asked. The girl had apparently died of consumption, and after a few more questions, Chris then asked the strange spirit where it was *right then*, at the very moment it was speaking with them. "The planchette began to spell the letters 'H-E-L.' Then I asked it, 'why are you in Hell if you died of Tuberculosis?' The letters 'I-K-I-L' were spelled, meaning *I kill*. I asked one final question: what are you? We watched as the letters 'D-E-M...' were spelled out, and sensing something truly horrific, my girlfriend and I moved the planchette up to 'goodbye' as quickly as we could.

"We never touched Ouija boards again after that."

Though Chris' story remains one of the most frightening first-hand encounters I recall hearing, not every instance I've had related to me has been quite so terrifying. Perhaps my very earliest knowledge of a Ouija board came from my mother, who talked about experimenting with one back in her teenage years, after school one day in the company of a friend. According to my mother's testimony, what she presumed to be the spirit of a young man named "Ralph" began to tell them how he died in a car accident a decade earlier. He told about driving a convertible, which rolled off a bridge and into a river, pinning him underneath. In addition to the details of his own demise, "Ralph" seemed to possess knowledge of things occurring in the lives of my mother and her friend; needless to say, they found it startling to be receiving such intimate details from a plastic cursor moving across a foldable game board. The experience frightened my mother so badly that she, too, swore she would never use Ouija boards again.

Strange interventions, which some credit to spiritual forces, have sometimes worked as strong deterrents for those who intended to use Ouija boards. Famous talk radio host Art Bell, creator of the late night radio program *Coast to Coast AM*, often cited an experience he had with a Ouija board as something he "tried to forget." Though he never divulged any specific details, he warned his listeners "never to use one... ever." As cryptic as his warning sounded, Art's advice apparently wasn't enough to deter his successor, George Noory, who in the summer of 2007 publicized that he intended to carry out a Ouija board experiment live on the radio, despite the objections of one of his in-studio guests, Jordan Maxwell. Other guests for the occasion, including writer Rosemary Ellen Guiley, Dr. Bruce Goldberg, and Jerry Edward Cornelius, author of the book *Aleister Crowley and the Ouija Board*, hoped to encourage George's participation. However, within the hours leading up to the broadcast, Noory claimed that "unfortunate events" had begun to plague his friends and family—even the family members of a Bishop he had consulted on the matter, who sustained serious injuries in a car accident. Taking the air that night, Noory said that the overwhelming response he had gotten from listeners (he claimed it was close to 90%) expressed opposition to the experiment. After recounting a near-death experience he had in 2000 and, citing the bad luck that many people close to him had suffered as further reason for concern, he canceled the experiment.

Paranormal researcher Jason Offutt describes Ouija boards as what he calls "active invitations" to evil and negative entities, whereas things so simple as alcohol and drugs might actually serve as "passive invitations" to the same (it is worthy of noting here that co-founder of Alcoholics Anonymous Bill Wilson was known to have used a Ouija Board to contact spirits frequently. Due to this, his participation in the AA program was hindered for a time, though Wilson claimed that he received the famous "twelve step method" directly from such spirit intervention). [8]

Similarly, writers Ed and Lorraine Warren warned that "Ouija boards are just as dangerous as drugs." [9] For decades, the Warrens famously expressed their belief that "séances and Ouija boards and other occult paraphernalia are dangerous because 'evil spirits' often disguise themselves as your loved ones—and take over your life." [10] This sensationalistic idea has been further popularized in fiction, mostly thanks to William Peter Blatty's *The Exorcist*, in which a young girl named Regan conjures an ancient Sumerian demon called Pazuzu. This, of course, is achieved through Ouija board communication with an entity she refers to as "Captain Howdy," who possesses her mortal body and causes a variety of horrific disturbances.

For such reasons, many have warned against the lure of the unsuspecting plaything, although the stereotypical evil associated with the Ouija board dates back even further. In 1924, Dr. Carl Wickland wrote that, "the serious problem of alienation and mental derangement attending ignorant psychic experiments was first brought to my attention by cases of several persons whose seemingly harmless experiences with automatic writing and the Ouija board resulted in such wild insanity that commitment to asylums was necessitated." [10]

Several decades later, paranormal researcher Martin Ebon probed the alternative notion that such occult means of divination actually tapped negative forces from the other side. His book *Satan Trap: Dangers of the Occult* warned, "it all may start harmlessly enough, perhaps with a Ouija board... (bringing) startling information... establishing credibility or identifying itself as someone who is dead." Ebon warns that it is common for individuals to feel "chosen" for a "special task." He continues, "Quite often the Ouija turns vulgar, abusive or threatening. It grows demanding and hostile, and sitters may find themselves using the board compulsively, as if 'possessed' by a spirit, or hearing voices that control or command them." [11]

Conversely, psychologists see the negative effects of Ouija board use as resulting from a dissociative state. In his book *Pseudoscience and the Paranormal*, author Terrence Hines argues that, not only is the physical act of unknowingly moving the planchette a result of an induced altered state, it is also the underlying cause for the negative reactions many have from prolonged Ouija board experimentation. "A dissociative state is one in which consciousness is somehow divided or cut off from some aspects of the individual's normal cognitive, motor, or sensory functions. These states can be found in differing degrees of severity and underlie such nonparanormal phenomenon as hypnosis, hysterical disorders, and the rare psychiatric disorder of split or multiple personalities. The dissociative state also explains several other impressive phenomena associated with the séance," Hines says, obviously alluding to things like channeling and possession. [12]

This notion of possession and other interventions perceived as "evil" taken into consideration, many would no doubt find it strange that Aleister Crowley, heralded during his lifetime as "the wickedest man alive," actually described ways one might protect themselves from such outlying forces. As described by occult researcher J. Edward Cornelius in his book *Aleister Crowley and the Ouija Board*, Crowley advised of Ouija board use that:

> There is, however, a good way of using this instrument to get what you want, and that is to perform the whole operation in a consecrated circle, so that undesirable aliens cannot interfere with it. You should then employ the proper magical invocation in order to get into your circle just the one spirit you want. It is comparatively easy to do this. [13]

As simple as Crowley made it sound, preparing a consecrated circle with intention of drawing in a single, desired entity might be more difficult than it sounds. In his book, Cornelius states that an inexperienced person sitting down before the Ouija board and merely asking, "Is someone there?" is a dangerous practice, and that "You must know exactly who is being summoned and from where. You do not want to blindly open a doorway into the lower astral plane." Doing so, he warns, only allows one to open themselves to communication from what he calls "a lower elemental" or lesser spirit, or perhaps even so little as "a lucid window whereby uncontrolled imagery from the subconscious mind is allowed to ramble forth, filtering into reality." [14] Cornelius also points out that, in spite of the dangers Crowley warned of, the magician did advocate the use of Ouija boards as implements in conjuring entities from other dimensions. Much like the bizarre "sex magick" that Crowley practiced, the taboo elements presented by spirit communication through magical means, as well as the apparent notion that people working together can more easily open a "doorway" to other realms, relates directly to the Ouija board.

ALIENS BY NUMBERS: CODED MESSAGES FROM OUTER SPACE?

The "spiritual pathways" believed to exist by Ouija board users aren't merely windows for spirits of the dead, or even disembodied spirits like angels or demons. In keeping with early twentieth century mediumistic pursuits that interchangeably sought to contact spirits and alleged "Space Brothers," some have even claimed that alien beings may occasionally use Ouija boards to transmit messages from other

worlds, or even the future. Gary Val Tenuta, author
of the book *The Secret of Nine*, described a strange
Ouija board experience he shared with his friend
Tom, whom he became acquainted with in 1967 at a
Military Serviceman's YMCA in Long Beach,
California. [15] After their time in the service together
ended, Tom came to visit one day—along with his
new Ouija board—at the apartment Gary and his wife
Edie had just rented. The first sessions the group
shared with the Ouija board were fairly typical,
involving various communications with presumed
spirits of the dead. However, during a later session a
list of strange words began to appear, leading the
three participants to believe they were receiving
direct communications from what, in their minds,
could only be extraterrestrials.

It began as an uneventful evening with the Ouija
board. Tenuta describes that he and Tom had nearly
given up, when suddenly the planchette began to
respond; strange words were soon appearing, the first
of which was "SPECTOR." After a brief pause, the
next word, "MIND", appeared, followed by "YOU"
and "EARTH." The final word in the strange series
was "GREK 5", which Tenuta describes as having
been "spelled" on the Ouija board with "a very
deliberate motion."

More words were eventually imparted, with many
of the phrases, especially "GREK 5" being repeated.
At one point, Tom began to recount a dream he
remembered having years prior to the experience,
which he had shared with Gary back during their
days at the Long Beach YMCA. In the dream, he was

being pursued by "something," and recalled hearing a voice shout that his pursuers were near. "It was the Greks!" Tom confided to Gary as they sat scribbling the words spelled by their Ouija board. "Look out! The Greks are coming!" Eventually, Gary and his company would come to interpret the bizarre information being related to them as a message from alien beings, living on a planet called Grek-5, in another dimension they described as existing "...in your future time."

What was the riddle of the messages the men received? Could something like contact from an alien intelligence *actually* be achieved using Ouija boards as a medium for communications from elsewhere in space... *or even time?* Or are such experiences purely a fanciful projection of science fiction, once again stemming from within the eye of the beholder?

For believers, the Ouija board, as well its mirror-gazing cousins like the psychomanteum, present a compelling arsenal of tools that may provide, as an Episcopal priest described to me once upon a time, "physical handles for spiritual realities that exist unseen." Skeptics, on the other hand, see such implements of the occult as windows into the deeper nature of the human psyche, rather than devices that can literally make contact with other realms.

Giving consideration to both perspectives, and the myriad mysteries presented by the inner-workings of the human mind, only fueled my growing interests. If other realms—or possibly infinite numbers of other dimensions—truly do exist, one almost can't help but consider what avenues would best lead to a deeper understanding of them. Specifically, I wondered if mysticism and meditation, as practiced by the monks and mystics of the East, could open similar paths to these "inner realms" which I sought, and perhaps allow people to train their minds to ease into these altered states over time. This, as opposed to the more forcible ritualism comprising what is traditionally called "magic," seemed to represent a maturation of thought over the ages, in relation to finding the *true* source of the mystical.

Indeed, powerful adepts of the magical arts like John Dee, Aleister Crowley, and others had once believed they could use the tools of magic to bring angels, demons, and possibly interstellar visitors into this realm. But what if the meditative and mystical arts, with their introspection, could present more lasting truths about the true nature of the mind... perhaps on some higher plane of consciousness?

PART TWO

MYSTICISM

CHAPTER FIVE

THE MYSTICAL OTHERS: A LOOK AT THE
DEVELOPMENT OF MYSTICISM

The most beautiful and profound emotion one can experience is the sensation of the mystical. It is the source of all true science.

-ALBERT EINSTEIN

So far as we have learned, man cannot escape the Other. Beyond even our highest resonating principles of religion and doctrine, we as humans strive to connect with something beyond, above, or "other" than what is visible to us in our daily lives. Scholars and sages alike have pondered this since time began, and for many, mysticism remains something that escapes us more today than at any point in our history. While the attainment of enlightenment through mysticism often seems intangible, perhaps the true goal of its practice is actually to find harmony and unity within the confines of the sacred journey itself, rather than to covet what may lie at its end. After all, one is considered lucky to merely be shown the "path"; to relish this and learn from it, however, is the key to enlightenment. Surely, this is best illustrated by the adage, "I know not where I am going, but I am on my way."

Around the time I began writing this book, I found myself in this intermediate area of discovering my "path," when I began studying mysticism as part of the research process. Initially, when I would focus on the term *mysticism*, I had no trouble associating it with things like meditation, yoga, or other things deemed to represent the "inner arts." However, trying to actually define "mysticism" presented an issue. The harder I tried to understand it as a concept all to itself, the further from it I seemed to get. As the mystic scholar Evelyn Underhill wrote, "Mysticism, in its pure form, is the science of ultimates, the science of union with the Absolute, and nothing else." [1] In Underhill's definition, her *Absolute* equals God, the creator. Indeed, here mysticism is perhaps best defined as the search for oneness with the great cosmic forces of creation, or a creator (which, in itself, could be considered as a sentient intelligence operating apart from humanity). Even still, attempts at defining the elements that unite to form the heart of mysticism resulted in the opposite of what I had expected, and presented a new string of questions, rather than the solid answers I hoped to find.

I became perplexed by this; how does one manage to describe something, when its elements are less concerned with "what is" than "what isn't?" Of equal profundity was the idea that, regardless of its ability to escape us when sought out, we all nonetheless seem to be "carriers" in a way, with the most basic components of true mysticism hidden within each of us, waiting to spring to life after being urged by some unseen force at the right moment in our lives. Being so fundamental to humanity, mysticism might act as a form of intermediary, I thought, utilizing common themes to bridge the subjective nature of our inner experiences.

Underhill so lucidly brought this to attention in her book *Mysticism: The Nature and Development of Spiritual Consciousness*, where she said that the mystic experience "forms a body of evidence, curiously self-consistent and often mutually explanatory, which must be taken into account before we can add up the sum of the energies and potentialities of the human spirit, or reasonably speculate on its relations to the unknown world which lies outside the boundaries of sense." [2]

I was fascinated by the idea that a *true* spiritual union between our inner selves, and perhaps things that stem from outside consciousness, could be more than just philosophical interpretations of shared human experience, written into world religions since ancient times. Instead, and in a very real sense, it became evident that an actual exchange between things both *inner* and *outer* lies at the heart of mysticism, and the essence of the mystical way shows us that separate manifestations of either of these, one without the other, could not exist.

EARLY DEFINITIONS: ANCIENT GREECE

Among the earliest attempts at capturing the essence of mysticism in writing appeared in Greece, during the classical period. Plato famously polarized these elements of the inner and outer consciousness in his dialogues *Alcibiades* and *Theaetetus*, in which the terms *ta eso* (inner things) and *ta ekso* (outside things) appeared respectively. [3] Both were likely precursors to *esoterikos*, a term that would appear more than five centuries later in acclaimed satirist Lucian of Samosata's work, *The Auction of Lives*. [4]

Ironically, Lucian was the first writer of his day, and perhaps even the first in Western thought, to predict travel to distant planets and contact with beings from other worlds. Today, such inclusions might be seen as early nods at what would later become science fiction; however, the genesis of esotericism (in language, at least) appears to stem from the creation of a word in one of Lucian's parodies. It is interesting to consider whether he also envisioned mystical practices that might open so-called *inner paths* to the cosmos, or other dimensions inhabited by alien life, and our proverbial mystical "Others."

Centuries after Lucian first coined *esoterikos*, Thomas Stanley would westernize the term somewhat, forming the word *esoteric*, which first appeared in his classic *History of Philosophy* as a reference to those in the mystery-school of Pythagoras who had been admitted into the "inner circle" of the religion. Various "mystery schools" of this sort, more commonly referred to as *mystery religions* or even *mystery cults*, existed in ancient Greece during the later periods of classical antiquity. [5] These included the Eleusian Mystery and various instances in the lineage of Socratic Mysteries, the precursors to our modern notion of "secret societies" like the Rosicrucians and the Freemasons.

The philosopher and mathematician Pythagoras is of particular interest here, due to the unusual mystique he commanded, as well as his perception of the unseen world that intrigued so many. Because of the manner in which Pythagoras used mysticism as a tool to make attempts at contacting beings from beyond the physical realm, Greek philosopher Aristotle went so far as to describe Pythagoras as actually being some sort of supernatural personage himself, maintaining that he possessed various signs of divinity that proved this. Among these signs were his "golden thigh," which Pythagoras was said to have shown during his participation in the Olympic games, as well as the notion held by many of his contemporaries that he possessed the literal ability to travel through space and time. [6]

As a word of caution, it goes without saying here that Pythagoras is seen as something of a mythical character himself, as evidenced by the feats attributed to him. For this reason, scholars have long cautioned against ascribing too much faith in the Pythagorean disciplines, as outlined here by Sir William Smith:

> The authenticated facts in the history of Pythagoras are so few, and the sources from which the greater part of our information respecting him is derived are of so late a date, and so untrustworthy, that it is impossible to lay down more than an outline of his personal history with any approximation to certainty. The total absence of written memorials proceeding from Pythagoras himself, and the paucity of the notices of him by contemporaries, coupled with the secrecy which was thrown around the constitution and actions of the Pythagorean brotherhood, held out strong temptations for invention to supply the facts, and the stories which thus originated were eagerly caught up by the Neo-Platonic writers who furnish most of the details respecting Pythagoras, and with whom it was a recognized cannon, that nothing should be accounted incredible which related to the gods or what was divine. [7]

According to the Pythagoreans, the concept of *Henosis*, a Greek word literally meaning "unity and oneness", detailed the concept of union with the *Monad,* or rather, man's connection with God and the totality of all beings. [8] Scholar Barry Sandywell effectively detailed in his book *Presocratic Reflexivity: the Construction of Philosophical Discourse c. 600-450 BC,* how the Pythagorean Mystery cults used number systems in formulating their basis for the creation of all things in the universe to illustrate this:

> Since things equal numbers, the first unit, in generating the number series, is generating also the physical universe. From this perspective 'the monad' or 'One' was readily identified with the divine origin of reality. [9]

Around the third century AD, the Syrian philosopher Iamblichus, who was also a Pythagorean philosopher, began to incorporate *Henosis* within the framework of Neo-Platonic philosophical teachings. Iamblichus first suggested that by providing services and other "divine work" dedicated to making the world better, we may get closest to the "One", or *Monad.* Thus, this unity with the "One" becomes the very essence of *Henosis.* [10]

Only through the process of *Henosis* are we able to "unlearn" and free our consciousness temporarily, enabling the silence of the mind required in returning to our fundamental *tabula rasa* state. Thereby, we experience a *no-mindedness* that brings us to what the Eastern mystics call *enlightenment,* or as the Greeks described, the point of deification where an individual may merge with the "One".

This "silence of mind", with regard to mysticism, is perhaps best described by author Jess Byron Hollenback in her book *Mysticism: Experience, Response, and Empowerment*, who describes a process of learning to turn off one's own inner-dialogue:

> This inner silence that mystics cultivate cannot develop unless the individual first learns how to tightly focus his or her attention so that the mind and the imagination no longer wander aimlessly from one subject, thought, or feeling state to another. [11]

According to Hollenback, when this mental "background noise" ceases, the mystic can better focus his or her attention; at this time, a dramatic change occurs, affecting the mystic's very mode of consciousness.

Hollenback further describes this as a change potentially greater than the shift between the waking-state of awareness into a dream-state, and actually defines mysticism as being this transfer of the waking consciousness—resulting directly from the act of simultaneous focus, and quieting the mind—paired with "responses in both thought and deed that it generates." [12]

MYSTICISM IN THE EAST

It is evident that the early Greeks had ideas that we today are quite familiar with, bearing similarities to a number of world religions. Specifically, the process of attaining *tabula rasa*, and quieting the mind in order to allow union with the "One" appears to be similar the Eastern idea of "enlightenment," as represented in Buddhism. Also, we see that the Greek concepts of performing "divine work" in order to reach oneness with higher powers as described by Iamblichus bears great similarity to elements within Buddhism's Noble Eightfold Path. The eight precepts taught in this path include *right views, right aspirations, right speech, right actions, right livelihood, right effort, right mindfulness, and right meditation*; all of which involve abstaining from unwholesome actions that may affect others negatively, much like the Neo-Platonic philosophers would later express in their teachings. [13]

The definitions of mysticism provided by the Greeks were choice for their time; however, it becomes clear through study of the parallels between Neo-Platonic mysticism and Buddhism that, in the Eastern world, these concepts were emerging and appearing even earlier, predating Plato's speculations regarding the inner and outer worlds by as much as a century. Siddhartha Gautama, upon whose life the principles of Buddhism are based, lived in the fifth century BC, and after reaching enlightenment via an intense, prolonged meditation lasting 49 days, he would spend the rest of his life teaching his "path of awakening," or *Dharma*; thus was born the way of Buddhism. [14] No doubt, Siddhartha was not the first to contemplate higher realities in such a way, but the lasting impression his insights have had on humankind remain key in understanding the modern concept of mysticism. Indeed, Siddhartha's story perhaps best exemplifies the universal concept of discovering "a new path," as well as the concepts of *enlightenment* or *ecstasy* resulting from achieving unity with the higher consciousness.

Siddhartha was not a mystic by birth, but instead had been born into wealth, living a life of relative luxury near Kapilavastu. According to legend, a hermit named Asita predicted on Siddhartha's day of birth that he would become one of two things in life: either a noble king, or a holy man. His father Suddhodana thus decided to shelter him from life on the outside world, instilling in the young Buddha a false sense of comfort and security by never allowing people of old age or those afflicted with illness to be seen on palace grounds. Nonetheless, most accounts tell that at the age of 29, Siddhartha left the palace in order to go and meet with his subjects, the common folk that resided outside his palace. Here, he first encountered old age and disease afflicting two men, as well as a decaying corpse; these encounters badly frightened and depressed him, being so alien to his previous understanding of the world. While outside the palace, Siddhartha also met an *ascetic*, that is, an individual who practices material abstinence to achieve higher spiritual disciplines. After this initial experience of confronting physical reality, Siddhartha left the palace, struggling with the acceptance of this new understanding that old age, disease, and death will one day overtake all living things. Thus, he began a new life of contemplation, aimed at discovering an end to suffering through the pursuit of enlightenment.

Siddhartha experimented with asceticism after his meeting with the man during his first departure from royalty. Siddhartha began to see sacrifice, self-mortification and fasting as being various means of attaining the inner peace and longevity he sought. However, the young sage, in his inexperience, had not yet learned the proper ways to maintain physical strength and care for himself while fasting, and nearly drowned after collapsing from exhaustion while bathing in a river. It was after this near-death-experience that his earliest epiphany occurred, in which Siddhartha found himself reflecting on a moment from his childhood when he entered a peaceful, focused concentration. This came about one spring afternoon as he sat, relaxing, and watched his father plowing a field. This would later be recognized as a sort of altered state of consciousness, which Siddhartha called the *Dhyana*, meaning a "blissful meditative state." [15] Eventually, it became evident that studying a "middle path" of meditation and moderation, as opposed to the unhealthy extremes of complete fasting and self-mortification yielded better results. Siddhartha would soon announce the beginning his legendary 49-day sitting, from which he vowed not to arise from beneath the Bodhi tree until he reached enlightenment and divine oneness.

As we focus on the profundity of Siddhartha's legacy and teachings, let us not overlook that it was in discovering the unpleasant truths of mortality that

Siddhartha was given his "initiation" of sorts. Once he had witnessed death and suffering, he could no longer live in the ignorant bliss of the physical world. However, he would learn that the unpleasantness of his initial realization worked very much to his benefit, acting as the inner-agent that would release the mystical body from within, sending him on his path to ultimate enlightenment.

Although those who heed the calling of the mystic way find themselves in continuous pursuit of the "eternal truth" or "ultimate reality," it is interesting to note that in his lifetime, the Buddha often would not address these or other metaphysical subjects. It is said, according to Buddhist scriptures like the *Pali Canon,* that Siddhartha would remain silent when asked questions regarding eternity, the separation of the soul and body (our modern notion of out-of-body experiences), the afterlife, and other themes commonly associated with mysticism, including those things which in modern times we might call "paranormal." One such instance, which appears in the Pali, describes a wanderer named Vacchagotta who meets the Buddha in a monastery at Jeta's Grove, Savatthi. He begins to ask his master a series of questions dealing with such themes, to which Buddha only repeatedly says "no." Vacchagotta, perplexed by this, then submits to answering questions Buddha proceeds to ask him regarding the nature of a fire that has been extinguished:

> "Suppose someone were to ask you, 'This fire that has gone out in front of you; in which direction

from here has it gone, east, west, north, or south?'
Thus asked, how would you reply?"

"That doesn't apply, Master Gotama. Any fire
burning dependent on a sustenance of grass and
timber, being unnourished — from having
consumed that sustenance and not being offered
any other — is classified simply as 'out'."

"Even so, Vaccha, any physical form by which
one describing the Tathagata would describe him:
That the Tathagata has abandoned, its root
destroyed, made like a palmyra stump, deprived of
the conditions of development, not destined for
future arising. Freed from the classification of
form, Vaccha, the Tathagata is deep, boundless,
hard to fathom, like the sea. 'Reappears' doesn't
apply. 'Does not reappear' doesn't apply. 'Both does
& does not reappear' doesn't apply. 'Neither
reappears nor does not reappear' doesn't apply." [16]

What Buddha asserts here is that, much like the
flame in his example that has physically gone
nowhere, and yet remains physically *gone*, the soul
does not leave the body and go to some other place.
Rather, it too is just *gone*, perhaps having left this
realm for a place so far removed from our
consciousness that to contemplate its existence
would only serve in countering the ultimate
simplicity Buddha hoped his followers would attain.
Indeed, many scholars and Buddhists today assert
that Siddhartha felt questions of this sort would only
distract from the true nature of the mystical

experience: to realize enlightenment and the end of suffering in a singular oneness with the creator.

Many modern mystics and practitioners of transcendental arts like meditation hold views similar to this. Lawrence LeShan, author of the modern classic *How to Meditate*, described the dangers associated with focusing too much on paranormal events that may occur as a result of meditation:

> Many people, when these events happen, get so interested in them and excited about their occurrence that they lose all their orientation to the real goals of meditation. They become more concerned with the paranormal than with their own development. [17]

When this occurs, the paranormal occurrence then becomes the focus of the meditation, rather than the true benefits one may gain from focused practice of the mystical arts. This seems to be in stark contrast with ancient Greek mystical practices, where many elements of their religion involved specific means aimed at making contact with both sentient non-human intelligences (gods), as well as the ability to use mysticism as a way to communicate with the dead.

Putting this into context, despite of the prescribed goals of Eastern mystic practices that LeShan points out that, which seem so different from what the Greeks hoped to achieve, Buddhism does have its exceptions. On example of this are occurrences called *siddhis,* which are "paranormal" manifestations that sometimes occur; various branches of Buddhism do use such mystical processes, with some intent focused toward contacting, and even manifesting, sentient intelligences (a good example of this would include the Tibetan monks and their concept of *tulpas*, which we will later examine more closely).

MYSTICISM AS A PROCESS

Another element common to numerous cultures regarding mysticism is that it is a *process*, rather than an object, tool, or singular act. The idea of mysticism, seen as a "process of becoming," rather than a mere aspect of a religion, is perhaps best illustrated in the work of Evelyn Underhill, where she broke mysticism down into five stages constituting "a single process of growth, involving the movement of consciousness from lower to higher levels of reality, the steady remaking of the character in accordance with the 'independent spiritual world.' " [18]

The first of Underhill's five stages is the *awakening* of one's consciousness to the existence of what she calls "Divine Reality". This is exemplified in the ecstatic "discovery" of the mystical way or path, marked with sensuality and intense emotions, especially "joy and exaltation." For many, this sudden awareness comes without warning and for no particular reason, sometimes leaving the individual who experiences it dumbfounded and confused, though nonetheless elated.

The second stage is that of *purgation,* described by Underhill as where "the Self, aware for the first time of Divine Beauty, realizes by contrast its own finiteness and imperfection, the manifold illusions in which it is immersed, the immense distance which separates it from the One." [19] Siddhartha's realization of these elements during his first visit with his subjects outside the palace walls is perhaps the quintessential depiction of this stage in the process. The response is typically a leaning toward self-discipline and mortification; a removal of any and all things that may form a barrier between union of the initiate with the One. The purgation period is characterized by pain and effort, much like Siddhartha's period of experimental asceticism following his Great Departure.

The third stage, *illumination,* together with the previous two stages is what forms "the first mystic life," being the final stage beyond which many mystics never go. "Illumination brings a certain apprehension of the Absolute, a sense of the Divine presence, but not true union with it," says Underhill. Artists and visionaries often reach this point in the process of ultimate awareness, a kind of re-visioning of our lives and the Earth around us. Underhill uses Plato's allegory of the cave, describing illumination along the lines of prisoners within the cave who have "struggled up the harsh and difficult path to the mouth of the cave," to behold the sun for the first time; the source of all shadows, as well as the symbolic evidence of true reality. It is interesting to note the parallel between this concept of Earth's sun, the source of all illumination (both literally, and symbolically) alongside the prevalence of "blinding light" at the heart of ecstatic mystical experiences.

In the New Testament, the apostle Paul described visionary experiences which might fit Underhill's notion of *illumination*. Though he refers repeatedly in 2 Corinthians to "knowing of a man" who was swept into a mystical state with Christ, most scholars agree that Paul is likely referring to himself, on account of references to a physical infirmity (he calls it a "thorn") which he had asked Christ about on three occasions. In this passage, it is also interesting to note Paul's reference to "the third heaven" in correlation with *illumination* being the third stage in Underhill's mystic process:

> I knew a man in Christ above fourteen years ago, (whether in the body, I cannot tell; or whether out of the body, I cannot tell: God knoweth;) such an one caught up to the third heaven. And I knew such a man, (whether in the body, or out of the body, I cannot tell: God knoweth;) How that he was caught up into paradise, and heard unspeakable words, which it is not lawful for a man to utter. Of such an one will I glory: yet of myself I will not glory, but in mine infirmities. For though I would desire to glory, I shall not be a fool; for I will say the truth: but now I forbear, lest any man should think of me above that which he seeth me to be, or that he heareth of me. And lest I should be exalted above measure through the abundance of the revelations, there was given to

me a thorn in the flesh, the messenger of Satan to buffet me, lest I should be exalted above measure. For this thing I besought the Lord thrice, that it might depart from me. And he said unto me, My grace is sufficient for thee: for my strength is made perfect in weakness. Most gladly therefore will I rather glory in my infirmities, that the power of Christ may rest upon me. [20]

In his book *Paul the Convert,* Alan F. Segal says that "Although the passage can be understood in other ways, Paul reveals modestly that he has had several ecstatic meetings with Christ over the previous fourteen years." [21] Segal points out that this is not strange at all for a first-century Jew, since ecstatic ascents into divinity were common among the mystical traditions in Jewish Hellenism at the time, and though the apostle carefully blankets his experience with modesty, "Paul's identity as the mystic seems assured, though his reputation has never featured ecstasy, perhaps because he opposed the excessive claims made by his opponents on the basis of his own ecstatic experiences described in this passage." [22]

Underhill describes the fourth stage as "the most terrible of all the experiences of the Mystic Way." Sometimes referred to as the "mystic pain" or "mystic death," mystics seeking true enlightenment will proceed beyond illumination to a fourth stage, which Underhill calls "the dark night of the soul" (an allusion to the words of St. John of the Cross). "Sooner or later," she writes, "psychic fatigue sets in; the state of illumination begins to break up, the complementary negative consciousness appears, and shows itself as an overwhelming sense of darkness and deprivation." [23] The loss of connection and unity with the One, God, or the creator, signified by a profound sense of withdrawal, also occurs during this stage. "The 'eye which looked upon eternity' has closed, the old dear sense of intimacy and mutual love has given place to a terrible blank." [24] This stage, more elusive than the previous three common to those travelling the path of the mystic, signifies complete purification, accompanied by elements of helplessness and confusion. During much of the latter half of her life, Mother Teresa described this same sense of withdrawal and emptiness, whereas she had once said she felt the presence of God very strongly. It is here that the mystic surrenders to the underlying intentions and divine purposes of the One, often with uncertainty as to whether their effort will be in vain.

The final stage is one of union, "the true goal of the mystic quest." Though many describe the state of "Ecstasy" as being the end of the mystic journey, Underhill argues that ecstatic states are instead perceived by mystics during the stage of illumination, which are characterized by a "short and rapturous trance—a state with well-marked physical and psychical accompaniments." This is also similar to Paul's numerous ascents to the "third heaven" where he described meeting Jesus on several occasions during out-of-body experiences, following Christ's Ascension. The true final stage of union differs from ecstatic states, in that it brings the mystic to a "permanent establishment of life upon transcendent levels of reality, of which ecstasies give a foretaste to the soul." Again, making the correlation with Buddhism, Underhill writes that the state of union "appears to differ little from the Buddhist's Nirvana, and is the logical corollary of that pantheism to which the Oriental mystic always tends." [25] On the other hand, the "ultimate union" Underhill describes may actually follow death, considering the Christian notion of heaven being where one is born into a new, non-physical body with Christ in the afterlife.

Paul's descriptions of union with Christ through ecstatic states may be among the most recognizable mystic experiences appearing in the New Testament. These meetings with Christ—via what could only be described as an altered state of consciousness—may also best exemplify Underhill's notion of union with the creator, as well as the notion of spontaneous travel outside the body to non-physical realms where we meet the "Other."

MYSTIC EXPERIENCES AND CONTACT IN OTHER CULTURES

This notion of Christian mystics having out-of-body encounters with the heavenly realms mirror several elements of culture already familiar to us. For instance, the classic near-death-experience (NDE) is often described as follows: the individual typically feels the sensation of leaving their bodies, which is often followed by an embrace or immersion in a "bright light." Once the individual reaches this state of peace and light, encounters with beings will often occur. These beings are most often deceased loved ones, though many people have returned from their NDEs to tell of sentient intelligences that spoke to them, and much like the apostle Paul described, they feel as though direct communication with God was achieved.

Author and mathematician Richard L. Thompson, Ph.D. describes similar concepts which can be found in the ancient Vedic texts of India, which describe beings called *Devas* who live in a place called *Svargaloka*, a Sanskrit word for "paradise" or "the celestial region". Thompson believes this refers to a "higher-dimensional domain that cannot be included in ordinary three-dimensional space," due to the fact that the Vedic texts appear to describe, with a great degree of clarity, methods of travel between places elsewhere in the universe. "I suspect that this idea brings us closer to the intended meaning of the Vedic texts than the idea of Svargaloka as an ordinary region of outer space above our heads," says Thompson. [25] Obviously, if this refers to a non-physical realm rather than some location in outer space, it could be likened to the Christian concept of heaven, or even the realm of light described by spirit-travelers during their NDEs. And what of these *Devas* the Vedic texts mention? If anything, the Sanskrit term serves as a perfect counterpart to our Western concept of "angels" and other heavenly deities. As discussed in Hinduism, *Devas* are not to be confused with "the One" or "Supreme God", similar to the way Christianity constructs a hierarchy of angels below God.

Many of the ancient Vedic texts describe travel to these heavenly realms by mortals, which may involve the use of unique flying craft called *Vimanas*. These ancient references to flying machines, described variously as looking like "wheels", "chariots", and "flying birds," have prompted some modern UFO theorists to assert that ancient civilizations may have commanded advanced aerial craft similar to the airplanes of today, or even more unusual aircraft resembling flying saucers. The term *vimana*, in literal translation, equates to "measuring out, traversing" or "having been measured out". [26] This translation from the Sanskrit contrasts with the definition of vimana when put into context, which according to the Sanskrit-English Dictionary describes, "a car or a chariot of the gods, any self-moving aerial car sometimes serving as a seat or throne, sometimes self-moving and carrying its occupant through the air; other descriptions make the Vimana more like a house or palace, and one kind is said to be seven stories high." [27]

Obviously, the characteristics of the vimana tend to vary greatly, although we can conclude that the modern association between these mythical aerial vehicles and UFOs has mostly to do with a controversial document called the *Vymanika Shastra*, which features references to vimanas, along with illustrations which seem to depict them—almost irrefutably—as being mechanical flying machines similar to airplanes. The document was heralded by many as final proof that advanced aircraft existed in ancient India during the height of the "ancient astronauts" craze in the 1970s (which, in recent years, has undergone something of a renaissance, due in part to television programs like History channel's *Ancient Aliens*). Pandit Subbaraya Shastry, a mystic from Anekal, apparently dictated the document to Sanskrit scholar Shri Venkatachala Sharma sometime after 1903. It came to attention again in 1952 when G.R. Josyer, Director of the International Academy of Sanskrit Research in Mysore, recovered it and began promoting its existence; an English translation finally appeared in 1973. [28] However, a paper by researchers with the Indian Institute of Science published the following year determined that the Vymanika Shastra was an unreliable source for claims that flying craft existed in ancient India. "It appears that his work cannot be dated earlier than 1904," the authors concluded, "and contains details which, on the basis of our present knowledge, force us to conclude the non feasibility of heavier–than-air craft of earlier times." [29]

Similarly, entities depicted in primitive cave art from around the world, dating back thousands of years, have been compared to modern images of space aliens popular in UFO literature. Some ufologists assert that these, and other representations of art from antiquity, resemble things like highly advanced spacecraft, or even "space suits" like those worn by NASA astronauts over the last several decades. It seems that it is difficult for the human mind not to make comparisons in this way, and at least for some, to project our modern spacefaring ideas onto the mythologies of ages past.

It is indeed unlikely that cultural representations of the past represent real-life encounters between ancient people and alien "gods." However, it isn't beyond the realm of possibility that some mystics in ancient cultures were able to become "spiritual vessels," in a sense. Perhaps, rather than travel to places beyond the known physical realm, these mystical practices allowed communion to occur via altered states, with varieties of consciousness in the deeper corners of the mind. Maybe some who had these experiences produced a record of their visions, and immortalized their experiences through carvings in stone, which seem perplexing to us today.

Whether we choose to call these places heaven, Svargaloka, the afterlife, other dimensions, or simply that which is not *here* is irrelevant. What seems most unlikely, however, is the notion that such places were ever accessible using ancient flying machines, or other vessels of the *physical variety*.

ULTIMATE LONELINESS

Slawek Wojtowicz is a medical oncologist, author, and science-fiction illustrator, originally from Poland and now living in New Jersey, who in his written work has observed and discussed the nature of the mystic experience in terms of meditation, as well as through the use of entheogens and psychedelic substances. During a conversation we had in August 2008 about his book *Inner Paths to Outer Space*, co-written with authors including psychedelic researcher Rick Strassman, Ph.D., I asked Slawek to give me an idea about his definition of mysticism.

"I'm sure that you've seen the film *The Matrix*?" he asked, to which I responded I had.

"You know, I think it's easier to discover a *mystic* than *mysticism*. A mystic in my mind is a person who realizes that there is something wrong with our world, kind of like Neo in *The Matrix*. He starts searching, and he will not rest until he will find an answer, or *the answer*. The *Truth*. I think that's the goal of mysticism, to discover the truth, and it has to be an experiential discovery. It's not enough to read about it. It's not enough to know about it from hearing about it from somebody else. It's something that has to be experienced personally, the *Truth*.

"I can tell you what that Truth is," Slawek said, getting a bit reflective. "The truth is that *each of us is God*. But it's meaningless unless you actually experience that. It is possible to experience, and meditation and other techniques lead to that. So in my mind, mysticism is something that outgrows religions. Each of the religions has roots and seeds of that mysticism within.

"You can argue that God actually created this world because he didn't want to be alone. That's another thing that has to be experienced, the metaphysical terror of experiencing ultimate loneliness. Of God being all powerful, and being completely alone." [30] I was familiar with what Slawek was describing, as many recollections of mystical experiences include a realization on behalf of the mystic at some point that they are alone. This is sometimes accompanied with visions of floating in the expanse of outer space, or by mere silence alone, the complete absence of all things outside the self. "That is *the worst terror*," Slawek told me, "the worst thing that you can experience. I think this is why some people who use psychedelics without preparation, or without a 'guide' or a shaman, jump through the windows! When you experience that loneliness, you may actually do that, because it's such a terrifying experience. It is part of the Truth. Yes, *you are God*, but there is nothing that exists... this is the ultimate truth. *You* are all that exists. You're not really the person who you think you are, you just *are*. And that's part of the deal, that God *needs* this universe, this reality, so that there will be others, and he created this world not to have zillions of worshipers who are going to fall on their face and worship him, but for each of us to *become God*. So this is a universe populated by zillions of gods, and that, basically, is paradise. That each of us will be all-powerful and perfectly loving, just like God that Jesus teaches about." [31]

Slawek effectively summarizes the notions expressed by not only Evelyn Underhill and her summation of union with the divine, but of countless others who came before her proclaiming the same realization. For Christians, this ultimate realization lies in Christ's fundamental teachings, that his followers are "of one body" with him, and in reaching unity with God on the most profound spiritual level, find themselves drawn into his body, and thereby becoming Christ themselves. Buddhists learn that seeking enlightenment may reveal a Buddha in any one of us, just as many Buddhas have existed over the ages since Siddhartha first discovered *himself* while meditating beneath the bodhi tree. The archaic rituals of the primitive world, still practiced today by the religions in Central America and Africa, among other places, lead their initiates to discover that the end of the mystical journey is not only union with the divine, but a more complete understanding and "discovery" of oneself; a lifelong dedication to living the shamanic life and continual deepening and understanding of the expanses within. In essence, through mysticism, our ultimate goal is to find *ourselves*. In reaching unity with the divine, we must venture through the terrifying expanses of emptiness that lay within us, but in doing so we learn not only that we are not who we initially thought we were, but that there are indeed others here with us; whoever, or wherever they may be.

It seems that humankind will always seek out this absorption into the divine; regardless of how we may go about finding it, or to whom we look when seeking. Still, one might conclude that it is this conscious attempt at seeking the mystical, our innate desire to connect with the hidden elements of existence, which further disassociates us. Perhaps only by "allowing" the energies and intelligences present in higher levels of consciousness to trickle down into our reality can we hope to make our ultimate union with our proverbial *One, God, Creator,* or *Other*. After all, there are many throughout the ages that have described finding themselves stricken without warning by the sudden, inexplicable nature of the mystical, regardless of any religious training, background, or prior inclinations to seek it out.

Occasionally, this perception of the divine, when we are unprepared, can surprise, or even shock us, leaving us unable to comprehend the religious or mystical elements we have been shown until much later in life. In such instances, those who have been set along a new path may begin to change aspects of their own lives in ways that remain invisible at the outset of the spiritual journey. The duality of the experience may be easily overlooked, whereas later our "inner" and "outer" selves combine somewhere along the way and, eventually, a complete union with the divine is achieved.

It seems that the seeds of mysticism are planted within each of us at the beginning of consciousness, resting dormant until given a need to awaken the mystical nature within at some point in our existence. Ultimately, we are shown the inner pathways to the outer realms of consciousness, where perhaps we are meant to discover, nonetheless to our astonishment, *that we are not alone.*

CHAPTER SIX

THE DOORS OF PERCEPTION: MYSTIC ARTS, MEDITATION AND OTHER METHODS OF ENTRY

I hoped to distill the essence of Shamanism, to track the Epiphany to her lair. I wanted to see beyond the veils of her whirling dance. A cosmic peeping Tom, I dreamed of confronting naked beauty.

-TERENCE MCKENNA, *Food of the Gods*

The mystical practice of perceiving the *self within oneself* is ancient; some call it magical, others call it finding a path to God. Within the sacred art of silencing the world around us, somewhere lays the summation of our collective memory of humankind as a species; an ancient prototype that, while lacking the technological advances and conveniences of modern humankind, in some circumstances was able to wield a sophistication long ago that rivals the greatest minds of today.

In some ways, it may actually be easier for us to imagine our ancestors being capable of doing such things, rather than people like you or me. After all, modern man is so easily distracted by the *physicality* of existence that things we recognize as "mystical" in nature often seem hard to grasp. We romanticize the ancient way of life, and imagine cultures more primitive than our own having to rely on innate senses and abilities, rather than tools and devices of the technological age. This has also led to speculation over the years that any psychic potential humankind may have maintained throughout history is only a watered down remainder of what our ancestors had— something that might have been vital to humans long ago, but which has atrophied, in a sense, as we've grown more dependent on external stimuli. If only we could assume that some semblance of our mystical attributes does still exist, and that humans could learn ways to harness it, then perhaps unlocking certain mysteries of our universe would seem more feasible.

Previously we have tried to examine what mysticism is, particularly in a historical sense, in order to better understand how people in the past have sought the "others" presumed to exist in realms beyond those known to us physically. Now, in an effort to better understand processes that would allow mysticism to be used to learn more about these perceived greater realities in the modern world, we will attempt to examine the individual methods mystics have employed to access higher planes of universal understanding. Rather than merely giving instruction on these practices (since untold volumes already exist on such things as yoga, meditation, and how they are best implemented), our examination will focus on their relationship to altered states, as well as visions or interactions with perceived entities during such experiences.

MEDITATION

In various parts of the world, there are shamans, seers, brujas, mages and mystics that still exist. However, the mystical arts, as they appear in the world today, have become less a way of life or a path to meaning than they once were. Often, the things we deem "mystical" have been diluted for consumption by modern minds, to provide escape mechanisms for people who, otherwise, may not be able to cope with the stresses of daily life.

I feel justified in saying this, because I can accept my own dependence, at times, on things I perceive to be "mystical," as far as being tools used for escapism. We have so many vices available to us today, ranging from potentially dangerous practices involving drugs, sex, and even violence, to the less physically damaging (but nonetheless distracting) escape we receive from sitting in a movie theater and watching films. Indeed, Hollywood has done a fine job providing a host of different varieties of mind-numbing entertainment. Even if we choose not to physically engage in destructive behavior ourselves, we can still partake in them vicariously through action heroes and flavor-of-the-month starlets with flaring attitudes and firm physical extremities.

Perhaps, at least in some capacity, this act of escaping does still maintain a mystical quality; it is almost meditative, in the way that the duality of the mind can be recognized. Author Lawrence LeShan expresses that, with meditation, what seems impossible with one circumstance may not be in another. In other words, when we "escape" to this hidden area in the mind, whether through film, intoxication, or by meditating, we do enter a different state of consciousness, with intent of using a particular *metaphysical system*.

"In the system one shifts to," LeShan says, "Extra Sensory Perception is permissible and 'normal'. It often does occur." [1] LeShan warns practitioners of the meditative arts against succumbing to fascination at the apparent occurrence of ESP or other paranormal phenomena. When these sorts of things happen to most people, "they get so interested in them and excited about their occurrence that they lose all their orientation to the real goals of meditation." [2]

This is not surprising, and though I don't wish to attempt to draw the practitioner of meditation away from the intended goals of such mystical practices, one must nonetheless ask, *how could somebody really be uninterested when "paranormal" things occur?* Having the ability to wield powers beyond the capacity of what we deem "normal" is merely a further realization of our Hollywood fantasies; most of us, at some point, have wished we could be mutants with superpowers, capable of thwarting bad guys and saving the day with abilities that exceed what we can do at our day jobs. To do so might not only provide us with the love, respect, and attention we desire from our peers, but it would also help us realize our *separation* from others, our uniqueness, in what we might expect to be a more positive way. Suppose, for an instant, that we could learn to accept the fact that our insecurities—the very things about ourselves we consider to be "flaws"—are actually most often the things that people dear to us love the most. Wouldn't we all be happier people, *without* wishing we were comic book characters with superpowers?

On the subject of unusual phenomena associated with meditation, in the last chapter we briefly mentioned ancient cave art, and other depictions of nonhuman beings in antiquity. There are a variety of explanations that provide feasible answers as to the identities of these "ancient aliens"; perhaps they were purely mythological in nature, the equivalent of our science fiction today. If there is indeed some factual basis for them, it could be that they represent entities met by shamans and mystics, either as a result of ingesting entheogenic compounds or, relative to the present discussion, met while exploring meditative states and altered consciousness. Scenarios like this outline for us ways that ancient man may have experienced encounters with "others" via mystical practices. However, considering such circumstances is particularly important in modern times as well, because of the experiences many people *continue* to report having with entities during altered states of consciousness. Whether these experiences stem entirely from within the mind, as is generally accepted, or they are representative of some element that is capable of being influenced by factors external to the mind, remains unclear.

Slawek Wojtowicz, M.D., who provided us such illustrative commentary on mysticism in the last chapter, also describes having had an encounter with a "being" while meditating, which he perceived as being hostile. While in school as a medical student years ago, Wojtowicz had regularly practiced meditation. During one session, he began to feel a sensation similar to an acute "expansion" of one's senses, allowing him to perceive a variety of sounds and other sensations outwardly spanning a radius around him, covering several miles. "Simultaneously, I noticed that my body felt like an empty shell, and I started shrinking within that shell, becoming smaller and smaller. At some point, I sensed another presence near me. I perceived it as dark and hostile, and it appeared intent on destroying me." [3]

Wojtowicz describes that he later recognized this as either "his shadow"—a rejected element of our psyche which we project upon those around us—or it may have been what he calls a "Threshold Guardian", an entity often described by Native Americans which guards the entrance to spiritual realms.

Similarly, in his book *The Disappearance of the Universe,* author Gary Renard described that after years of practicing meditation he was finally able to reach the point of "ultimate silence" described by practitioners of advanced meditation. On one occasion, he described emerging from a meditation session to see, to his surprise, a pair of strangers sitting in the room with him. Over time, these individuals began to teach Renard about various spiritual, religious and interpersonal relationships, even allowing him to travel through time. The beings were alleged to have confirmed for Renard things like the Roswell UFO crash of 1947, in addition to a variety of doomsday prophecies related to the year 2012 that, fortunately, didn't come to pass. [4]

American anthropologist Hank Wesselman described similar occurrences in his book *Spiritwalker: Messages from the* Future, where in addition to receiving communications from beyond space and time, Wesselman claimed to have also "lifted into space and traveled to a number of other planets." Wesselman described details such as "two suns in the sky" at one of these locations, witnessed at one of the many alien worlds he claimed to visit. [5]

Such claims, as we have observed already, are actually commonplace in a variety of cultures. In his book *Easy Journey to Other Planets,* A.C. Bhaktivedanta Swami Prabhupada describes how "yogis can travel to all the planets in the universe." Though there is certainly some degree of question as to what metaphysical Hindu perceptions of *planets* may be (see Chapter One), the specific wording here denotes "all the planets in the universe," which seems to indicate very clearly terrestrial bodies in our solar system and beyond.

Prabhupada tells us that yogis can train themselves to block their *vital force* from exiting their eyes, ears, nose and mouth in achieving what he calls "the seventh orbit", by way of learning to suspend air in their bodies. "The yogi then concentrates the vital force in the middle position, that is, between the eyebrows." From here, a yogi can apparently focus on any planet they wish to "enter" after leaving their physical body. Prabhupada compares a capable yogi's ability to achieve this to being as ordinary as a "man's walking to the grocery store." [6]

Taking this concept one step further, Prabhupada also says that at the time of death a yogi can concentrate their vital force between their eyebrows in this way and, if he so chooses, leave the material world "in both finer and grosser forms". The spirit moves to the topmost portion of the skull from which, apparently, it is able to ascend through a hole the Hindus call the *brahma-randhra*. [7] Prabhupada says, "This is the highest perfection of the practice of *yoga*." Among other things, to equate spiritual escape at the moment of death to being "perfection" in the art of yoga illustrates the division between the Eastern and Western minds; primarily as it relates to traditional practices that combine elements of meditation with ecstatic body postures.

Yoga and Ecstatic Body Postures

As early as the 1960s, Dr. Felicitas Goodman began performing groundbreaking research into ecstatic body postures, using university students as test subjects. [8] While trying to stimulate the mind in various ways to induce mystical experiences among her subjects, many students did report some degree of success in reaching altered states of consciousness. Nonetheless, Goodman found the apparent lack of similarity between experiences frustrating.

Around this time, Goodman also began to uncover research that indicated how postures of the body, especially in meditative practices, seemed to be able to initiate physiological changes under certain conditions. Thus, Goodman began looking for similar ways that specific postures might work with her research. A survey of illustrations depicting small statues and cave art, dating back thousands of years, seemed to hold the key to what became the foundation for her "ecstatic postures," which were later successful in helping bring about altered states of consciousness in several of her test subjects. Goodman likened their effectiveness to being a gateway into an alternate reality, where ecstasy could be achieved. [9]

Somehow, ancient cultures were able to discover the use of supplemental postures in their meditative practices. The question remains, however, as to exactly *how* practices involving body postures used to evoke altered states were ever devised; commonly referred to today as *yoga,* their history and origins welcome further inquiry.

Yoga and its development are indeed somewhat mysterious. Though it is traditionally said that yoga was revealed to sages during enlightened meditation as a "divine science of life," archaeological evidence suggests that it was likely in practice prior to India's Vedic Era. Sanskrit texts during this period began to illustrate the foundations of yogic practice in written form, and beginning around the third century BC, texts involving the Raja Yoga Sutras and Haltha Yoga, the precursors to modern yogic practices, began to surface. However, yoga is not exclusive to Indian traditions, and is shown to have connections to ancient Buddhist, Jain, and Sufist ascetic traditions. [10]

By looking at the Sanskrit etymology, we find that yoga has several meanings, having been derived from the original Sanskrit word *yui,* which translates to mean "control". Other meanings include "to yoke" or "unite", as well as "to join" and "conjunction". As indicated by these translations, yoga's underlying purpose focuses primarily on the union with oneself, or as described in the East, "reuniting the individual self (jiva) with the Absolute or pure consciousness," the latter representing the Hindu god Brahman. [11] In certain Hindu denominations, Brahman is joined by two other deities, Vishnu and Shiva, together representing the *Trimurti,* or three primary aspects of the divine; Brahma being the creator, Vishnu the preserver, and Shiva representing the destroyer.

In conjunction with his role as destroyer, Shiva is also lord of the dance, and is commonly depicted in one of two unique poses; the first depicting him in mid-dance with one foot raised. According to legend, once Shiva allows his raised foot to rest on the ground, the universe will cease to exist, thus fulfilling his role as "destroyer." Interestingly, it is Shiva that is also traditionally regarded as the original founder of yoga, which explains the second of his unique postures, often depicting him in deep meditation. Devotees of Shiva aim to release their souls from the bonds that hold us to our mortal existence, and it is believed that through yoga, in addition to ascetic practices including penance and renunciation of worldly views, one can achieve *shivata*—thus acquiring the nature of Shiva themselves.

In the ancient Sanskrit *Mahabharata*, Shiva was depicted in the midst of one such state of meditative isolation, a sort of spiritual "retreat" someplace in the vast Himalayas, where the hero Arjuna meets him while following his own ascetic path. Shiva manifests to him as Pashupati, a hunter-god who commands elements of life, death, and time. An epithet for Shiva, Pashupati was recognized not only as "The Divine Hunter", but also "Lord of The Beasts", specifically cattle. [12]

This notion of a god who protected cattle draws an interesting parallel with psychedelic entheogens, since ethnobotanist Terence McKenna actually proposed that the mystic traditions of many ancient civilizations might have been influenced by psychedelic experiences. The rationale for this has to do with the fact that psilocybin mushrooms (*Psilocybe semilanceata,* among other genera) commonly grow on cattle waste; the existence of "cattle cults" in many ancient civilizations, McKenna thus argued, indicated that these cultures looked at their bovine brethren as a sort of "provider" of these magical mushrooms, revered by mystics then, and now, as fascinating spiritual technologies capable of elevating the mind to higher levels of existence. [13]

TULPAS: EXTENDING BEYOND THE MIND

Though psychedelic substances indeed may have influenced the ancients, many traditions, particularly in the Eastern world, believed that meditation alone could achieve similar altered states of consciousness. Along these lines, another interesting byproduct of meditation in Eastern mysticism has to do with the notion that one may be capable of learning to project their thoughts *beyond* the confines of the mind, resulting in the manifestation of physical "Thought-forms." Tibetan Buddhists call such manifestations *tulpas,* which are essentially physical projections that are believed to occur in conjunction with the intense meditations performed by yogis.

Esoteric though the idea of a "tulpa" may seem, this concept has received a remarkable amount of attention over the years, having been borrowed by countless paranormal enthusiasts that have employed it as a sort of "catch all" for explaining various types of unexplained phenomena. From UFOs and ghosts, to alleged appearances of water monsters, or even the "ape men" that exist in folklore from around the world, virtually *anything* could be accounted for under the "tulpa" theory, so long as it can be fathomed by the human mind.

That's the *theory*, at least, although the question remains as to whether things like focused meditation, or certain psychosocial and behavioral phenomena, could *really* explain any of nature's anomalies. However, in the next chapter we will delve into just how strange the human imagination can get, and learn what odd realities may truly exist behind Huxley's proverbial "doors of perception."

CHAPTER SEVEN

THOUGHTFORMS: MYSTICAL MANIFESTATIONS, SENTIENT BEINGS OR PSYCHOLOGICAL AGENTS?

Tibetans believe that advanced human minds can manipulate... invisible energies into visible forms called tulpas, or thought projections.

-JOHN KEEL, *The Mothman Prophecies*

In the early 1920s, camped out in the remote highlands of Tibet, explorer and mystic Alexandra David-Néel claimed to have her first encounter with a most unusual apparition. Between 1914 and 1924, the author and spiritualist made several ventures into the then forbidden land of Tibet, peacefully invading its borders in search of something she had begun at an early age; her own search for the mystical, and the pursuit of freedom and enlightenment at nearly any cost. The fact that Tibet was forbidden to foreigners at the time did little sway her convictions, and disguised as pilgrims, Alexandra and her companion, Aphur Yongden, a young monk from Sikkim, near the Tibetan border, travelled together to Lhasa on several occasions.

It was on such an occasion, while camped among other travelers in the Tibetan highlands, that she was visited by a young painter, with whom she had become acquainted during one of her trips to Lhasa. The artist had always shown particular reverence and fascination with one specific Tibetan god, featuring this deity profusely throughout his many paintings over the years.

Upon entering the camp where Alexandra was staying, she had noticed his arrival, and reported seeing a "cloud-like apparition" following behind the painter in midair; a misty representation of the very god upon which the man had focused so intently in his art. Alexandra became fascinated with this bizarre apparition, recalling a belief among the Tibetans that during the final stages of a Yogi's meditation, one could focus intently on the deity from which he wished to receive instruction, thus externalizing the meditations into what is called a *sprul pa*, or as Alexandra chose to write it, "tulpa." This physical manifestation of the entity would thereby instruct the Yogi in the completion of his training.

Alexandra, in addition to her observations, later reported being able to create a "tulpa" of her own, by experimenting with intense meditations and focusing on creating forms from the extension of thoughts. With time, a regularly occurring manifestation began to appear, which had taken the appearance of a jovial monk resembling "Friar Tuck".

Her earliest visions of this character had stemmed from meditation sessions, but with time she was able to "summon" the monk with ease, which would seem to "appear" before her as though projected onto her surroundings from within her mind. Alexandra continued to experiment with summoning the monk into existence, and soon not only did the friendly friar begin to appear without Alexandra concentrating on him first, but strangely, it also seemed to alter its appearance. Losing weight and obtaining a sly expression, Alexandra's harmless tulpa began to appear regularly, as though the result of some will other than hers, and to her astonishment Alexandra soon began to hear others in the encampment discussing "the strange little lama" frequently seen moving about. This brought the ultimate realization that her creation must be destroyed, a process which she described as arduous, and taking time and great effort. [1] Alexandra David-Néel went on to describe similar instances of tulpa activity during her lifetime, in books detailing her many adventures in the Far East.

★   ★   ★

Moving forward, our focus here will be an analysis of these apparition-like manifestations, referenced occasionally in esoteric literature. These occur, it is believed, as a result of powerful projections from within the human mind, and are most commonly referred to as a *thoughtforms*, though we will also use the terms *tulpa* or *projection,* when expressing similar concepts stemming from various cultures, regions, and available literature.

As the reader will see, these thoughtforms, with their roots in Tibetan spirituality, have everything to do with mysticism as we understand it thus far. However, to give a complete and thorough analysis, we must begin to depart somewhat from the view of thoughtforms and similar alleged "manifestations" solely in relation to the mystical; it seems that this subject has as much (or perhaps more) to do with the nature of human psychology, evoking consideration for psychosocial factors that may be involved, and other behavioral and cultural concepts.

A History of Thoughtforms

The general concept behind thoughtforms can be, at times, somewhat convoluted. Thus, for our purposes, the discussion of thoughtforms in relation to folklore and other literature here will deal with the specific appearance of *apparitions or other apparently physical phenomena, that are alleged to appear, externalized, as the result of powerful projections from within the human mind.*

In a historical context, the term *thought form* has also been used by the likes of theosophical societies and spiritualists, pertaining to the appearance of nearly any vivid thought in conjunction with stimulus like sound, color, smell, and other sensory functions. [2] In these instances, thought forms don't necessarily have to appear anywhere but in the subjective view of the individual who perceives the manifestation. Since the kind of manifestation discussed in this chapter refers instead to an objective, external phenomenon (i.e. several individuals in an environment are capable of perceiving it), the more modern term, *Thoughtform*, will be used instead, except with the occasional use of *tulpa* where best suited.

The experiences David-Néel recounted from her travels in Tibet were by no means the only references to this sort of phenomena. In fact, other writers of the early twentieth century began to discuss the notion that thoughts could possibly be projected from within the human mind around the same time. Prior to David-Néel's encounters, in their short book *Thought Forms* written in 1901, authors Annie Besant and C.W. Leadbeater had been the first to articulate the concept of a thoughtform, where they described two different effects thoughts can have, these being "a radiating vibration" and a "floating form." [3] Both authors were members of the popular Theosophical Society based out of New York during the early 1900s, and had studied the ways they believed music, emotions, and colors could effect and enhance human thoughts.

Interestingly, Besant and Leadbeater's ideas on the harmonic conditions that affect thoughts seems to correlate well with another of David-Néel's encounters, where a "snake of fire" was said to have emerged from the mere *sound* of a ceremonial cymbal she had witnessed a Tibetan priest using. [4] As recounted in her book *Tibet, Bandits, Priests and Demons*, Alexandra had entered a monastery, where at the time the Bonpos within had been conducting a ritual. At this moment, a peasant guide who had followed shortly after her found the ritual that was taking place unimpressive, and began making abusive statements. After being asked to leave, this peasant guide was said to have shouted that the sacred torma cakes used by the Bonpos used no special recipe at all, but were in fact merely common bread. Suddenly, the Bonpo conducting the ceremony grasped a small cymbal called a chang, and struck the instrument, producing what David-Néel described as "strange, savage sounds... with a tidal wave of vibrations." [5] The irreverent peasant recoiled in horror, and left the monastery in a hurry, to the astonishment of many present, including Alexandra.

"What had happened?" the author recounted, questioning the sudden departure of the peasant. "I hadn't noticed anything, except for that extraordinary sound. I went outside and asked my bearers. The troublemaker who had disturbed the sacred ritual had lost his bravado." The peasant was insistent that "a snake of fire" had come out of the chang wielded by the priest. "Didn't you see it?" the bearers asked Alexandra, who surmised that they had "dreamt it."

Alexandra never claimed to have seen the manifestation they described, though her bearers would confess to seeing "flashes of light shoot out of the chang." All parties nonetheless agreed that something incredible had occurred, and David-Néel wrote that everyone present had indeed seen something; even stating "they had all been witnesses to a miracle." [6]

The Bon who had created the snake of fire, considered to be a White Priest, discussed how the sound of the chang itself had caused the "snake" to emerge. However, in spiritualist literature that would follow David-Néel's account, many interpreted the specter that chased the rude peasant from the monastery to be a modern written account of a thoughtform.

GHOSTS, UFOS, AND PSYCHOLOGICAL ARCHETYPES

The idea of thoughtforms having connections with ghosts and other paranormal phenomena would eventually gain popularity in the west. Famous ghost hunter Harry Price had said that once an idea is formed, "it is no longer wholly under the control of the consciousness which gave it birth," but may operate independently on the minds of other people, or even physical objects. Psychologists would also borrow the idea, especially prevalent in Carl Jung's concept of *Active Imagination*, where one interacts with thoughtforms of the subconscious mind. Jung believed Archetypes, or varying "models" of human behavior, were actually thoughtforms themselves. Still, his approach to Active Imagination differed from the spiritualist concept of thoughtforms, in that the latter may be created intentionally whereas, just as Jung's description suggests, a "subconscious" thoughtform would seem to extend only from the *subconscious* mind. Nonetheless, both perspectives clearly illustrated that thoughtforms were not always believed to be dependent on specific sounds, colors, or other external factors in order to manifest subjectively, but instead that the human mind seemed capable of producing fantastic "specters of the imagination" which, sometimes, were alleged to be more than just pure imagination.

In his book *Flying Saucers: A Modern Myth of Things Seen in the Skies*, Jung supposed that UFOs and flying saucers were a similar extension of mankind's deeply rooted psychological fear of death and annihilation during the Cold War era. [6] However, in a 1951 correspondence, Jung also seemed to question whether the appearance of UFOs could be mere rumor, or based on facts that could be validated:

> I'm puzzled to death about these phenomena, because I haven't been able yet to make out with sufficient certainty whether the whole thing is a rumor with concomitant singular and mass hallucination, or a downright fact. Either case would be highly interesting... The phenomenon of the saucers might even be both, rumor as well as fact. In this case it would be what I call synchronicity. It's just too bad that we don't know enough about it. [7]

Jung supposed in *Flying Saucers* that UFO sightings may indeed be *projections* of some sort; psychological agents which stem from the subconscious:

"The plurality of UFOs... is a projection of a number of psychic images of wholeness which appear in the sky because on one hand they represent archetypes charged with energy and on the other hand are not recognized as psychic factors." [8]

Jung also states that although these "psychic images" may not be recognized as factors, "if it is a case of psychological *projection*, there must be a *psychic cause* for it." He continues, "Though visionary rumors may be caused or accompanied by all manner of outward circumstances, they are based essentially on an omnipresent emotional foundation, in this case a psychological situation common to all mankind." [9]

Specifically, the psychological reason Jung puts forth results from "collective stress or anger," stemming from "the strain of Russian policies and their still unpredictable consequences." [10] Taking into consideration Jung's concept of *projections*, one might surmise that at any particularly critical period in history, whether it involves war, political unrest, religious persecution, or other factors, the human consciousness may be capable of "projecting" its hidden desires and fears into the world around us, the result of intense mass-focus and strong emotion connected with whatever circumstances are then present.

A different approach to Jung's idea that a physical Thoughtform might stem from intense emotion or other built-up psychic potential involved author Walter Gibson, creator of the classic pulp novel and radio character The Shadow. Researcher and author John Keel described how residents living in Gibson's former home years later had witnessed an apparition fitting the description of Gibson's fictional character. Keel asked, "Why would a Shadow-like apparition suddenly appear in an old house? Could it be some kind of residue from Walter Gibson's very powerful mind?" [11] Keel supposed that this might have been an example of tulpa activity; referencing again the similarity to eastern traditions in his supposition that Gibson had actually created the ghost future residents would later report seeing.

It is interesting to note that tulpas occasionally appear to be likened to being "omens." This appears to correspond with Keel's own thematic use of omens and prophecy in what is, arguably, his best-known book, *The Mothman Prophecies*. This tells of a modern legend involving a series of sightings of a strange "monster" in West Virginia during the late 1960s, which seemed to lead up to the devastating collapse of the Silver Bridge, a large structure which closed the gap between the West Virginia and Ohio sides of the quaint country town of Point Pleasant. [12] Could there have been a strange, foreboding anticipation on behalf of people in the region, perhaps derived from some fear or unrest, which coincided the Mothman creature's appearance? If so, what were the deeper psychological stresses that "manifested" the likeness of this winged harbinger of doom?

THE GOLEM OF PRAGUE

Widespread collective unrest often appears to be a factor coinciding with periods where peculiar cultural legends are born. Such may have been the case in another early reference to a thoughtform or tulpa-like entity, this time during the Middle Ages, and having to do with an earlier Jewish mystic tradition.

According to legend, the Rabbi Yehuda Loevy ben Bezalel the Maharal, a famous rabbi and Jewish mystic who lived in Prague during the late sixteenth century, had gone to extraordinary means defending his fellow Jews against anti-Semitic attacks called "blood libels," made frequently at the time. These blood libels often involved the killing of non-Jewish children, and even the planting of their bodies among homes in Prague's Jewish ghettos (especially around the time of Passover). Gershon Winkler, a traditional rabbi and practitioner of Jewish Shamanism, detailed in his book *The Golem of Prague* how the Maharal went about trying to dispel the rumors regarding blood libels:

> In 1572, when the Maharal of Prague, R. Yehuda Loevy ben Bezalel, assumed the rabbinate of Prague, his immediate goal was to make an end to

the frequent blood accusations usually instigated by local parish priests. (He) took the initiative and personally requested of Cardinal John Sylvester that... a debate be arranged immediately. [13]

The cardinal was apparently impressed by the Maharal's arguments, sending information along to Emperor Rudolph II of Hapsburg. Rudolph met with the Maharal soon afterward, and immediately issued a royal mandate requiring fair trials for any Jews in Bohemia accused of ritual murder. Nonetheless, in spite of the Maharal's efforts, persecution through blood libels continued. In order to protect his people once and for all, the Maharal resorted to focused prayer and meditation. Using a procedure known as *sh'elath halom* (a "dream request"), he was given permission to use of his kabbalistic skills for intervention. In the spring of 1580, the Maharal gathered his two closest disciples, R. Yitzchak ben Shimshon HaKohen Katz (his son-in-law) and R. Yaakov ben Chayyim HaLevi Sasson, and working under cover of darkness, together they created a "man" from the mud of the Vlatava River near Prague.

The ancient Kabalistic incantation said to have brought the golem, which the Maharal had called "Yossele," to life involved the inscription of the word "emet", meaning "God's truth", on the creature's forehead. At the end of its service (which in some traditions coincided with the golem becoming violent and non-submissive to the Maharal), it was destroyed once the Rabbi erased the first letter of this word, creating a new word, "met", meaning *death* in the Hebrew language. At the time of its destruction, the golem was laid to rest beneath a pile of Hebrew manuscripts in the attic of the Old-New Synagogue in Prague; an ancient building that remains a popular landmark to this day. It was said that no one entered the attic for centuries thereafter, lending further to the mystique of the golem legend.

However, one reputable individual *is* said to have ventured into the attic. In 1909, the prolific author R. Yudel Rosenberg of Warsaw, a renowned master of the Torah and consultant on Jewish legal issues, printed a revision of an ancient document written by the Maharal's son in law, R. Katz, who according to legend had witnessed the creation of the golem firsthand. The original document was discovered in the Main Library in the city of Metz in Northeast France, where it had remained for centuries after the Maharal's death.

Rosenburg, upon obtaining it, printed it under the new title *Niflaos Maharal: HaGolem M'Prague* (The Wonders of the Maharal: The Golem of Prague), and gave the following account in the introduction:

> It is a known fact that when the great Gaon, HaRav Y'chezkel Landau served in the rabbinate of Prague, he revived the authenticity of the matter. He personally testified to the certainty that in the attic of the great synagogue of Prague, lies the Golem which the Maharal had made.

As is known, HaRav Landau once decided to go up to the attic and verify the tradition. Before he went up, he fasted and then immersed himself in the *mikveh* (ritual pool). When he was about to go up the stairs, he instructed ten of his pupils to recite Psalms on his behalf. He then wrapped himself in a prayer shawl and put on his phylacteries and walked up the stairs.

At the top of the staircase, HaRav Landau hesitated for several moments. He then came back down the steps, trembling with fright, his face pale with shock. He announced to those present that he was re-enacting the Maharal's original warning about going up to the attic. [14]

Due to so many of its fantastic details, the story of Yossele the golem is generally accepted as myth, in spite of the historical truths that surround it. If anything, the idea of a man springing to life from a clay figure sounds outlandish to the modern thinker. According to Jewish tradition, the creation of a Golem is described as the result of "an intense, systematic, mystical meditation." Rabbi Shlomo Yitzchaki, an early Jewish scholar living in Northern France during the tenth century, wrote what is considered the definitive Jewish commentaries on the Babylonian Talmud and the Bible. In his writings, he also said that instructions for the creation of a Golem could be found in a text called *The Book of Formation*. Here, it is suggested that the creation of a Golem was, in fact, not so much a *physical* procedure as it was "a highly advanced meditative technique" involving the chanting of certain letter arrays together with that of the "Ineffable Name", the most powerful and important name of God in the Torah, *YHVH*. In this manner, one could create in their mind a vivid mental image of a human piece by piece, formed with intense focus, and once a non-physical golem had been created, this thought projection could then be manifested within the clay body and activated, by inscribing holy letters on its forehead.

As the Maharal and his students had gathered together in the cover of darkness to create the golem from mud by the shores of the Vltava River, their minds would certainly have been focused intently on the rigorous purification and demanding meditations involved in its creation. Their intricate knowledge of the Kabalistic magic they performed made each man a perfect fit for the idea of "advanced human minds" capable of such intense meditative prowess. Also, much like Carl Jung's theory that emotional tension as a result of collective distress or danger serves a "vital psychic need," perhaps the Maharal and his disciples also were able to harness the fear and concern of their brethren, whom they were afraid may succumb to persecution if some action weren't taken. Whether or not, of course, an actual golem was created in doing so, is another matter entirely.

WRITERS AND THEIR TULPAS

Thinking back on the "ghost story" of pulp fiction novelist Walter Gibson, and how he might have brought to life his most famous character within in his former residence, it is interesting to note that Gibson is not the only author said to have created thoughtforms as a result of his work. William Dudley Pelley, a psychic researcher and controversial political activist during the 1930s and 1940s, also believed that a psychic friend of his was once able to recognize a thoughtform he created subconsciously as a result of focusing intently on a character from a novel he was writing around the time, as told in a recorded speech from the period:

> One night while writing my fourth novel, "Golden Rubbish", I went out to spend the evening with an extremely capable psychical lady who could see thought forms with her naked eye... and there is such a thing as what the Scots call "second sight." But during the course of the evening she leaned across the table and whispered to me, "Who's the pretty lady who seems to be following you about so closely?" I wasn't aware of any such person, and said so. Then, my psychical friend turned my blood cold, by listening a moment and then volunteering to me, "She says her name is Louise Garland," and then proceeded to describe her minutely as she appeared in the physical. Louise Garland was the name of the heroine of the story I was then writing day after day in my apartment down on West 53rd street! According to the data which developed, I gathered the astounding impression that, thinking of this imaginary 'story girl' day after day over so long a period, had given her literality in the astral immediately above me. To carry out the idea I'm trying to convey to you, suppose a mediumistic

person had been present to cloak Louise Garland, my story heroine, with "teleplasm", wouldn't I have created a literal woman to all intents and purposes in the flesh; at least, temporarily? [15]

Similar instances have been reported over the years by authors like Norman Mailer, who recounted how he was seemingly driven to include a Russian spy as one of the characters in his second novel, *Barbary Shore*. After publication, he was surprised to learn that within the boarding house where he resided (upon which he based the novel), U.S. Immigration Services actually did arrest a suspected Russian spy, who had been living just above him. Such historic coincidences are hard to overlook in relation to the almost "meditative" qualities of the writing process itself, and the focused act of creation it involves.

TULPAS AND PARANORMAL PHENOMENA

For years, especially after John Keel referenced tulpas in his written works, paranormal researchers have drawn correlations between thoughtforms and tulpa activity in conjunction with bizarre unexplained occurrences, as discussed in books like researcher and historian Jerome Clark's early collaboration with Loren Coleman, *The Unidentified*. [16] Even the late Dr. J. Allen Hynek, who served as scientific adviser to the government UFO research studies like *Project Blue*

Book and *Project Grudge,* wrote in his book *The UFO Experience: A Scientific Inquiry* that "we have all kinds of UFO and alien theories revolving around lost civilizations, time travelers, evolved dinosaurs and sea mammals, tulpas, collective projections, hostile takeovers, demonic and angelic forces, and on and on." [17] Certainly, with so many competing theories in relation to the unexplained, thoughtforms and their related phenomena will be thrown into the mix from time to time.

In keeping with the aforementioned notion that the "collective consciousness" somehow ties into all this, appearances of strange phenomena often seems to be representative of the perceptions and traditions of collective groups of people. Cultural influences, ranging from the advent of religious belief systems, to the widespread implementation of technology, may play a role in "filtering" people's perception of such things. A classic example is the associations between "ghost lights" and faeries, having been prevalent in Europe in the nineteenth century, compared with modern phenomena like UFOs seen today. Many suppose, in fact, that UFOs are actually a sort of modern equivalent to the once-popular belief in spirit folk and fairies; in either case, different kinds of cultural belief in the supernatural, relative to things existent at different periods in history, might have been attributed to certain kinds of "anomalous" phenomena in nature. Today, the once mysterious "ghost lights" are understood as being everything from natural plasmas, to the ire invoking "swamp gas" first referenced by J. Allen Hynek in relation to

UFO sightings occurring over Michigan in the 1960s. While certainly not the *only* explanation for anomalous aerial phenomena, with little doubt, plasmas and "swamp gas" are probably still mistaken for UFOs, on occasion.

Author and researcher Nick Redfern has spent years chronicling reports, spanning several decades, of what British locals have called the "Man-Monkey", a sort of spectral Bigfoot-like creature said to haunt the Shropshire Union Canal's Bridge number 39. Of course, England isn't large or remote enough to hide creatures of this size, let alone entire clans of them, whether below bridges, in forests, or in subterranean caves. Even still, encounters with these, and other "mystery beasts" persist frequently throughout the UK, and other parts of the world.

What, if anything, might the appearance of strange entities like this have to do with the idea of mystical projections of thoughtforms? Or, in terms of modern psychological studies, could there be some element within various cultures—a sort of "wild man" archetype—that is conducive either to mass panics and other social phenomena, or even a sort of *cultural memory*, either embodied and carried along within representative members of these cultures, or stemming from aspects of their history that live on through heritage and ritual?

The British Isles also incorporate similar "wild men" into their legends in the form of the *Woodwose*, which some scholars compare to the North American creature called *Sasquatch*. Similar iterations of these "wild men" occur in all parts of the world; despite the general scientific attitudes toward the existence of such creatures today, it would be foolhardy to think that we have managed to map and account for *all* of the members of the animal kingdom extant today. Nonetheless, the literal existence of such feral beasts resembling humans in the modern world remains a hard pill to swallow for most. Perhaps the idea of psychological or cultural reasons for their endurance in our myths and legends over the centuries should at least be considered.

A striking incident occurred in 2001 around Delhi, India, which involved several appearances of a monkey-like creature that attacked several residents in the region. Initially described as resembling a monkey, descriptions of the creature soon began to relate a much larger creature; within days, the "animal" had begun to take on a more manlike appearance, which led to the creature being dubbed, appropriately, the "monkey man." [18] The saga of the shape-shifting monkey man only became stranger in weeks that followed, as people's descriptions of the creature became more elaborate. Soon, the creature was said to leap across the tops of buildings, and had acquired a metallic helmet and claws that it used to further ravage its victims. Curiously (and despite the separation between cultures), this description shares a remarkable similarity with accounts of a phantom attacker called "Spring Heel Jack," said to haunt parts of London and surrounding areas in the 1830s. [19]

While such widespread incidents are nonetheless deemed to be the result of social and behavioral phenomena, the anomalous occurrences at the heart of these "panics" no doubt seemed real to those who experienced it firsthand. Though a literalist interpretation of strange phenomena may be appealing to us, at times, we must give equal consideration to the deeper workings of the human mind as well, and ask ourselves whether the *real* mysteries of human perception, along with some of the most unusual circumstances in the history of human experience, aren't actually rooted in things occurring *within*, rather than as a result of things going on in the world around us.

The mind is, after all, a complex structure, and it ultimately serves as the filter for all things perceived in our daily experience. It is an entertaining thought, to say the least, to consider what kinds of human experiences might result almost entirely from the ways our minds perceive various stimuli, or react in response to its apparent presence. In equal measure, the idea that aspects of our reality might "manifest" as a result of how we think, and what we choose to believe, provides us with unique implications for the cultural varieties of the human experience.

Thus, "I think, therefore I am," may in some cases effectively become, *I think, therefore it is.*

CHAPTER EIGHT

MYSTICAL MISDIAGNOSIS: CHEMICAL CONNECTIONS TO ALTERED STATES OF CONSCIOUSNESS

"There is a kind of religion in science... this religious faith of the scientist is violated by the discovery that the world had a beginning under the conditions in which the known laws of physics are not valid, and as a product of forces or circumstances we cannot discover."

-DR. ROBERT JASTROW in N.Y. Times Magazine, June 25, 1978

On at least two occasions in my life, I have had personal experiences with what is known as "sleep paralysis." On both occasions, I can say with particular relief, the events that took place weren't overtly strange or frightening, as is often reported by those who suffer from episodes with such "Night Hags," to borrow another popular name for the experience. However, unlike many individuals who have had these experiences without prior knowledge of the phenomenon, upon awaking into a state of apparent dreamlike paralysis, I merely concentrated on moving the digits of a single hand, then the entire hand, and the forearm thereafter; and at this point I immediately "snapped out of it." This was a trick I had learned after reading of a similar experience years earlier, during which one particular individual claimed to have been "paralyzed by an evil presence in the room." After having my own experience, I remain convinced that what occurred was neither evil, nor particularly unusual.

The same cannot be said for many others who have experienced sleep paralysis or *SP*. Many describe seeing ghosts, demons, and strange creatures that float around the room, often interacting with them in strange ways—even sexually. Louis Proud, author of *Dark Intrusions: An Investigation into the Paranormal Nature of Sleep Paralysis Experiences*, speaks almost apologetically for his strange encounters:

> Some of them, I'm almost embarrassed to admit, were of a highly sexual nature. Unbelievable as it sounds, I had sexual intercourse with female spirits who visited me in the middle of the night. This happened on several occasions. [1]

As strange as Proud's assertions may sound, many people have described having such experiences, and remain convinced that their encounters pertain to actual interactions they have had with strange beings.

SCIENCE OF MISDIAGNOSIS: ALTERED STATES AND PSYCHOSIS

In early 2009 I became acquainted with Dr. David Hufford, an expert in Sleep Paralysis and Professor of Medical Humanities at Penn State College of Medicine. Since 1979, Hufford has taught courses in spiritual belief and alternative medicine, with his research centered on, "the ethnographic and phenom-enological study of the beliefs of ordinary people— especially as those beliefs that are in competition with the positions of official institutions." [2] Hufford has long argued that there is reason behind the persistence of strange, often psychic and spiritual phenomenon in various cultures throughout history, leading him to propose "an experiential grounds for spiritual beliefs," and the pursuance of studies in, "the role of reason in their development and persistence." [3] In essence, Hufford asserts that many widespread spiritual beliefs are empirically founded, and draw from people's rational experiences, rather than delusions and "psychotic episodes."

Sleep paralysis is also considered one of these rational experiences. Hufford had his own strange encounter with SP while he was in college. It was near the end of an exam period, and a few of his friends had decided to go have dinner together.

Exhausted from his study schedule, Hufford decided that he would rather lie down and take a nap. A few minutes later, he heard his door open. "I thought it was someone coming in to ask if I wanted to go over to the student union building and have dinner. I tried to turn on the light but I couldn't move, and then I felt someone climb up onto the bed and kneel on my chest. I was being crushed, and I thought I was being killed! I couldn't move, so I struggled, and when I finally *could* move, I leaped out of bed, turned on the light, and there was nobody there. I ran downstairs, and nobody there had come into the room. I even asked the landlord, and he said nobody had come into the house. So I never told anybody about it, for the same reason nobody else does: I didn't want them to think I was crazy." [4]

Sadly, this seems to be the primary deterrent that keeps people from sharing their experiences. Those participating in Hufford's research over the last several decades almost unanimously said things like, *I didn't want people to think I was crazy*, when discussing their experiences. Almost as widespread as people's fear of being labeled "crazy" were the experiences themselves. "I found them in the high Arctic, West Africa, Southeast Asia, South America... literally everywhere. The pattern is always essentially the same, with this terrifying 'intruder' often pressing on the chest." [5] An astounding eighty percent of those Hufford interviewed described this scenario, almost precisely, in addition to things like footsteps, voices, and even the sound of doors opening and closing.

"We understand a lot about what produces the paralysis," Hufford says. "There's a mechanism in the brain stem—what's called the reticular activating system—that is a bio-chemical mechanism operated by the cholinergic pathway, which produces a paralysis during dreaming sleep. REM sleep, or dreaming sleep, is what produces the paralysis during sleep paralysis also." Critics of SP phenomena have said that Hufford's description indicates that the hallucinations that occur are the result of a dreaming mind controlling a body that is, in essence, half awake and still unable to move. "The puzzle," Hufford argues, "is why they all seem to be dreaming the same thing. That's very, very peculiar, and that's what makes this so tantalizingly interesting." [6]

During the interview, Dr. Hufford expressed to me with a degree of urgency the fact that SP was once often misdiagnosed as a serious psychiatric symptom, "simply because many people in the medical community do not know that this pattern of the threatening presence in the experience is there, and don't know that afterwards it is normal for people to be convinced that it was real." He warns that, "In the modern world, particularly in the US and Western Europe, if you describe something like this and you say it seemed real, you're at great risk of being diagnosed with a psychiatric illness." [7]

Sleep paralysis isn't the only state of altered-consciousness under which people have claimed to experience strange phenomenon, making it only one of many types of experience the modern psychiatric community would likely consider a form of "mental illness." David Ritchey is an independent psychological researcher with a particular interest in altered states of consciousness and transpersonal, metaphysical and paranormal experiences. In his book *The H.I.S.S. of the A.S.P.*, Ritchey discusses an excerpt from *The Diagnostic and Statistical Manual of Mental Disorders—Fourth Edition (DSM-IV)*, which states the following:

> (The primary) questionnaire used to assess schizotypy reads "do you believe in telepathy?" ...Schizotypal personality disorder is characterized by... belief in clairvoyance, telepathy, or "sixth sense." [8]

"Defining and pathologizing a belief in Extra-Sensory Perception as the primary symptom of a mental disorder appeared to me to be a way of brushing ESP under the rug," Richey says, "and precluding, by dismissal, any study of ESP that might lead to a better understanding of it." [9] Indeed, both Hufford and Ritchie note that the overwhelming response to mystical states and altered consciousness by the mainstream medical community is rejection and dismissal, with the potential for even putting one's mental health at stake. "Perhaps the adherents of this approach were not so much trying to understand ESP as they were trying to debunk it—so as to bolster an entrenched worldview that did not allow for the possible genuineness of such experiences," Ritchey says. By labeling experiences with ESP—or any other mystical state—as mental illness, Ritchey argues the authors of the text on mental disorders excerpted above merely seek to protect themselves from an alternative worldview, so as not to have to face something they fear and misunderstand.

This calls into question a 1976 report by psychologist Jane Murphy, who in her studies of native practices around the world, found that shamanic cultures among the Eskimos and the West African Yoruba tribes both possess a cultural concept that is identical to being "crazy" or mentally ill by western clinical standards. However, these cultures nonetheless separate the mentally ill from those they believe to be *actual* shamans or mystics that possess paranormal abilities. For instance, the Eskimo word *nuthkavihak* pertains only to a person who carries on conversations with themselves or who refuses to speak at all, to which delusions and a variety of other abnormal behavior are also attributed. Along the same lines, the Yoruba tribes of Africa have the word *were*, which denotes a condition almost identical to "nuthkavihak". [10] In both cultures, shamans and their perception of entities and other visions from beyond are considered to be very distinct from what is viewed as a counterpart to our definition of being mentally ill.

Of even greater interest is how, much like Dr. Hufford found while researching traditions involving sleep paralysis around the world, there is continuity between these cultures and their interpretation of strange phenomena, as well as its distinction from mental disorders. These cultures seem fully capable of distinguishing between a dysfunctional mind, and what they argue to be real experiences (we'll look at how this study pertains to the use of psychedelic drugs by shamanic cultures later on).

Similar to mystical experiences, scientific studies have been carried out in relation to the phenomenon of out-of-body experiences (OBEs), and the unique relevance they share with situations that present life-threatening stress. In 1984, a study appeared in *The Journal of Nervous and Mental Disease* titled *Hostage Hallucinations: Visual Imagery Induced by Isolation and Life-Threatening Stress*. The author, Ronald K. Seigel, Ph.D., argues that eight people out of 31 case studies experienced "hallucinations," some of which included disassociation and traditional OBEs. The article's abstract explains that victims the study included were "ex-prisoners of war and victims of rape, kidnapping, terrorism, robbery," as well as "UFO abductions." All eight who seemed to experience hallucinations had also been subjected to some form of isolation and/or life-threatening stress. [11]

Among the types of hallucinations that occur, Siegel lists appearances of "long-forgotten childhood friends," in addition to other manifestations that include the appearance of a variety of bizarre, flashing geometric patterns, particularly among blindfolded subjects in sensory isolation studies. Drawing obvious similarities to other known altered states of consciousness, Siegel also lists reports of experiences by survivors of near-fatal accidents, which are known to literally paralyze their victims with fear, "or catapult him or her into a state of mystical consciousness." [12] Of all the varieties of altered states related to trauma listed here, it is strange to note that this final variety of hallucination, which Siegel says, "cause those who see them to respond as if they were real," appears to bear remarkable similarity to sleep paralysis experiences.

The hallucinations described by those eight victims who endured isolation and threats of death again show many consistencies. All eight individuals described seeing flashes of light, geometric patterns and shapes, and "tunnel forms." Seven described "tactile-kinesthetic hallucinations," and five claimed to witness "complex visual imagery" that included beings they often recognized from past memories. [13] One particularly fascinating account the study details deals with a 23-year-old gang member who, after being taken hostage by a rival gang, was tied to a chair in a warehouse where he was beaten and burned with cigarettes during captivity. When such torture was being inflicted upon him, the man often said he felt no pain, as though he had been under the influence of drugs like phencyclidine. In one instance he even described floating to the ceiling of the warehouse, where he watched his captors as they tortured his body several feet below. At other times, he experienced vivid recollections of past events, and bizarre imagery involving "devils and cops and monsters." [14] A similar revealing case dealt with a 61-year-old grandmother who was locked into a small closet in her home by an invader, where she remained gagged and bound for four days. At one point during her captivity, she described how she felt "invisible" and, floating out of the closet, wandered around her house as though she had stepped right through the locked closet door and out of her physical body. [15]

Arguably, some of the strangest descriptions of any phenomenon included in Siegel's study have to do with reports of alleged UFO abduction, as well as the varieties of hallucinatory elements experienced by purported abductees. One case dealt with testimony provided by a 52-year-old man and his 24-year-old son, both of whom described vivid recollections of being abducted by a UFO craft while driving across the Arizona desert. At noon on the day they of the incident, they recalled hearing a "strange mechanical noise", and after stopping to inspect the cause, witnessed a UFO hovering above them. A brilliant light blinded and paralyzed them, at which point the father described dizziness, muscle tremors, and hearing "voices" in his head. The son described only the dizziness. Both men described floating above ground and being levitated into an opening in the UFO, continuing to float down a long metallic tunnel inside the craft. Within, they encountered humanoids bathed in a bright light, and both men reported a "flash of their past lives" on a screen before them (it is presumed this meant life experiences, rather than "past lives" in the sense of reincarnation). Finally, the screens displayed the two men stopping their car in the desert earlier that day. They saw themselves sitting in the car, and shortly thereafter regained a normal state of consciousness. To their surprise, seven hours had seemingly passed, and it was now dark outside. [16]

This case, in the context of an examination of hallucinatory experiences, presents us with a number of questions. First, which set of circumstances, precisely, describes the "hallucination"? Do we focus on the flashes of past memories and other visual stimuli both men described, or the abduction scenario itself? The report illustrates for us that "the propensity of long distance drivers to hallucinate as well as the role of optical phenomena created by the sun in generating UFO reports suggest possible stimulus conditions here." [16] Siegel also points out that neither of the men described seeing one another during their experiences, although their reports were almost entirely similar. The hallucinatory elements described (i.e. sunlight, driving for long periods, etc) might indeed evoke strange, or even psychedelic experiences that involve colors, patterns, tunnel-like imagery, and other related visual phenomena, similar to those reported by other hostages in the study. However, isn't it odd that the two men would recall an identical series of events that transpired, while apparently "hallucinating" together in the desert? Both recollections involved a UFO craft (and its presumed occupants) capturing the men, from which they both appeared to emerge seven hours later with memories of bright lights, tunnels, and other images commonly reported by those who have entered altered states of consciousness. If not an encounter with some variety of objective, external phenomenon, how could separate hallucinatory experiences specific to the two men have managed to influence each other in a way that resulted in so many similarities?

It is interesting to note that the father's medical records showed "a previous diagnosis of paranoid psychosis two years before the UFO abduction." Given Dr. Hufford's earlier warning of misdiagnosis pertaining to those suffering from sleep paralysis, one is tempted to wonder about what predisposition may have led to this diagnosis; of course, due to medical standard practice, further information regarding the condition is withheld. However, the mental state of the man's son is given, and it is stated explicitly that "the co-hostage in this case tested within normal ranges on all measures," although both father and son were said to have maintained belief in "various paranormal phenomena" prior to their abduction. [17] The experience related by both father and son does share many similarities with sufferers of sleep paralysis and OBEs. But again, the similarities in experiences, contrasted with the differing medical backgrounds of both men, make chalking it up to previously diagnosed psychosis difficult, at best.

Since the article appears to take the traditional scientific stance that hallucinations of the variety discussed here only *appear* to be real, it is strange that the many references to UFO activity made throughout the report are done so rather matter-of-factly. Along with two instances of hallucination resulting from alleged UFO abductions described in the study, Siegel also references the Biblical account of Ezekiel in the historical background he provides, citing it as the earliest hallucinatory experience pertaining to a hostage experience in history. Siegel even takes into consideration "contemporary interpretations" of Ufological perspectives insinuated over the years:

> To my knowledge, the earliest account of a hostage experience was given in 593 B.C. by the Babylonian priest Ezekiel who described (as reported in the Bible) an abduction by "creatures" in a flying round bronze object.... Ezekiel's account details shock, feelings of floating, and perceptions of lights, colors, and mystical visions of God. [18]

Siegel's analysis had been willing, at very least, to reference various cultural interpretations of strange phenomenon in a historical context; it also lends a bit of much-deserved credence to the notion that people from different walks of life seem to be capable of interpreting strange phenomenon with consistency—whatever the underlying causes may actually be.

A unique study carried out by psychiatrist Devon E. Hinton in 2003 suggested that there may be a link between sleep paralysis sufferers, and those diagnosed with post-traumatic stress disorder (PTSD). In his study, Hinton observed that forty-two of 100 Cambodian refugees he surveyed discussed having SP experiences, and that forty-five had also been diagnosed with PTSD. Thirty-five of those who battled PTSD also described regular experiences with SP. Additionally, Hinton's research indicated that many sufferers of PTSD relived the events that led to their diagnosis through their paralysis episodes, during which a variety of strange images and sounds were often described. [19] This calls into question again whether altered states possess some capacity for helping people alleviate problems resulting from extreme stress, isolation, and other factors.

SOUNDS OF CONSCIOUSNESS: THE PSYCHEDELIC CONNECTION

In his book, *Dark Intrusions*, author Louis Proud relates the strange story of "Mary," a woman of Polish decent who suffered from bouts with sleep paralysis. After visiting a doctor and complaining about strange "buzzing noises" she had heard prior to, and during her experiences, she was diagnosed with a variety of mental illness and prescribed medication. This had no effect on the experiences she was having, and she continued to describe hearing loud buzzing, as well as "chirping" and even sounds like "someone breathing" during her ongoing experiences. Proud quotes Mary, who told him, "The sound of insects is often very strong, as if the whole room is filled with them." [20]

Mary isn't the only individual that has described strange auditory occurrences similar to these. Proud's research led him to the discovery of a whole range of sounds that, according to research conducted by the University of Waterloo, can be classified under one of three types: *elementary, technological, and natural.* Furthermore, these categories elicit different sounds that constitute loud vibrations, ringing, roaring, rushing, screeching, squeaking, and buzzing (similar to swarms of insects gathered together, or cicadas singing on a summer night). Grinding noises, machine-like humming, whirring, or whistling, and other noises also occur. Proud explains:

> According to psychologist Allan Cheyne, these elementary sounds "are often described as being very loud and mechanical," and "are sometimes accompanied by bodily sensations described as 'tingling,' 'numbness,' or 'vibration.'" One SP sufferer reported hearing "a high, humming sound that gets louder the further I fall into the 'trance.'" [21]

Accompanying these sounds are also *physical sensations* that involve intense vibration, as well as the feeling of "being electrocuted slowly." Technological sounds might include sirens, or whirring similar to "air entering a vacuum." Another sound Proud notes that SP sufferers describe often is static, or the sound of "a radio being heard from another room in the house." This reminds me of a momentary blackout that occurred immediately after a car accident I was in several years ago, during which I recall a dreamlike sequence that involved a small room with a table, upon which sat a radio playing classical music. Just before I regained consciousness, I recall the classical music beginning to get louder, turning into static, as though the radio dial had been changed to "white noise" between stations. The next sounds I recall hearing were the voices of the emergency response team shouting as they pulled me out of my battered pickup truck.

Despite my own experience with "noise" of this sort, there are far more interesting parallels that exist between the sorts of sounds Proud has documented in his research, especially when paired with clinical studies involving drugs like *dimethyltryptamine*, or DMT as it is commonly known. Dr. Rick Strassman describes in the book *Inner Paths to Outer Space* a variety of effects this especially potent drug can have on those who take it, and mentions specifically the building of a "high-pitched whining, ringing or cracking sound." [22] Earlier, in his book *DMT: The Spirit Molecule*, Strassman went into far greater detail regarding the variety of sounds that accompany the DMT experience, but due to the fact that they are all nearly identical to those described by Proud in the excerpt above, there is little need to detail them here. The important factor, instead, has to do with *why* there is such consistency between the experiences.

In addition to the "mechanical" or "buzzing" sounds DMT users and SP sufferers both encounter, visual distortions, contact and communication with beings ranging from deceased loved ones, to aliens and monsters, as well as geometric or kaleidoscopic patterns, are all relative to both experiences.

The obvious connotation here is that, somehow, the same sorts of mystical occurrences that transcend consciousness and elude understanding are present in altered states of consciousness like sleep paralysis and OBEs, as well as induced psychedelic states using substances like DMT. In a final example of possible connections that may exist between the two, Strassman mentions a handful of participants from his DEA-approved study who experienced virtually no effect from taking a large dose of DMT:

> One of these three was a former monastic who had a meditation-induced mystical experience... The former monastic's experience was tentative support for a corollary of my hypothesis that endogenous DMT is involved in spontaneous mystical experiences. [23]

Strassman's research, in essence, suggested that DMT is produced within the human pineal gland (as described in chapter three), and that people who study mysticism through meditation and deepening themselves spiritually could, in theory, actually learn how to instigate DMT-fueled "endogenous" mystical experiences, which he supposed was the case with his monastic volunteer.

As we have now seen, clearly there must exist some association between the mystical experience, and chemical workings of the mind when entering mystical states of altered consciousness; however, all-too-often the medical community is more willing to buffer and silence claims that seemingly broach the extraordinary or divine, leading to the misdiagnosis of illness, and thus, the unnecessary prescription of medication to otherwise healthy individuals.

The mystical way outlines yet another powerful tool we can use in the ultimate quest for realization of our inner selves, as well as the potential discovery of what may exist beyond the confines of our psyche. However, to truly understand all the implications of magic and mystical practices—as well as how they pertain to expanding our notion of the universe around us—we must also study mysticism's possible molecular attributes. The strange inner-world of psychedelic molecules like DMT awaits, and despite their apparent simplicity, they exist in tandem with the spiritual realities we seek... capable of dictating, on a molecular level, the essence of the mystical experience.

PART THREE

THE
MOLECULE

CHAPTER NINE

ENTHEOGENS: "GOD RELEASING" PLANTS AND SPIRIT MOLECULES

To the ancients, trees were synonymous with truth, and more specifically, sitting under a tree was an avenue to discovering truth. Some say this is the symbolism of the Christmas tree, and the gifts beneath it. For under a tree is where you find a gift, including one of the greatest gifts of all—truth.

-KEN KORCZAK, *The Fairy Redemption of Jubal Cranch*

Mystic scholar Evelyn Underhill wrote in her exhaustive *Mysticism: The Nature and Development of Spiritual Consciousness*, that "The spiritual history of man reveals two distinct and fundamental attitudes towards the unseen; and two methods whereby he has sought to get in touch with it. For our present purposes I will call these the 'way of magic' and the 'way of mysticism'." [1] To add to this, I must argue that for the present purposes illustrated in this book, there is a third conduit which man uses to make the unseen visible: "the way of molecules," which contain mind-altering substances, or *entheogens.*

True, many would try and lump the use of *entheogens,* a term literally meaning "God releasing" substances, in along with what Underhill, among others, have outlined as mysticism over the ages. However, it seems to be the case that those things "purely mystical" by definition, specifically the use of meditation, prayer, and "inner arts" to reach ecstatic states and enlightenment, are separate in nature from the breathtaking, full-force "launch" into altered states of consciousness that entheogens seem to allow. Granted, not any random, molecular cluster could elicit such powerful insights; the specific molecules to which I refer are hallucinogens, particularly psychedelic substances like psilocybin, LSD, and perhaps most mysterious of all, the "spirit molecule" known as DMT.

Indigenous cultures predating the emergence of Western views toward magic and mysticism by several centuries had incorporated powerful, mind-altering chemicals into their religious ceremonies. Many of these ancient practices were only discovered and chronicled in modern pharmacology within the last century. In addition to their "newness" in terms of modern study, the suppression and demonization substances like these makes it even less surprising that so little is known about them, how they work, and how long they may have been in use.

Perhaps the earliest suggested evidence of entheogen use was discovered in the Tassili National Park in Algeria. There, a variety of cave paintings dating back as far as ten thousand years exist, which depict characters like the *Grand Dieu de Sefar*, meaning the "Great God of Sefar"; or the "Great Martian God", a being very reminiscent of a spaceman clad in a suit and helmet. But perhaps most curious—and telling—among the characters decorating the cave walls at Tassili is the "mushroom-man", a likely tribute to the psychedelic mushrooms that later became the focus, in part, of ethnobotanist Terence McKenna.

It was McKenna who first supposed that many ancient cultures—the same who formulated religions around cattle they domesticated—might have done so partially due to an interesting by-product of herding the creatures. Since psilocybin-bearing mushrooms grow on cattle waste (as touched upon in earlier chapters), McKenna guessed that early cattle-rearing cultures may have tried eating these mushrooms, and were thus introduced to their mind-altering effects. Looking at the historic record, this might have occurred even earlier than the creation of the paintings at Tassili, predating them by as much as

7000 years in parts of Egypt, where evidence of cattle worship has been discovered during the unearthing of ceremonial buildings, gravesites, and artifacts. [2]

Early cultures migrating into Europe around 4000 years ago are also believed to have partaken in psychedelic fungi growing in the wild, specifically the *Amanita* variety. Since it cannot be cultivated, the Amanita had likely been most accessible to nomadic Indo-Europeans in their wanderings. [3] Later, between 1700 and 1000 BC, among the Vedic epics being authored in India was the *Rig Veda*, which dedicates an entire chapter to *Soma*, a liquid that priests and initiates ritually prepared and drank. Believed to have psychedelic properties, it is interesting to note that a common theme of immortality emerges in the Vedic literature regarding the use of Soma, which parallels other ancient literature. The following passage from the *Rig Veda* illustrates this belief in immortality:

> King Soma!... O [Soma] Pavāmana, place me in that deathless, undecaying world wherein the light of heaven is set, and everlasting lustre shines.... Make me immortal in that realm where happiness and transports, where joy and felicities combine. [4]

The Epic of Gilgamesh also describes a plant that can bring immortality. Flourishing at the bottom of the ocean, the plant is believed to have been similar to *boxthorn*, a cousin of the poisonous *Solanaceae* or nightshade. [5] Elsewhere, Archaic Period hunter-gatherers who flourished in what is now Utah State as early as four thousand years ago depicted strange beings in their rock art, which was very similar to those found in the caves at Tassili. It is believed that these entities may have been first witnessed by shamans, while experiencing altered states of consciousness triggered by the use of entheogens like peyote, in addition to psychedelics like mescal beans, psilocybin mushrooms, morning glory seeds, and Salvia divinorum, which would begin replacing the powerful peyote cactus in North American ritual use as late as the 19th century. [6]

AYAHUASCA: ENTHEOGENIC HERBAL TEA, PASSAGEWAY TO OTHER REALMS

One of the most curious entheogenic substances, and perhaps one of the most popular thanks to New-Age movements today, is the herbal tea known as *ayahuasca*. Of South American origin, early missionary diaries and other writings included information on the brew, although ayahuasca wasn't fully recognized in the west until the 1950s. At this time, it was often referred to as *telepathine*, for the strange, seemingly psychic effects professed by the shamans who drank it (today, *Harmine*, one of the chemical elements of ayahuasca, is still referred to occasionally by the name *telepathine*). [8] For such reasons, the Catholic Church began attempting to eradicate the use of this ceremonial tea, believing its powers were demonic.

Though *ayahuasca* is the popular term used today, other regional names throughout South America include "yage", "natem" or "caapi" after the official name of its active ingredient, *Banisteriopsis caapi*. It is this element, taken from the vine of the Liana plant, when paired with plants which may include *Psychostria viridis* and *Diplopterys cabrerana*, that create the psychedelic effect found in ayahuasca tea. In essence, the combination provides both the active hallucinogen, dimethyltryptamine (DMT), with MAO inhibiting harmana alkaloids which allow the DMT to become active before being broken down in the stomach when ingested. [9]

Many consider the Banisteriopsis vine to be the "spirit" of ayahuasca, a sort of gatekeeper who guards access to unseen realms it harbors. In discussing the seemingly "conscious" aspects of the plant itself, it is also interesting to note that many who have taken the brew describe the strange, almost intelligent effects it seems to have on the body. In some capacities, ayahuasca is used as a medication to purge the body of tropical parasites. Author Daniel Pinchbeck described his experience with ayahuasca healing in his book *Breaking Open the Head: A Psychedelic Journey into the Heart of Contemporary Shamanism*, during which the powerful entheogen coursed through his body like an "alien intelligence" fixing small problems within:

> It was like I was a computer and ayahuasca was a program performing scans and repairs. When it had done its work, I threw up—the vomiting was like the beep at the end of a program. [10]

Apart from its purely medical effects, ayahuasca is primarily renowned for the visionary experiences it provides. One noteworthy experience of this variety involves anthropologist Michael Harner, who decades ago had been working with the Amazonian Conibo Indians in Peru when he tried ayahuasca for the first time:

> For several hours after drinking the brew, I found myself, although awake, in a world beyond my wildest dreams. I met bird-headed people, as well as dragon-like creatures who explained that they were the true gods of this world. I enlisted the services of other spirit helpers in attempting to fly through the far reaches of the Galaxy. Transported into a trance where the supernatural seemed natural, I realized that anthropologists, including myself, had profoundly underestimated the importance of the drug in affecting native ideology. [11]

After his experience, Harner related his encounter with the "dragons" to a blind shaman, who calmly told him, "they're always saying that, but they are only the masters of outer darkness." [12]

Dennis McKenna also described an experience he had with ayahuasca, in which he said the plant itself spoke directly with him. "Somehow I understood—though no words were involved—that the Banisteriopsis vine was the em-bodiment of the plant intelligence that embraced and covered the Earth," he said. Before the experience ended, a voice he could only interpret to be the plant itself spoke to him:

Suddenly again from behind my left shoulder, came a quiet voice. "You monkeys only think you're running things," it said. "You don't think we would really allow this to happen, do you?" and somehow, I knew that the "we" in that statement was the entire community of species that constitute the planetary biosphere. I knew that I had been given an inestimable gift, a piece of gnosis and wisdom straight from the heart/mind of planetary intelligence, conveyed in visions and thought by an infinitely wise, incredibly ancient, and enormously compassionate "ambassador" to the human community. [13]

Here, an interesting association could be made with other varieties of meditative altered states, in that people emerging from conditions like sleep paralysis, etc, often hear voices speaking to them *just prior* to emerging from the experience.

PLANTS AS ALIEN SIGNAL RECEPTORS?

In 1971, an electronics engineer named L. George Lawrence had been conducting experiments in Oak Grove Park near Temecula, California, in which he used living vegetal tissue shielded behind a Faraday tube capable of screening even the slightest electromagnetic interference to record biological radiations transmitted by nearby plants. By adjusting the aperture of a lens-less tube, living tissue in Lawrence's setup was able to detect directional signals from other plants receiving remote-controlled electrical stimulus up to one mile away. [14]

One day, Lawrence had stopped to have a snack, while leaving his apparatus aimed randomly at the sky above. Suddenly his instruments, which normally gave a distinct, constant whistling sound, began to pulsate evenly. This lasted for half an hour, and with his lens focused only at the wide empty space of heaven above, Lawrence was forced to consider whether the source of the signal might have been extraterrestrial.

With a background in laser engineering, as well as having authored the first book on such technology to appear in Europe, Lawrence reasoned that *Ursa Major* had been the direction from which the signal had arrived. For his second attempt at receiving these mystery signals using his biological plant apparatus, Lawrence drove to the center of a huge volcanic butte, the Pisgah Crater, located in the heart of the Mojave Desert, so as to rule out any influence from nearby vegetation (since detecting vegetation was the intended use of his equipment). Lawrence aligned his telescope, along with the Faraday tube, a camera, and an EM interference monitor, and his trademark plant tissue chamber, at the general location of Ursa Major; a biological call-back, of sorts. Lawrence was indeed successful in recreating the effect, which he later would liken to being "transmissions between (alien) peer groups,' suggesting that our ignorance of such broadcasts is due to our limited use of radio signals in attempts to detect intelligent signals from outer space. "Because we don't know anything about biological communications we are simply excluded from these 'conversations'," he said. Lawrence was so convinced that he had uncovered an organic means of receiving cosmic signals that he mailed a seven-page report on his findings to the Smithsonian Institute. [15]

Could it be that plants might not only harbor certain degrees of awareness, but that they possess other innate abilities which allow them to communicate—perhaps even with humans—or act as receptacles for passing knowledge, as Lawrence's findings suggest? Just within the last two decades, research into plant communication has established that plants possess a remarkable degree of awareness. Michael Pollan, a researcher in the relatively new field of plant neurobiology, argues that plants are more perceptive than many would think:

> They have analogous structures... They have ways of taking all the sensory data they gather in their everyday lives... integrate it and then behave in an appropriate way in response. And they do this without brains, which, in a way, is what's incredible about it, because we automatically assume you need a brain to process information. [16]

There are many instances where scientists and engineers have described using psychoactive drugs to stimulate their problem-solving abilities, and claimed to receive insight in the form of "communication". Several individuals have described being shown complex solutions that brought them to a greater understanding of the knowledge they sought while under the influence of entheogens. For instance, while visiting an Amazonian shaman, anthropologist Jeremy Narby brought with him three European molecular biologists. The biologists took ayahuasca, and were directed to try and communicate with the spirit of the plant. In doing so, each individual described receiving insights and knowledge from "responses" issued by the plant. Two of the three even went so far as to say they felt an "independent intelligence" had communicated with them directly.

Indeed, available literature would, at very least, suggest that psychedelic compounds and/or the plants that contain them might convey information in some way with humans that have used them. I would later discover instances where people had also described having premonitions or "callings," which occurred *prior* to ever testing the hallucinogens they would later develop affinities for; a notable example of was Albert Hoffman's discovery of LSD. One could reason, in fact, that at some point the same must have taken place, in order for Amazonian natives to successfully learn of the ingredients and processes which created ayahuasca, allowing the hallucinogenic DMT molecules to remain active when consumed orally.

Could there be as-yet unrecognized ways that interspecies communication might occur, perhaps through a medium provided by altered states of consciousness?

CHAPTER TEN

DMT, DREAMS, AND THE SEROTONIN BLUES: ENCOUNTERS WITH SAMURAIS AND OTHER ENTITIES

The various 'other worlds' with which human beings erratically make contact are so many elements in the totality of the awareness belonging to Mind at Large... Temporary by-passes may be acquired either spontaneously, or as the result of deliberate 'spiritual exercises'... or by means of drugs.

-ALDOUS HUXLEY, *The Doors of Perception*

My fascination with psychedelics—particularly DMT—seemed to emerge overnight during the summer of 2007. Looking back on this period of my life, these interests might have seemed pedestrian, compared with some of the subjects and locales that my research has taken me since then. Yet, with little doubt, at the time it must have seemed strange, since most that knew me were aware I had never been a "user" of these kinds of substances. On our way back from a fishing trip one evening in early July of 2008, my friend John Anderson, a radio announcer and producer in Asheville, North Carolina, expressed his own concerns to me after a brief discussion about Dr. Rick Strassman's book, *DMT: The Spirit Molecule.*

"DMT isn't the same as your typical happy, mood-altering hashish and the like. That stuff takes you to a different place. We're talking the land of the fractal mantoids, here."

"Fractal mantoids?" I exclaimed. "Then you *must* be aware of Terence McKenna?"

"Well, in passing," John admitted. "But anyway, I'm going to give you a piece of advice about this, and just take it for what it is. If you ever *do* decide to go and experiment with this sort of stuff..."

My laughter cut him off. "John, come on. You know I'm only interested in the research. I've never tried it before and I don't plan on trying it... *any of it,* anytime soon."

"Well, maybe I'm just saying what needs to be said aloud is all," John surmised. "But either way, if you ever *do* decide to try messing with this stuff, get a buddy; preferably somebody who's tried it. Get somebody to hang around and babysit, too. Like I said, what you're talking about isn't the same as the simple little weeds that make you enjoy stuff a whole lot. On the other hand," John added, changing his tone slightly, "a lotta folks would say you might owe it to yourself to try it at least once if you're going to write about it. Sometimes it helps to have *been there.*"

On our ride back into Asheville, I pondered what John said. It was interesting how, metaphorically or literally, John didn't refer to trying drugs as going into a particular altered state of mind. Instead, he had likened the entire experience to going someplace, as though it were actually a location you could hop in your car and go visit. True, if taking mind-expanding drugs were as simple as a Sunday drive, I might be more inclined to "go there." However, impediments ranging from illegality, to other dangers, restrained me. I didn't have to dig very deep to find the big one: *What if I go "there" and can't get back?* I couldn't count on one hand the number of personal friends I had who had tried psychedelics like LSD and other things. A number I *could* count on one hand, however small, were the friends whose minds had been permanently changed, and often not for the better, through recreational use of such substances.

Not two days before John and I left town for this fishing trip, I had called to check on a friend named Justin who, after various bouts with depression and anxiety over the years, had recently checked out of one of the area hospitals after a brief psychological evaluation. Having battled depression for quite some time, Justin had shared with me a number of strange synchronicities over the years that seemed to involve his unique state of mind, as well as a history of drug use. One that stood out in my memory had occurred during the summer of 2003, shortly after his family doctor suggested he undergo an evaluation. Fearing that he displayed characteristics that, in a clinical sense, resembled schizophrenia, Justin described waking from a deep sleep in his room one evening to find a "samurai warrior" standing before him. The figure was clad in dark, bloody armor resembling classical images of a *kappa,* an evil spirit prevalent in Japanese legends. Another strange item had been a "washboard hanging from a chain or rope around his neck." Needless to say, Justin was startled at the apparition, but finding himself paralyzed, he was unable to move. Suddenly, the menacing figure pointed at him and told him the serotonin in his brain wasn't being produced correctly. At that moment, the eerie phantom vanished, and Justin was again able to move his body. Leaping out of bed, he was badly frightened, confused, and left wondering what the monster had meant by its statement. Even more strange is how, at the time, Justin claimed to have had no knowledge as to what serotonin was, nor what functional purpose it had.

It seemed obvious that Justin was describing an episode of sleep paralysis, and remembering my own somewhat mundane experiences with it, I asked if he was familiar with the term. Not only was he aware of what sleep paralysis was, he shared that his family on his father's side had a history of experiences with it. I suggested that the apparition had likely only been one of these "specters of the mind," and that he not put much stock into believing that the warrior had actually appeared before him with some evil, foreboding, or other underlying purpose. Then Justin told me the rest of the story: shortly following his "encounter," he had gone in for the scheduled evaluation, only to be diagnosed with what his doctors believed was a serotonin deficiency. Depleted levels of naturally produced serotonin within the brain have been linked with depression and other psychological disturbances in the past, including insomnia, fatigue, anxiety, and even low self esteem; all of which Justin had been battling at the time. Still, he claimed that he hadn't known prior to his diagnosis (or the sleep paralysis experience, for that matter) exactly what serotonin was. Had there indeed been some purpose behind the appearance of this frightening entity?

SEROTONIN, TRYPTAMINES, AND THE STUFF OF NIGHTMARES

Serotonin is a neurotransmitter responsible for creating calming feelings of comfort and wellbeing. [1] In a nutshell, it helps us relax. This is why decreased levels of serotonin have so much to do with the onset of depression and anxiety. Though serotonin is created naturally in our bodies, the source for its creation is tryptophan, serotonin's biochemical precursor and one of the 20 standard amino acids, meaning it must be ingested by an organism to become present in their body. [2] It is probably most famous for its association with "Thanksgiving napping", due to the high levels of tryptophan found in turkey meat. Without getting into things on a molecular level, tryptophan's involvement in the production of serotonin can be summed up as follows: we consume things like turkey and receive tryptophan, which then is synthesized in our bodies into the mood-altering serotonin. The process may not be complete at this point however, since serotonin can then be converted into melatonin, a naturally occurring hormone in our bodies that controls our sleep schedules and other biological functions. Melatonin also happens to be in the same tryptamine family as DMT, and bears a close molecular similarity to its hallucinogenic cousin. Along these lines, it's interesting to note that many people who have used melatonin as a dietary supplement or sleep aid since its release to the public for over-the-counter sales in the United States in 1993 have described an increase in vivid dreams.

I discovered this unique quality which melatonin possesses quite by accident, though only second hand. Several years ago after moving into my first home, I found that the transition into living alone in a house in the middle of a strange neighborhood had the natural effect of causing me difficulty in sleeping at night. One morning in particular I had arrived at the news-talk radio station where I worked at the time, only to have our program director walk into my office, take one look at me, and say with due reverence, "man, you look like shit." A few minutes later, our business manager's assistant, Debra, caught me in the hall outside her office and asked me why I looked so down. I explained that I wasn't "down" so much as I was just very tired! She suggested that I buy a bottle of melatonin, which I confessed I had never heard of.

"Oh honey, it's a sleep-aid is all" she told me. "You can buy it at any drug store. I used to give it to the kids when they'd have trouble settling down before bed."

That afternoon I went straight out and purchased a bottle, and tried it that night right before I went to sleep. Aside from a mild calming sensation, it seemed to have little effect on me. I continued taking the small 3-milligram tablets, which lasted for about three nights before I ended up visiting Joshua P. Warren at his house one evening. It was there that he, our mutual friend Casey Fox, and I discussed something about the seemingly harmless sleep-aid of which I had been previously unaware.

"Oh man," I remember Josh saying. "If you've not been sleeping well, *and* you're suffering from all this anxiety, I don't think melatonin is the stuff you need to be taking. Haven't you ever heard about the bad dreams it causes people to have? It caused me to have all kinds of strange, really vivid nightmares."

Casey agreed. "Yeah, I took that stuff years ago, back when a single tablet contained a lot more than your standard 3 milligram dose. Man, I'd go to sleep and wake up thinking I'd been tripping all night." Casey described some of the bizarre things he'd encountered in his dreams while taking melatonin, and then I asked Josh what his dreams had been like. He told me there had been "entities" present.

"What kinds of entities?" I asked.

"They were from hell," he said staring at me, "and they were after me."

Soon after this most encouraging conversation, I gave up on melatonin, and left the bottle sitting on the shelf in my medicine cabinet where it would remain forgotten, for a while at least. I had decided, at that most delicate point in my life, that the idea of being pursued by demons from hell every night while I slept would have done little to help the growing stress and sleeplessness I had begun to experience. Later on however, I would return to the concept of using melatonin, this time specifically for the purpose of trying to enter some sort of an "altered state," even if it could only be entered through dreaming. This seemed much safer than gambling with the variables I'd tucked away in my subconscious that involved *real* psychedelics; the hardcore entheogens and substances like LSD, peyote, and yes, DMT, our friendly spirit molecule.

Nonetheless, I would soon find that I didn't have to take melatonin to encounter all kinds of strange things while in dreamland. If anything, it began to seem like all the reading and researching I had begun to do with regard to psychedelic substances and their ability to connect us with other worlds was literally permeating my consciousness. I began finding myself in bizarre scenarios within my dreams nearly every night, in which people, or sometimes other weird beings like robots and aliens, would hand me little "samples" of the very substances I would read about during my waking hours. In one particular dream, I had been performing at a strange venue with an imaginary band, and while retrieving equipment from my car before the show, a couple of weird looking kids came up and handed me a reefer, inviting me to smoke it with them before we played. I accepted it from them with haste, shoving it into my pocket, eager to smoke it later. This never occurred, however, as it seems that before the band and I ever got to perform, I had been transported elsewhere, as is often the case with dreams.

Now, we found ourselves in a setting similar to that of a festival I actually *had* played with one of my bands, near Loganton, Pennsylvania, just a few weeks beforehand (as a professional guitarist, during the summer months I do tend to travel around the Southeast a good bit, performing with various folk and Bluegrass acts). It was at this point in the dream that I discovered a strange magazine sandwiched in a stack of old books, still wrapped in plastic as though it had been shipped from the publisher, containing a small sample container with the letters DMT marked on the side. Before I could ever use the stuff, I lost the weird looking periodical. Then, after dodging into a comic book shop to try and find it again, I woke up.

What had been the meaning of these dreams, if any was intended at all? Was my subconscious playing tricks on me as I slept, or was I just reading too much about this subject; and then subsequently reading too much into the dreams that resulted? In a sense, I could liken this to feeling like someone, or maybe *something*, had been trying to encourage me to experiment with these substances, or had been taunting me subtly from someplace outside my own consciousness. Could the allure of psychedelics reach out to us in this way, even in the absence of their use?

THE PSYCHIC EFFECTS OF PSYCHEDELIC DRUGS

This notion seems ridiculous at a glance; however, I certainly wouldn't be the first person that has described this sort of thing. Many people involved with the use and production of psychedelic substances in the past have described a strange attraction or "calling" to them. In his book *LSD: My Problem Child*, Albert Hoffman described his own strange instance of being lured back to the otherwise uninteresting synthesis of a useless drug he had named LSD-25 while pursuing medically useful derivatives from the parasitic fungus Ergot:

> I could not forget the relatively uninteresting LSD-25. A peculiar presentiment—the feeling that this substance could possess properties other than those established in the first investigations—induced me, five years after the first synthesis, to produce LSD-25 once again so that a sample could be given to the pharmacological department for further tests. [3]

Hoffman notes that this was all but forbidden in his practice; after all, experimental substances, as a rule, could not be resubmitted for what would amount to potentially costly testing, especially when they were understood to be "lacking in pharmacological interest." Whatever the case, Hoffman followed his intuition, and in the spring of 1943, synthesized yet another batch of the peculiar LSD-25.

It was around this time Hoffman discovered LSD's strange chemical attributes. Somehow, he had managed to get a very small amount of the stuff on his fingertips during the purification and crystallization process. He described feeling "a remarkable restlessness, combined with a slight dizziness." Later at home, he lay down, closed his eyes to block out the "unpleasantly glaring" light from outside, and was treated to an "uninterrupted stream of fantastic pictures, extraordinary shapes with intense, kaleidoscopic play of colors," which lasted for two hours. Interestingly, the heading in Hoffman's book directly prior to recounting this information is titled *Discovery of the Psychic Effects of LSD*. It is likely that this referred simply to the effects of LSD on the human psyche, although it seems plausible that Hoffman might have truly felt that the unordinary circumstances leading to the discovery of the drug, and the experiences that would follow, were indeed psychic in nature. [4]

Similarly, as I described in the last chapter, many indigenous cultures use the potent tea called *yage* or *ayahuasca* derived from the liana vines, *Banisteriopsis caapi*, that grow throughout South America. The hallucinogenic compound active in ayahuasca is DMT (though it should be noted that not all varieties of ayahuasca are hallucinogenic). As we know, DMT's hallucinogenic properties aren't present when taken orally. This is where it gets interesting; the ayahuasca brew is also very rich in *beta-carbolines*, a kind of alkaloid that can be hallucinogenic by itself, though only at near-toxic amounts. In the smaller, less-toxic doses present in ayahuasca, the active *beta-carboline* harmine has the peculiar ability to inhibit enzyme systems in the body that prevent DMT from causing its psychedelic effects. In essence, the brew includes a unique chemical mix of harmine and DMT, which together break down monoamine oxidase inhibitors in the body that keep the psychedelic DMT from becoming active when taken orally. [5]

Somehow, the South American natives figured all this out on their own, having used ayahuasca in their shamanic practices for some time—perhaps centuries or more—before western anthropologists first observed them using it in the 1950s. The question of how they discovered the correct mixture of native plants remains a mystery, which involves another ingredient in the ayahuasca tea: the leaves of the *chacruna* plant.

"Chacruna leaves contain DMT. (Natives) mix chacruna leaves with ayahuasca, which contains several substances that inhibit the stomach enzyme," says anthropologist Jeremy Narby, who has studied psychedelic shamanism for decades. "How could they have discovered this recipe when we know there are

80,000 species of evolved plants in the Amazon? Any given combination would give only a one in six billion chance of finding it." [6]

On the subject of psychic phenomena with regard to discovering psychedelic drugs like LSD and even DMT, I must again draw a few relevant parallels between the strange relationships these drugs, and altered consciousness that results from their use, share with mental illnesses like schizophrenia. Much like the circumstances my friend Justin experienced where the weird "samurai" appeared to warn him of his serotonin deficiency, schizophrenia is often characterized by delusional behavior that sometimes includes the appearance of beings or entities. Unlike my friend's circumstances, in the schizophrenic patient this occurs while they are awake and aware, whereas Justin's entity appeared in the altered state present during his sleep paralysis.

Still, in drawing comparisons to the appearance of entities in both drug-induced and psychotic states, I discovered references to studies conducted in the 1950s with schizophrenia patients where they were administered DMT in order to see how similar the "DMT state" may be to their descriptions of schizophrenic hallucinations. The article appeared in the *Journal of Mental Science* in 1958 under the title "Dimethyltryptamine Experiments with Psychotics," where Stephen Szara had described how one of the patients in this study had been aware of "strange creatures, dwarves or something," at the beginning of an administered DMT trip. [7] A 1959 study tried similar experiments with ten schizophrenic patients, who were injected with DMT; only one was able to recall anything of her experiences afterward. This woman also described inhuman entities that were hurting her. "I was living in a world of orange people," she said of her experience. [8]

In these studies, the schizophrenic patients described these instances of encounters with "beings" only during their DMT trips. Similarly, in many shamanic practices by native cultures, DMT or other psychedelics might be introduced using things like the *ayahuasca* tea to induce their visions, though some visions may still occur using methods other than those involving psychedelic substances. As a result of the many parallels between mystical states similar to the DMT experience and documented schizophrenic hallucinations, it has been suggested of shamanic visions that *cultural relativism*, where foreign definitions of abnormality would differ from our own due to varying cultural and social norms, might cause these shamans to be labeled the same as schizophrenics in western society.

Again, let us return to the 1976 report by psychologist Jane Murphy, regarding Eskimos and West African Yoruba tribes making distinctions between altered states of consciousness and "being crazy," as might be the case with one suffering schizophrenia. As noted previously, the Eskimo word, *nuthkavihak*, describes one who may carry on conversations with oneself, or one who refuses to speak altogether, as well as noting delusions and other erratic behavior. Similarly, the Yoruba people refer to this as *were*, a condition almost identical to its Eskimo counterpart. Both cultures treat these as what we, in the West, might call schizophrenia, while separating shamanic visions altogether as something controlled and wholly spiritual.

Another instance where the parallels between DMT trips, alleged contact with entities and the descriptions of schizophrenic patients have been noteworthy involves the research of psychologist Wilson Van Dusen, Ph.D. Van Dusen conducted a fascinating study with hundreds of schizophrenic patients and individuals suffering from hallucinations where entities would appear before them. Attempting to better understand the nature of schizophrenia, he decided he would try and interact with the hallucinations described by his patients, and by finding individuals who were able to distinguish between their own thoughts and those presented by the hallucinations, Van Dusen hoped to establish a relationship with both the patient and the "entities" they described, with the patient acting as a sort of interpreter.

During the interview sessions, Van Dusen treated the hallucinations he wished to speak with as though they were real, much as his patients believed them to be. Often speaking directly to the entities, he asked the participants to dictate their replies to him word for word. By doing so, Van Dusen was exposed to bizarre instances of dialogue, sometimes held for long periods, which often appeared to be symbolically (and literally) beyond the comprehension levels of the patients themselves. Many of the patients even said they felt that their encounters with the beings were some sort of contact with entities from other places, rather than being mere hallucinations. [9]

Supposing that his patient's interpretations may be of some merit, Van Dusen believed that there might be a connection between these entities, and other types of phenomena, like possession and other instances of paranormal contact with beings like ghosts, spirits, and demons. Though most in the clinical world would never consider a source for this kind of interaction beyond fragments of the patient's own unstable mind, Van Dusen questioned whether the entities he interacted with might "really be spirits or pieces of one's own consciousness?" [10]

Though Van Dusen's fascinating research didn't involve administering drugs to his patients, the similarities between his work and the previous studies with DMT being administered to schizophrenic patients, as well as the entities encountered by patients of a sound mental state during DMT studies like those of Dr. Rick Strassman in the 1990s, are hard to ignore.

Whether the circumstances represent a natural chemical imbalance, or an experience is instigated from external sources or stimuli, could there be a way that certain molecules act as "keys," opening the human mind as though it were a doorway to other worlds? And if not other worlds, what deeper realms of *consciousness* might await the intrepid psychonaut, should they aspire to reach further depths beyond the known areas of the human mind? Rather than aliens and otherworldly beings communicating across space and time, what if the deeper mysteries of humankind reside within our minds... in a realm inhabited by archetypes and symbols that have guided us along since the beginning of time?

CHAPTER ELEVEN

THE INHABITANTS OF INNER-SPACE: DMT ENTITIES AND SPACE ALIENS

What happens when the spirit molecule pulls and pushes us beyond the physical and emotional levels of awareness? We enter into invisible realms, ones we cannot normally sense and whose presence we can scarcely imagine. Even more surprising, these realms appear to be inhabited.

-DR. RICK STRASSMAN in *DMT: The Spirit Molecule*

It was September 21, the Belizean Independence Day, when my group and I arrived on land at the former colony of British Honduras. Festive crowds moved with the late summer heat as we made our way from the pier, stomping along several blocks of narrow sidewalks to the area where our bus waited. It would carry us to an embarkation area, and from there, a half-hour speedboat ride upriver would bring us to *Lamanai*, the ancient Mayan City of the Sunken Crocodile.

Belize is one of several countries in the region that had once comprised the center of the Mayan civilization. Today, more than 900 Mesoamerican archaeological sites exist, with many having become renowned tourist attractions. Wandering along the jungle paths toward Lamanai, the eerie taunting of howler monkeys echoed from trees around me. Despite this, I found peculiar comfort in recognizing the vines dangling overhead as a variety of *liana*, whose cousins further south are the primary ingredients in many of the regional varieties of ayahuasca brewed in South America.

Joining me on this adventure was a friend and former intelligence officer, operating under the self-ascribed nickname "MacAlias," who occasionally offers me advice and guidance regarding my news and current events podcast. Also with us had been Neil Stickel and his wonderful girlfriend, Jaime, who over a lunchtime discussion just one day earlier had shared their personal experience traveling to Peru a few years ago, and undergoing an ayahuasca ceremony; it remains, without contest, one of the most striking ayahuasca experiences ever related to me.

Neil and his girlfriend had not been users of psychedelics, or any other kinds of drugs, in the past. However, Neil, whose father passed away at an early age, had long battled with the pain of losing his parent, and maintained conflicted feelings about the relationship for many years afterward. After hearing about the healing effects described by many users of ayahuasca, he and Jamie decided to make the journey to Peru, where they would visit a retreat center, and participate in a supervised ayahuasca ceremony.

The ayahuasca experience is not a pleasant one, as most who drink the tea are stricken with nausea and sickness for the duration of the time the ingredients are active in their bodies. Neil and Jamie had been no exception, and each of them, while in separate parts of the lodge (so as not to become a distraction to one another) were gifted with the full effect of the ayahuasca "cleansing." Each recalled having a number of unique visions, which included one synchronicity the couple shared from their separate areas in the lodge that was seemingly telepathic in nature. However, the most striking experience was a personal recollection Neil recounted having late in the evening of their stay.

"I was having a very hard time," Neil told me. "I was very sick, and at one point I was so exhausted that I could barely move any longer." It was at this point that Neil became aware of three soft, glowing lights in the distance ahead of him. Through the haze of the ayahuasca subspace, Neil saw three forms—each were masses of golden light that were vaguely human in their general shape—moving slowly toward him. Once they finally reached his area, Neil then observed a column of light descending from above, encasing him and the three luminous forms that were now directly before him. "I was so amazed and excited that these beings were with me that, at first, I didn't even notice a fourth source of light had appeared in the same direction they came from." Once he became aware of this new light, which was a soft blue color, Neil felt distracted by it, as though the approaching glow were preventing him from being able to focus on the golden "beings" within the encircling light formation.

"The blue glow kept moving toward me for a long time," Neil said. "Finally, it was just outside the circle of light, and then it entered the circle with the golden beings and me. But by that time, I could recognize the glow."

It was Neil's father.

Neil was able to interact with this bluish glow for some time, and experienced an energetic exchange with it that indicated, beyond any doubt, that his father was being allowed to interact with him, almost as though interacting on an immaterial plane between the worlds of life and death. Then, at one point the blue light moved closer, and actually *entered* Neil, filling him with an incredible sense of love, comfort, and recognition.

"After some time, I finally felt that I had been able to reconcile with my father," Neil told me, as I sat across from him and Jamie, enthralled by his memory of this experience. "I managed to get one of the chaperones over to help me, because I felt at this point that I had to get outside." The guide helped Neil—who was crawling at this point—allowing him to safely reach a stone step where he could sit outside the lodge.

Once he was alone again, Neil looked up, his eyes focusing on the gleaming stars overhead. He lifted his hand, and watched as the blue light emerged, passing right through his fingertips, and steadily rising away toward the dark evening sky. The light moved quickly upward, and disappeared, with the strange, cosmic reunion between father and son now behind them.

"The experience absolutely changed me," Neil said. "I didn't feel the anxiety, or the confusion about my father's passing any longer after that, and I truly believe that what I experienced was, in some way, a reunion where my dad was able to come back, make peace with me, and tell me that he loved me."

As experiences like Neil's help illustrate, there is probably no hallucinogen more powerful, or profound in effect, than DMT. Though we've discussed some of its unusual effects already throughout this book, DMT will be the sole focus of the remainder of this chapter, due to several peculiar traits it possesses that makes it hard to compare with other psychedelic drugs. Studies and literature pertaining to DMT experiences recount a number of consistent features, which include encounters, often frighteningly real, with what could only be likened to "alien" beings. These often occur in environments that at least appear to maintain a degree of continuity from one account to the next. Also, DMT, unlike other psychedelic compounds, is already present in our bodies; one might even argue that this makes it the most readily available drug of its sort.

So far as its composition, dimethyltryptamine is among the simplest of all psychedelic molecules; maybe surprisingly so. DMT is a member of the tryptamine family of drugs, which are derived from the amino acid *tryptophan*. A tryptamine molecule basically consists of two clusters of carbon atoms; one is a six-membered *benzene* ring, which is fused alongside a five-membered *pyrrole* ring containing a single nitrogen atom. These two carbon clusters are also surrounded by numerous hydrogen atoms, which altogether form what is called an *indole*. An indole can be produced when naturally present bacteria begin breaking down tryptophan. With the inclusion of a second nitrogen atom conjoined by a chain of two carbon atoms stemming from the pyrrole ring, the simple indole then becomes a tryptamine molecule. Finally, the inclusion of two more methyl groups (carbon atoms) stemming from this second nitrogen atom, which is then called the *amine* nitrogen atom, results in the formation of the DMT molecule. [2]

Now, I'm aware that I said DMT is the simplest of all the psychedelic molecules, and I certainly just gave you an eye-full with the "simple" description above. For the sake of simplicity, just remember that essentially all you need is an *indole* molecule joined with one of those little *amine* nitrogen atoms, which is all DMT really is. Easy, right?

As stated earlier, DMT is already in our bodies since it is a natural by-product of tryptophan, just like serotonin. However, in spite of its "availability", DMT is not produced in large enough amounts within our bodies to evoke psychedelic experiences, though in theory there may still be ways that various stimuli can (and sometimes will) cause a larger endogenous release. The trick seems to be learning exactly what kind of stimulus this would involve, which became the focus of Dr. Rick Strassman, M.D., one of the only true medical pioneers in DMT research. In his book *DMT: The Spirit Molecule,* Strassman describes how he believes that the DMT produced in our bodies may actually stem from the pineal gland within our brains, an area first referred to by French philosopher Rene Descartes as "the seat of the soul," and having been long believed to possess mystical properties.

THE SPIRIT MOLECULE

These ethereal properties associated with the pineal gland bear strong resemblance to several ancient mystical traditions, namely that of the Tibetan Buddhists. In the classic funerary text the *Bardo Thodol,* most often referred to in the west as the *Tibetan Book of the Dead,* it is interesting to note regarding Tibetan concepts of reincarnation that forty-nine days is the period of time a spirit that has passed into the afterlife must wait before it may re-

246 Magic, Mysticism and the Molecule

enter a mother's womb for birth. Interestingly, there is a biological counterpart to this; the pineal gland becomes visible in the developing fetus at *exactly forty-nine days*, a date which also marks the clear indication of gender. Might this be a coincidence, or is there indeed special relevance between the appearance of the pineal gland and Eastern mystic traditions of the soul entering the body?

The *Tibetan Book of the Dead* also describes what is called the *chikhai bardo* or "bardo of the moment of death." *Bardos* are intervals described throughout the text, the word literally meaning "transitional state", and at the moment of death the *chikhai bardo* is associated with what is called "The Clear Light of Reality":

> At this moment, the first (glimpsing) of the *Bardo* of the Clear Light of Reality, which is the Infallible Mind of the *Dharma-Kaya,* is experienced by all sentient beings. [3]

Of course, this persistent notion of "going toward the light" at the time of death has become one of the signature elements of the near-death experience. Their similarity to ecstatic states, brought about by the altered consciousness that occurs during use of psychedelics, is remarkably similar. Rick Strassman, who had long wondered about the parallels between psychedelic visions and mystical experiences, was fascinated by this, and after years of interest in the pineal gland and its role in human development, he began to wonder if some biological agent could be associated with the pineal gland that might be responsible for triggering mystical experiences at key times throughout our lives.

Early tests ruled out substances similar in makeup to DMT, including Melatonin, as far as having any psychedelic properties. Though the direct associations between DMT and the pineal gland remain inconclusive even today, Strassman nonetheless felt that DMT's appearance in our bodies, as well as similarities between its chemical precursors in relation to brain activity and the role of the pineal gland, made it a likely candidate for what he dubbed "the spirit molecule." "Both Western and Eastern mystical traditions place our highest spiritual center within (the pineal gland's) confines. I therefore wondered if excessive pineal DMT production was involved in naturally occurring psychedelic states."

THE DMT EXPERIENCE

Strassman's research is well known today in various circles, ranging from topics as varied as transcendental meditation and clinical pharmacology, to the more bizarre reports of alien abduction phenomenon. By obtaining DEA approval for clinical research with DMT, between 1990 and 1995 he performed an extensive study at the University of New Mexico with sixty volunteers, where he was able to observe and record the profound effects DMT has on the human mind.

The nature of the DMT experience was often frighteningly real to the participants of the study, who described bizarre encounters with a variety of beings in colorful, illuminated environments consistently described as resembling "docking areas," nurseries, medical environments, and other clinical settings. In a typical encounter, participants would describe beings including insect-like humanoids (specifically resembling praying mantises), cactus-like beings, shadow people, clowns, elves, reptilians (often resembling crocodiles, or even dragons), and bizarre geometric stick figures. Sometimes these beings would appear surprised or even startled to "find" the participants in their environment; other times they were described as seeming to have been expecting them. During portions of Strassman's study, which were intended to test participant's tolerance levels to the drug, some people said that subsequent doses sent them back to these locations repeatedly, where they were greeted by the same beings and "welcomed back." [4]

In some cases, a prevailing sense of friendship and brotherhood seems to resonate from these beings during the DMT hallucinations. "Cassandra," one of Strassman's volunteers, described being loved by what she called elves:

> I saw and felt myself as a good person, as loved by the DMT elves... there was a sense of many visitors, all of them jovial, and they had a great time giving me the experience of being loved. [5]

A similar recollection provided a description of an entity that resembled a honeybee, who gave off a "sensual energy" as it showed its visitor the hive-like community where it lived, saying "this is the future of mankind."

Not all DMT experiences shower the participant with love, and feelings of happiness and all things good. At least a few experiences are very upsetting, sometimes including personal invasions that may affect the participant for some time (not surprisingly, a similar small percentage, around 15%, describe "hellish" events during near-death experiences). For instance, one participant actually described being sexually assaulted by two crocodile-like creatures, while others described "sinister" beings, and a sense of some presence "taking control," which some participants expressed a desire to protect themselves from.

Also common to the DMT experience, as well as many shamanic mystic journeys, is the experience of disembodiment, where the physical body is "stripped apart" in order to allow the freedom of moving about in a spirit-form. In shamanic traditions, this usually concludes with the process of being reassembled, a sort of "initiation" into the role of the shaman, but for many in the West, this seems to be less easily understood for its spiritual symbolism, and many describe the experience as terrifying.

Similar to this disembodiment are the reports of people's bodies being tested, probed, or otherwise subjected to medical environments, which lends itself very much to an idea Strassman proposes: that a common link between alien abduction and the DMT experience should be further explored. [6]

ALIEN ENCOUNTERS WITH DMT BEINGS

Fortunately, in spite of the occasional negative encounters, most participants did feel their experiences were positive in nature, and that they stood to gain from the experiences they had. But regardless of the positive or negative effects, perhaps what is most striking about the experiences is the consistency between "alien" aspects recounted during DMT trips. This pertains not only to the physical characteristics of the entities themselves, but also the way the DMT seems to "present itself." As Terence McKenna put it, "its seeming accentuation of themes alien, insectile, and futuristic," has led some to believe that the drug itself might act as some strange, alien presence, "come to give humanity the keys to galactarian citizenship." [7] Strassman even seemed to indicate that he felt DMT might have gone about "showing" its users things which, in some way, they may have "needed to see," as if carried out by some sort judgment existing beyond what the individual themselves expects or hopes to find. "DMT seems to have its own agenda," Strassman surmises. On another occasion he asks, "What was the spirit molecule trying to tell us?" At one point, he even states, "I could not ignore the message the spirit molecule was giving us." [8]

If indeed the experience were purely hallucinatory, it would be easy to assume that encounters would vary according to the physical environment, the mindset, and the history of each participant. Instead, the consistency of alien aspects reported during the DMT trip includes the aforementioned varieties of beings that were frequently encountered. Among these, strangely enough, are "elves", both those of the classical description, as well those like Terence Mckenna described: the "Self-Transforming Machine Elves" of his own DMT experiences. McKenna alternately referred to these entities as *Fractal Elves, Self-Dribbling Basket Balls,* and *Tykes* as well; in some cases, he seemed to almost struggle to relate the innately indescribable elements of the DMT landscape to his audience:

> So you burst into this space. It's lit, socketed lighting, some kind of indirect lighting you can't quite locate. But what is astonishing and immediately riveting is that in this place there are entities—there are these things, which I call "self transforming machine elves," I also call them self-dribbling basketballs... it's a jeweled self-transforming basketball, a machine elf. [9]

Perhaps stranger than the amorphous "machine elves" which McKenna described are the *actual elves* that sometimes appear. Let us recall "Cassandra" from Strassman's study, who described being "loved by the DMT elves." Indeed, though it is possible that knowledge of McKenna's references to elves might have been available at this time, Strassman argued in a 2008 interview that "Terence McKenna's descriptions of the machine elves and the dwarves and the pixies hadn't really come out yet... and not that many people were really familiar with Terrence in the early nineties in the first place." [10]

Author Daniel Pinchbeck described his own encounter with elves as "so embarrassing that I hesitate to tell it." One night while in Palenque, Pinchbeck combined mushrooms (which don't contain DMT, though the active agents in these fungi, psilocybin, is a tryptamine also) along with moclobemide, an antidepressant that inhibits monoamine oxidase, the enzymes that break down DMT when taken orally. After a few minutes of watching what he described as "rapid bands of green and yellow flimmering" behind his closed eyelids, the colorful images began to "sharpen into focus", resulting in a group of giggling elves standing together in a line. "There were many of them," Pinchbeck said. "A mob of little people in traditional green outfits and peaked caps. They were jumping up and down and they were cheering." Pinchbeck described the elves as being as clear as "film images" during the trip, and even supposed that there was a possibility that McKenna's "Elf Archetype" may have influenced him also, though he mentions that these friendly elf-folk "were not transforming and not at all machinelike. They were just normal, garden variety elves." [11]

As described earlier, Elves aren't the only entities reported consistently by DMT users during their experiences. Reptilian humanoids and creatures that resemble insects are also prevalent, both of which bear a remarkable similarity to certain varieties of alien occupants in UFO and abduction literature. Remember Michael Harner's account from two chapters ago of dragon-faced reptilians claiming to be "the masters of outer darkness," the same which a blind shaman seemed to recognize? It is interesting to note that aliens described as being reptile or dragon-like are often described in various UFO-related conspiracy theories. Some of these, pertaining to such things as a proposed "Planet X" or *Nibiru*, as it is often called, involve parts of our solar system (or places further beyond) that, very appropriately, could be likened to "outer darkness."

Of even greater intrigue than hostile reptilian aliens wavering between outer space and the DMT state are the "mantises." These represent intelligent insect-like alien creatures, described frequently by alien abductees and psychonauts alike. Greg Bishop, author of the book *It Defies Language!*, once ruminated over this same parallel at his *UFO Mystic* blog:

> What is at the root of our perceptions that makes both UFO witnesses and DMT (and other psychedelic substance) trippers hook up with this particular insect? The answer may lie in areas that most UFO researchers do not care to tread, namely, that some of the same brain circuits are

being lit up in the altered states that both experiences may induce. This leads us to the possible conclusion that the ufonauts are using parts of our brains that most of us never access in order to get to us.

Similarly, in his book *Sex, Drugs, Einstein, and Elves,* Clifford Pickover ponders the same: "Why do so many people using DMT see insects? The DMT insect race comprises 'larval beings,' 'alien space insects,' praying-mantis entities and so forth." [12] Daniel Pinchbeck describes a similar experience a friend of his had after a powerful DMT trip that involved meeting a praying mantis creature with "whirring legs." Strangely, Pinchbeck's friend claimed he "recognized" the entity:

He told us how he had set free a praying mantis when he was five. The praying mantis had turned to look back at him before it hopped away, and at that moment he knew, with complete and utter certainty.
He knew that the mantis knew him. [13]

But how could this be? Indeed, Pinchbeck's friend seems to have related something wholly metaphysical in nature. However, Ufologists like John Lear report a very different kind of scenario. Apparently, Lear claims to recall becoming fascinated with UFOs after learning from intelligence sources during his time with the Air Force that Germany had recovered a crashed "flying saucer" as early as 1939. More alleged saucer crashes were said to have occurred in the

United States after World War II, which Lear was told had been piloted by "ugly praying mantis creatures" that were far more advanced than humans.[14] Mantises appear yet again in what is arguably one of the best-known popular accounts dealing with alien abduction, Whitley Strieber's 1987 book *Communion*. The famous cover of Streiber's book has long been considered among the most widely recognized representations of a 'gray' alien in popular culture today. [15]

Though the majority of Strieber's experiences involved these well-recognized "grays" popularly associated with UFO abduction since the 1970s, at one point while undergoing hypnosis he did recount something a bit different. Recalling a camping experience from his childhood, Strieber describes something resembling "a skeleton on a motorcycle" interrupting him and his sisters at their campsite outside their grandmother's house. He also seems to remember a "horrible" being that pursues him, and admits that it "scares him to death." Suddenly, he gets a closer glimpse of the entity: "A praying-mantis is what it looks like." Strieber marvels over the insect-like creature, asking, "How can it be so big?" just before Strieber recalls feeling the creature "working something into his hair." [16]

Many of the peculiar, dream-like elements in Strieber's recollection of encountering a mantis-like alien do seem to parallel reports chronicled by DMT researchers Rick Strassman, Slawek Wojtowicz, Luis Eduardo Luna, and Ede Frescka in their book *Inner*

Paths to Outer Space: Journeys to Alien Worlds Through Psychedelics and Other Spiritual Technologies. Frescka notes in the book that such encounters aren't necessarily a recent phenomenon, stating that, "In ancient Greek mythology, there are Titans, godly beings who descend from heaven and who had sexual intercourse with earthly women. Interestingly, the Greek word *titanos* means 'gray', a term sometimes used to describe mantis-like aliens." Frescka also mentions a detailed description of ritual entities, depicted in plaster statues found at the 'Ain Ghazal excavation site in 1983, as dictated by Steven Mithen, Professor of Archaeology at the University of Reading:

> They have flattish bodies, elongated necks, large round faces, and wide-open eyes with deep black centers. The noses are molded stubs; the lips hardly exist at all. The plaster is pure white. [17]

This description does sound very much like alien "grays," although Frescka points out that Mithen originally interpreted them as representing ghosts. "Controversial and contradictory as it may sound," Frescka says, "we conceptualize them differently: they were "real" extraterrestrials—though not necessarily from outer space. Instead, these ancient gods—possibly the teachers of agriculture—were DMT entities that emerged from inner space." [18]

Indeed, a variety of reports from both UFO abductee lore and the realm of the psychedelic seem to detail encounters with these creatures, variously reported as grays, elves, mantises, reptilians, and other strange anthropomorphic forms. Though there appear to be obvious parallels—connections so apparent that they practically beg to be analyzed further—it seems that our efforts to interpret, classify, or draw conclusions can sometimes lead to false categorizations, or conclusions which may be altogether misleading. Still, it is difficult to ignore the prevalence of the mantises—and other consistently reported DMT entities—among these various related fields of study. It is equally difficult to discern what their presence may indicate. Perhaps it is intended that the mystery of these subspace entities be left to the individual; indeed, everyone seems to bring back his or her own interpretations of the experiences they had while meeting these beings.

In spite of the sense of newness, learning and discovery the DMT experience often provides, there is also a sense of familiarity that is frequently described. For instance, one of Rick Strassman's volunteers, "Sarah," admitted that she had somehow always felt that humankind wasn't alone in the universe:

> I thought the only way to encounter them was with bright lights and flying saucers in outer space. It never occurred to me to actually encounter them in our own inner space. I thought the only things we could encounter were things in our own personal sphere of archetypes and mythology.

Of course, many argue that this notion of "archetypes" forms the very essence of the DMT beings: rather than being aliens, perhaps they are a culmination of our cultural beliefs, our deepest longings, and our greatest fears. This is easy to surmise when giving rational consideration to the DMT experience, but the testimonies of those who have visited the wild and colorful DMT landscape differ on this interpretation. As Daniel Pinchbeck puts it so eloquently:

> It seems absurd to propose that the dismissed and disgraced psychedelic compounds might be real doorways to neighboring dimensions, and within these other realms there are beings we can contact who are waiting to welcome us with disconcerting glee. It is even more absurd to suggest that some of those beings resemble our folkloric archetypes, because they are the source for those archetypes in the first place.

CHAPTER TWELVE

FROM BEYOND: TESLA, LOVECRAFT, AND HIGH-TECH SHAMANISM

Belief is the enemy.

-JOHN KEEL, *The Mothman Prophecies*

On many occasions, Serbian inventor Nikola Tesla described how he thought the electrical potential created by his inventions, namely the Tesla coil, could be used as a "resonant receiver" capable of communication with the inhabitants of planets. "The possibility of beckoning Martians was the extreme application of (my) principle of propagation of electric waves," Tesla told *Electric World* Magazine in April of 1896. "The same principle may be employed with good effects for the transmission of news to all parts of the earth... Every city on the globe could be on an immense circuit. (Thus) a message sent from New York would be in England, Africa and Australia in an instant. What a grand thing it would be." [1]

Indeed, it would certainly have been grand if Tesla's applications had provided global communication of this magnitude by the early twentieth century. Of even greater importance might have been Tesla's success in establishing a SETI program so early in the game, although it is known that Tesla did, in fact, spend a good bit of the remainder of his life working on the creation of a unique device, sometimes referred to as the *Teslascope*, which was intended for such cosmic communications. Though the brilliant inventor would claim to have received radio signals from deep space on many occasions, modern researchers like Kenneth and James Corum have suggested that what Tesla may actually have detected was purely natural. Rather than being dispatches from aliens, Tesla's radio communications might have stemmed from natural radio emissions like those created by Saturn's magnetic field, known as the Saturn Kilometric Radiation; or even the Jovian plasma torus signals emanating from Jupiter and other distant locales. [2]

Whether or not he was accurate regarding the nature of the radio emissions he monitored, perhaps there were greater implications hidden within Tesla's body of work. Though the methods he ultimately chose for use in contacting other worlds may have yielded limited results, Tesla nonetheless seemed to have other ideas that kept him in the cosmic ballpark, so to speak. For instance, in addition to his theories about resonant reception, Tesla had also discussed how the effects of "other dimensions" might become visible in the resonant field of a Tesla coil. In other words, Tesla seemed to feel that the appearance of interdimensional oddities could result from being in the presence of intense electricity gathered in one area.

It is questionable whether or not this would indeed be the case, at least in terms of high-powered Tesla coils producing rifts in the fabric between two dimensions; especially considering the fact that many since his death have continued to experiment with Tesla's designs. However, along these same lines, there is at least evidence that suggests that more subjective anomalies—those triggered within the human body instead of in the space around us—may still occur in the presence of intense electric fields. Interestingly, during such experiences, people have not only described strange hallucinations, but even the appearance of strange, alien entities very similar to those from the DMT experiences described earlier. In essence, Tesla's research may have offered the first glimpses of evoking altered states of consciousness by implementing technology, particularly that which involves exposure to intense electric fields.

FROM BEYOND

More bizarre, perhaps, than the notion that Tesla had hoped to contact extraterrestrials is the fact that the renowned author of the macabre H.P. Lovecraft expressed similar concepts in one of his short stories, *From Beyond*. Literary critic S.T. Joshi points out that most of the philosophical elements portrayed in the story can be attributed to Hugh Elliot's book *Modern Science and Materialism*, published in 1919, which Lovecraft is known to have read. It deals with themes that include the fallibility of human senses, colors imperceptible to the human eye, and matter consisting primarily of empty space; all things that later became a hallmark of Lovecraft's unique style. [3]

There is no question regarding the fact that Lovecraft's brand of fiction was weird. However, in the particular case of *From Beyond*, we seem to catch a glimpse of Lovecraft's ability to detect elements of the human physiology, psyche, and spirit—as well as his aptitude for melding them together strangely in his stories—that nearly approaches the precognitive. Indeed, Tesla had predicted that strange things might occur in the presence of powerful electric fields, but Lovecraft somehow manages to take it a step further in *From Beyond*, predicting the exact mechanisms of the human body which may act as receptacles for interdimensional phenomena. It is hardly surprising that Lovecraft's receptor to other worlds was the very same organ Descartes called "the seat of the soul," and what Dr Rick Strassman has identified as the lonely manufacturer of his long-sought "spirit molecule" DMT: the pineal gland.

From Beyond tells the story of Crawford Tillinghast, who has managed to create an electronic device that emits a resonance wave capable of stimulating the pineal gland of people nearby. This, much in the same way Tesla described, allows the subject to see aspects of parallel worlds that exist outside the scope of accepted reality, only not quite in the same literal fashion that Tesla had predicted. The narrator in the story, a man who is concerned about the dangers involving Tillinghast's experiments, begins to perceive an alien environment that overlaps with our own dimension. Tillinghast then reveals that the effect the machine creates will work both ways, allowing the creatures from alternate dimensions to perceive humans as well. This, it turns out, resulted in the killing of two of Tillinghast's house servants by an otherworldly creature. At the climax of the story, Tillinghast points out to the narrator that he sees him trembling with fear. "Why don't you move, then," Tillinghast asks. "Tired? Well, don't worry, my friend, for they are coming... Look, look, curse you, look... it's just over your left shoulder..." At this moment, sensing the creature moving in from behind him, the narrator desperately reaches for a revolver and shoots the machine, destroying it. Police later investigate the scene, where Tillinghast is found dead.

At one rather revealing moment of dialogue early in the story, Tillinghast discusses the role the pineal

gland plays in the workings of his machine, referring
to it as a dormant sensory organ:

> You have heard of the pineal gland? I laugh at the
> shallow endocrinologist, fellow-dupe and fellow-
> parvenu of the Freudian. That gland is the great
> sense organ of organs—I have found out. It is like
> sight in the end, and transmits visual pictures to
> the brain. If you are normal, that is the way you
> ought to get most of it... I mean get most of the
> evidence from beyond. [5]

Lovecraft, through the diabolical character of
Crawford Tillinghast, effectively seems to anticipate a
few of the strange, paranormal aspects that would
later be associated with the pineal gland, though he
wasn't the first to correlate it with metaphysics.
Many ancient cultures took meaning from its location
deep in the brain, creating a perceived notion among
philosophers of its importance. The pineal gland was
often called a "mystery" gland, associated with myths
and a variety of paranormal theories surrounding its
purpose and function. René Descartes dedicated a
good bit of his philosophical meanderings to the
study of the pineal gland, calling it the "seat of the
soul," and believing it was an intermediary between
the spiritual and the physical realms. In the eastern
meditative traditions, it is regarded as critical in the
function of yogic and ecstatic body postures, and
traditions around the world attribute it to being a
literal "third eye" or guide for spiritual insight. [5]

THE SPIRIT GLAND, OR THE
PSYCHEDELIC PINEAL?

These metaphysical elements would not be considered scientifically until much later, as indicated particularly in Rick Strassman's book *DMT: The Spirit Molecule*. To my knowledge, Strassman had been the first to ruminate over whether the pineal gland had unexplained capabilities that may be proven through scientific testing. In 1982, while undergoing clinical pharmacology research training at the University of California in San Diego, Strassman began to consider whether the pineal gland might be able to produce psychedelic compounds, or whether it could even "mediate" between spontaneous psychedelic states. Under the right physiological conditions, it seems that if DMT is indeed produced within the pineal, it could be released in varying amounts into the body, causing a variety of perceptible mystical states ranging from the meditative, to the psychedelic.

In fact, Strassman argues that the gland's known primary function, the secretion of melatonin, doesn't explain effectively the pineal's positioning within the emotional centers of the limbic system, above direct access to cerebrospinal fluid "from the roof of a fluid-containing ventricle." Melatonin, since its psychological effects are comparatively "insignificant," as well as the fact that these effects develop over days and weeks after its release, make it an unlikely cause for the pineal's unique placement. If DMT were indeed the active ingredient in question, pineal access to ventricles containing cerebrospinal fluid would be far better explained, since the active period of DMT after synthesis is very short. In this way, DMT could be routed quickly to the visual, auditory, and emotional centers, which the pineal nearly touches anyway. This implies that the gland's placement in the human brain is intended for just such purposes. [6]

The only problem is that we have yet to figure out how a pineal release of DMT, large enough to be a psychedelic dosage, might be released by our bodies. Theories as to how this could occur (aside from DMT releases at the time of birth and death) include intense stress or trauma, or even learned methods of "short circuiting" the pineal via meditation, yoga, tantric sex, or other spiritual practices. Considering whether trauma or stress could also cause an endogenous DMT release to occur, I began to wonder if something along the lines of an intense electrical shock might do the trick; or, taking into account Tesla and Lovecraft's notions, whether exposure to an intense electrical field would achieve the desired effect.

As mentioned toward the end of the *Magic* portion of this book, during my interview with Dr Rick Strassman I made certain to ask him about this theory. "There are some electromagnetic field data studies on pineal," he said, admitting that he hadn't followed the technological aspects of pineal research very much since leaving the field to pursue DMT studies in the 1980s. "At that time anyway, it seems as if the data were suggesting the electromagnetic fields reduce pineal melatonin production. This being the case, it's possible to *speculate* that other pineal metabolic pathways that are latent become more active, and the *hypothetical* formation of DMT by the pineal could be one of these latent pathways." [7] Previously, I had misunderstood this to mean that, if indeed electric fields caused hallucinations or other strange effects, it was due to a temporary breakdown of the blood-brain barrier. However, since the pineal gland isn't actually "behind" the blood brain barrier, and is able to secrete melatonin directly into the systemic circulation, it stands to reason that DMT could do the same thing. Thus, Strassman's theory regarding "latent metabolic pathways" becoming more active in the absence of electrically affected melatonin production might indeed be the key to understanding how an endogenous pineal release of DMT might occur.

In various branches of paranormal research, what is variously referred to as a "Fear Cage" or a "Haunt Box" details a focused area in which strong electromagnetic fields (EMFs) are gathered, with intent of creating perceived effects that resemble supernatural experiences. Michael Persinger of the Consciousness Research Lab at Laurentian University in Ontario, Canada, has conducted a variety of experiments that involve EMFs used to induce effects similar to paranormal phenomena. In his studies, Persinger hoped to correlate EMF exposure to the right temporal lobe of the brain with strange, inexplicable sensations described by some of his subjects, which they likened to feeling a "presence" in the room with them. In order to achieve this, Persinger had his subjects enter a soundproof chamber, where they wore a helmet covered in electromagnets that directly placed electric fields in close proximity to the right temporal lobe. The results included decreases in melatonin levels in the brain (just as Rick Strassman had described). Tiny epileptic-like seizures were also believed to be a byproduct of this procedure, which in some cases could also produce hallucinations. But what, precisely, was the source of the hallucinatory experience? Might we speculate as to whether DMT being released into the blood stream played a role?

According to Persinger's research, over 80% of subjects reported "feeling a presence in the locked room with them," although Persinger himself does not claim that what the subjects were experiencing were necessarily hallucinations. "Although these results suggest that these apparitions are an artifact of an extreme state-dependence," he said, "the possibility that they are associated with transient, altered thresholds in the ability to detect the normally indiscriminable stimuli cannot be excluded." [8]

The work described here was outlined in-depth in Persinger's 1993 paper, "Average Diurnal Changes in Melatonin Levels are Associated with Hourly Incidence of Bereavement Apparitions: Support for the Hypothesis of Temporal (Limbic) Lobe Microseizuring." It is hard to interpret this in a way that doesn't exclude the possibility that Persinger thinks exposure to EMF fields in this way could a) allow us limited perception of *actual presences* that may exist around us, which b) are otherwise imperceptible without the aid of such stimuli.

THE QUANTOCK HORROR

Separate from Persinger's research, there have been studies that also show that stimulation of the temporal cortex has a tendency to evoke "infantile memories," which has been correlated with the fetal imagery commonly associated with Alvin H. Lawson, Ph.D.'s *Birth Trauma Hypothesis*. This supposes that many claims of alien abduction and close encounters of the third kind actually stem from archetypal fantasies involving belief or deception, in which the subject's birth memories play a central role. However, outside the lab, there are other instances where electrical stimulation of the brain seems to evoke frightening imagery, which nonetheless calls into question the possibility that a variety of stimuli are sometimes interpreted as being "alien beings." If we can suspend our judgment, it might be worthy of consideration that such encounters may only be perceptible in altered states of consciousness, created under very specific environmental conditions.

The case of Mr. Tony Burfield of Somerset, England, is famous among the annals of British Ufology. His encounters with strange phenomena began occurring in 1988, while walking with his camera among the Quantock Hills near his home. At some point, an airborne object appeared in the distance, and as it flew closer to Burfield, he was able to make out what appeared to be a complex machine with bat-like wings. There even appeared to be an entity on the rim of the craft, which Burfield, armed with his camera, was able to photograph, resulting in a series of several images detailing the object.

Later, UFO researcher Albert Budden was able to review the photographs, which seemed to show nothing more than a black dot vaguely resembling, if anything, a hang glider. During his investigation, Budden asked Burfield why he felt compelled to visit the Quantock hills on this particular day. Apparently, the witness suffered from an intense allergic sensitivity to various things in his home. To help alleviate the discomfort, Burfield would go for walks in the nearby countryside, but after his encounter with the winged "horror," his symptoms worsened, with the inclusion of a sudden inability to eat solid foods, complaints of a metallic taste in his mouth, and most interesting of all, extreme sensitivity to electrical equipment. Bright light, particularly a car's headlights, caused blinding pain, as well as strange after-images. But perhaps strangest of all was the appearance of "little men" in his home, who Burfield claimed would occasionally appear, and blast him with "painful rays."

While investigating environmental causes for this strange array of manifestations, Budden observed that Burfield's home was very close to a row of high-tension electricity pylons. He began to wonder if the witness might suffer from a rare condition called Electrical Hypersensitivity and Multiple Allergy

(EHMA), and that the apparitions he had witnessed might be his attempts at interpreting the strange, almost dream-like disturbances caused by intense electromagnetic fields near his home. It came as no surprise to Budden that the encounter with the winged object took place between two rows of intersecting pylons carrying high-tension cables, in addition to the fact that it was later revealed that Burfield had experienced a traumatic electrical accident earlier in life.

This, Budden believed, may have initiated his hypersensitive state, which had worsened with time, climaxing at the site of the Quantock hills encounter. "My own research has shown that individuals who experience these bizarre high-strangeness encounters have usually had a major electrical event in their formative years," Budden says, "which acts as an initiation for electrical hypersensitivity later in life." According to his research, most cases where such strange phenomena are reported "occur in locations where the environmental electromagnetic fields are elevated... The encounters can take the form of vivid hallucinatory visions induced by the effects of electrical fields on the brain, and are symptoms of EHMA."

As Budden indicates, circumstances like this do seem to suggest that various powerful environmental stimuli may cause vivid hallucinations for some individuals. The mysterious aspects surrounding such cases form the basis of two possible explanations, both of which require further inquiry:

- If the images are hallucinations, what aspect of the human mind causes aliens and humanoid entities to appear so often, as opposed to merely visual distortions, colors, etc?
- On the other hand, if certain conditions allow humans a limited perception of otherwise undetectable phenomena (i.e. alternate dimensions, etc), what is the role that electricity and exposure to powerful electric fields plays in doing so?

Arguably, there are also instances where the perceived effects of such conditions as those described here can lead to radical, even destructive belief systems, if not perceived with logic and reason. To give an example, years ago I visited two women who lived a good hour's drive from my residence in Asheville, North Carolina. The two ladies told me via email that, or years now, they had been experiencing a variety of strange paranormal phenomena at their secluded home. A mutual friend of ours—a UFO investigator I had known previously—finally called us together to meet at their property and discuss the disturbances.

When we arrived, the women welcomed us into a small cottage down the hill from their actual home, where they made tea for us and began to describe a variety of the strange things that had occurred over the last decade, which seemed to have increased in destructive force within the months leading up to my visit. In particular, lightning from a series of intense thunderstorms had wrecked thousands of dollars worth of utilities and other possessions on their property, and their desperation finally prompted them to call our mutual friend, the UFO investigator, to see if he could determine any "otherworldly factors" which might be affecting them. As he then explained to us, with the help of a psychic he had worked with on previous cases, our friend had come to believe that "an ancient extraterrestrial presence existed on the property, and it wanted them gone." Therefore, our friend admitted that he had brought us together to tell the owners of the property—to his visible distress—that they must now abandon their home of twenty years.

I was shocked by this, and found it hard to believe that, in addition to basing his judgment on what psychics had told him about UFOs and aliens operating in the area, he would be so brazen as to advise the property owners to leave their home. Therefore, I decided to ask a few questions regarding the various phenomena that had been plaguing the residents, hoping that a less extreme alternative to moving away might be reached. Over the course of the discussion, I was fascinated to learn that one of the ladies suffered from a condition that sounded very much like EHMA. When I had asked her about certain "discomforts" she kept describing, she told me that all the electrical appliances in their home had to remain on the farthest side of the house from where their bedrooms were, or she wouldn't be able to sleep at night due to the disturbance she felt from EM fields. Not to my surprise, the woman who shared this information had also been the one who had described having paranormal occurrences on the property in previous emails; in particular, she described that on many occasions she had "felt a presence" nearby, even when she knew she was alone (which reminded me of the effects described by participants in Michael Persinger's studies). In addition to intense electrical sensitivity, she suffered from a variety of allergies involving fungus and bacteria, so in order to prevent rotted wood and other bacterial havens from developing in their home over the years, the building had been constructed entirely upon a metal frame.

For me, this presented a very logical explanation for why repeated lightning strikes had occurred on the property. Rather than the angry, "ancient alien" hypothesis, simpler, well-known natural occurrences had been making life a living hell for the couple. On the way to my car after the meeting was over, one of the ladies walked with me, expressing further concern about whether they should abandon their home. "I just don't know if that's something we can bring ourselves to do, after all the time, money, and effort we've put into keeping this place."

With the bad luck they had experienced, these women seemed to exemplify questions like, "why do bad things happen to good people?" Floods had occurred and had washed away portions of the landscape, rockslides had followed due to the erosion that resulted, and of course, the lightning strikes had rendered many expensive electrical devices useless time and time again. These people had certainly been given a hard time with this place, I thought. But was there really anything sinister or "paranormal" about what was ailing them? Could I leave and allow them to continue to wrestle with the growing fear that the worst was yet to come, all the while knowing that most—if not all—of the seemingly "paranormal" aspects could be very easily ruled out? At that moment, I looked up and saw the concern on the face of the woman standing before me, as if she hoped silently for me to give her some kind of answer to all their problems.

"If I can say one thing to you about this discussion today," I began, "it is not to believe everything you hear."

At that moment, I was reminded of the words of John Keel, who once warned us about committing ourselves to belief for the sake of belief alone:

Belief is the enemy.

Maybe Keel had never meant to suggest that strange things, and even certain "paranormal" phenomena, simply don't exist. Instead, his intention seems to have been to illustrate that we should learn to remove ourselves from the belief systems that are built around the unexplained, and the inevitable control mechanisms that begin to emerge thereafter. Whether this control stems alleged paranormal forces themselves, or from people who would harness our fears and lead us by them—building on false hopes we hide within ourselves that our troubles may eventually be carried away—the necessity for learning to keep an objective perspective of all this had never been more apparent to me.

Humans, however, have evolved over time to spot what appear to be patterns, and to categorize and collate information in ways that make sense to us. With time, we have collectively learned to become more discerning, and recognize the crucial reality that correlation does not imply causation. We're human, in other words, and sometimes we become prone to believing things that are purely illogical. Still, one might argue that belief is something we are innately drawn to: how else can we expect to cope with the knowledge of endless possibilities extending before us into the infinite? The human mind simply was not designed to comprehend such realities.

Perhaps this would be the goal of the "sentient others," if they do actually exist: to attempt to bring us bits and pieces, one at a time, so that we may learn about these things, from minds, or at least from forms of consciousness, that are more experienced than we are in such things.

I later decided to bounce some of my ideas regarding the parallels between the "sentient others" and their various appearances in magical, mystical, entheogenic, and electrically altered states off of Joshua Warren. On the evening Joshua and I met for drinks after his radio show, he had just interviewed Dr. George Freibott, a man who capitalizes on what he calls holistic "ozone therapy," first proposed by Nikola Tesla as early as 1896. In the past, Joshua had interviewed a variety of other guests on his program, *Speaking of Strange*, whose research dealt with the bizarre angle I was taking. One that came to mind was Canadian inventor John Hutchinson, who in 1979 claimed to have observed a variety of strange phenomenon in the presence of strong electric fields while also trying to duplicate some of Tesla's experiments. Sadly, neither Hutchinson—nor anyone else—was ever successful in reproducing the effects he claimed to have created. However questionable the science surrounding his so-called "Hutchinson effect" may have been, in all likelihood it was Hutchinson's research that first triggered the notion in my own mind that bizarre phenomenon *might* occur in the presence of electric fields, albeit differently from the effects Hutchinson claimed to have caused. Having now traced the monster back to its proverbial lair, it came as no surprise that I too would ultimately be led to Tesla's experiments, just as so many before me had.

"It's funny you mention *From Beyond*, because that film also got me thinking strange dimensional things might happen around electric fields," Joshua told me (in fact, I hadn't known about Lovecraft's tale until Joshua first showed me the 1986 horror film based on the story, citing it as one of his favorites). "Sure enough, on one occasion years ago, I was working with a bunch of electrostatic generators all in one room, trying to build a massive charge in a low-humidity environment. At one point, I remember feeling kinda drained, and then my vision seemed to get a little blurry. In the near darkness I had been working in, I remember at one point I began to see a swirling, bluish movement in the air around me, and it kind of reminded me of the weird little 'leeches' that appeared in *From Beyond.*" Joshua figured these were something natural, suggesting they may have been wisps of ionized particles or something else with mild luminescent properties. "Regardless, I started wondering, like yourself, if there might be ways that electric fields could somehow open gateways to other realms."

Who knows what kinds of unusual effects electrical stimuli might have on the brain, when utilized in circumstances such as those Joshua and I discussed. Similar to this, I found that the modern concept of *techno shamanism* employs similar ideas, to aid in achieving certain altered states via what is called cranial electro-stimulation (CES). This puts minute electrical currents through the brain at specific frequencies, resulting in conditions described as "profoundly relaxing", and supposedly has positive long-term effects on mental and physical health. This, of course, is meager compared to the amounts of electricity produced in high-powered EM fields the likes of which we discussed previously. In addition to the unforeseen effects of EMFs on people's conscious states, there may be unexpected health complications that arise, too. Certainly, if one were to experiment with such things, extreme caution must be exercised, much like experimentation with powerful, potentially dangerous drugs like DMT.

As time goes on, our view of life on Earth, and the prospects for finding similar things elsewhere in the cosmos, continue to expand. Perhaps one day we will discover new ways humankind may be able to achieve contact with nonhuman intelligences, whether it occurs through our existing SETI programs, or perhaps with the help of controlled use of mind-altering technologies, as we have surveyed here.

If contact with intelligences from beyond is in our eventual future, will humankind be able to do so responsibly, and will the result of that cosmic communion be for our betterment as a species?

CONCLUSION

"In shamanism, the classic theme is death and rebirth—you are reborn in a new configuration. The neuroscientific interpretation is exactly the same: the default-mode network is disrupted, and maybe things that were mucking up the works are left behind when everything comes back together."

-DENNIS MCKENNA, *The New Yorker*, 2016.

For centuries, our ancestors would gaze at the evening sky, and while staring into the dark vastness of the cosmos, they probably never considered things so obvious, or simple, as why the sky appears black at night. It might have seemed logical to them—especially considering the perspectives of

ancient cultures that worshipped celestial bodies—
that since the sun brought light, the moon should
bring darkness. All things appear to contrast this way
in nature: man and woman, heat and cold, even life
and death. Why should day and night be any
different?

However, little did our ancestors know that the
blackness of the evening sky apparently defied
observation; after all, once we later began to discover
the physics that maintain such delicate balancing
forces as night and day, we also learned that our
universe was ever-expanding, infinite and uniform.
Thus, it became evident that light from an infinite
number of stars that exist throughout space should,
in theory, be bombarding us constantly, blanketing
the night sky in white light. On further reflection, it
would indeed seem strange, to say the least, that the
night sky still appears black in spite of this.

Though the universe itself may be infinite as far
as we know, when taking into consideration the not-
so-infinite life span of stars, we are able to predict a
"cut-off" to the light sources we had once assumed
should be blasting us constantly from deep-space,
courtesy of our modern big bang theories. Therefore,
the evening has been awarded its right to display
darkness; a winning bid in a cosmic exchange so vast
and great, and yet one that existed unbeknownst to
humankind for thousands of years.

Today, it may still be the case that obvious things
around us hold secrets that manage to evade
understanding, or even perception. There are some
today who believe that virtually any phenomenon

around us that can be observed can also be explained scientifically *at present*. We think, for instance, that the summation of our understanding of electricity lies in the electron, whereas in reality this is only one half of the equation. The late NASA engineer Charles Yost, co-creator of the popular "memory foam" used on mattresses today, often pointed out in his scientific publication *Electric Spacecraft* that a negative charge never exists without its opposite polarity, the positive charge. Yost stated that our present fixation on the electron is "a most simple and convenient model, but can lead into the never-never land of delusion." Yost also argued that attractive forces must always exist between a negative and a positive charge, calling into account "lines of force" which always connect positive and negative charges. "In this context," he said, "the charge (of the electron) is always a dual entity; a polar entity."

Surely, by expanding on this notion of the duality of subatomic particles and their relationships with one another, on a grand scale it becomes easier for us to consider our own relationships with other worlds, or even our singular connections to entities that may inhabit them. Once considered mere speculation, the modern concept of what we call the "multiverse," having to do with the existence of multiple different universes apart from our own, is now accepted as a likely potential, though still lacking ultimate proof. Nonetheless, several branches of physics now incorporate the idea of a multiverse, as a means to help explain a variety of theoretical principles such as *inflation theory*, which involves how a rapid expansion of our universe could start, and then in theory, stop again. String theory also incorporates the multiverse heavily, as well as M-theory, which considers whether parallel universes might actually collide with one another from time to time. The multiverse is also used as rationale for explaining the *Anthropic Principle*, which according to some, looks rather philosophically at multiverses as evidence of a creator. After all, the synchronicities that begin to mount as one considers all the factors involving maintenance of the delicate life on Earth—let alone living beings like us who have evolved to think rationally—are innumerable. Could utter chaos have somehow aligned itself so well, so *exactly*, to allow for the existence of humans on a planet like Earth? Even in the event that this miraculously occurred somehow by chance alone, what would be the chance that it could ever occur again?

In pondering such things we arrive at the sobering realization that our ever-growing understanding of nature and the cosmos simply is not yet capable of explaining *all* observable phenomena. And yet, in spite of thousands of witnesses coming forward each year to tell of their encounters with what we might suppose to be "paranormal" occurrences, many logical thinkers unabashedly exclude the reports of ghosts, UFOs, and other things that, outwardly, seem to defy our present understanding of science. Greatly limited by our own humanity and the limitations of our sensory perception, one might argue that we keep ourselves in a veritable dark age of the mind, where those things we cannot classify, quantify, or explain objectively, we shun altogether, perhaps out of an innate, or even a *repressed* inner fear of the unknown.

We must learn to accept that our knowledgebase in the present day has rather obvious limitations. However, taking into consideration things so strange as the existence of beings from other worlds, does this rule out the notion that past attempts at explaining strange phenomena using science can be applied to our expanding knowledge? For instance, in the case of supposed tulpas and thoughtforms, can we not consider the paradox of Schrodinger's cat, where the two primary ways of solving the paradox involve a) assuming that consciousness determines existence, freeing us to the possibility that virtually anything might exist if it can be perceived, and b) assuming that an infinite number of parallel worlds do exist? Does this apparent set of resolutions carry over into the realm of such things as ghostly apparitions, or even reports of UFOs, allowing us to consider the even stranger possibility that entities existing in parallel worlds might somehow be capable of bridging the gap between our dimension and theirs, whether physically, or by utilizing abstruse modes of consciousness which remain undiscovered? If these entities were doing so, would we even recognize them for being what they are?

Or, would we have elevated them throughout time as deities, totems, and symbols, around which the vast mythologies of human culture the world over have kept since time immemorial?

Rather than accepting that science will never be able to explain certain phenomena, perhaps it is more likely that scientific knowledge, as we know it at present, is incomplete, and hasn't reached a point at which things we call "paranormal" can be defined and explained. Indeed, a variety of favorite arguments have risen over the years, used by "believers" to exemplify humankind's past arrogance in our knowledge of the world around us. These range from the skepticism that once surrounded reports of "manlike beasts" alleged to have existed in Africa (later proven to be mountain gorillas), to "living fossils" like the coelacanth. These odd-looking fish were once believed to have died out by the end of the Cretaceous period, but were later rediscovered in December of 1938, still living in deep waters off the coast of South Africa.

Time and time again we have been proven wrong, made to feel foolish by our own arrogance, having learned that we simply don't know as much as we thought we did. This prompts the question, "when will we ever *really* learn?" How often must we continue to wield our arrogance like a sword, cutting down open-minded observation of things we deem "strange" from our limited perspectives, for the sake of maintaining a Napoleonic claim on our perceived mastery of nature?

The well-known and respected "physicist of the impossible" Michio Kaku wrote in his book *Parallel Worlds: A Journey Through Creation, Higher Dimensions, and the Future of the Cosmos* that humanity is, "making the historic transition from being passive observers to the dance of nature to becoming choreographers of the dance of nature, with the ability to manipulate life, matter, and intelligence." Indeed, the more we learn, the more it appears we can do; and yet so many elements already available to us that may yield the fruit of discovery are systematically ignored. Many western religions today scorn and decry the use of anything magical as being demonic, warning that our mortal souls will burn in hell for all eternity if we should choose to think outside our often narrow spiritual upbringings. Eastern religions that focus on mystical traditions are wrongly labeled as "godless." And most unfortunately, indigenous cultures that incorporate centuries of combined knowledge of entheogenic substances for religious purposes are marginalized, and seen as anachronisms in a modern era in which the gods of the old world are long dead; some are even made to fight federal regulation that has rendered the implements of their spiritual practices illegal.

The parallels that exist between those things we call magical, mystical, and entheogenic—as well as their mind-expanding ramifications—are more than merely obvious. The continuities existing between the various schools of study discussed in this book are also, at times, difficult to ignore. Sadly, in spite of all our sophistication and scientific knowledge, we have yet to recognize the true potential such spiritual sciences may afford us in the betterment of our understanding of consciousness. If anything, we continue to fear them, having failed to see past the stigmas that prevent us from understanding ways they might be beneficial to us.

Many tout the notion of a "new paradigm" that has steadily been approaching for some time now. Predictions include such things as a widespread expansion of global consciousness, as well as changes ranging from things which structure society, to even the rate at which we evolve. If our species is indeed changing and evolving at a quickened rate, of primary concern is whether or not we are *growing* also, and bettering ourselves in doing so. Will the changes we make today affect the people we become years from now, and if so, will it be for better or for worse? More importantly, will the repression we have used to separate the mystical elements of existence from our daily lives eventually come back to haunt future generations?

Despite the concerns concomitant with our modern existence, these times in which we live are exciting. The rate at which our technology continues to grow is amazing, if not alarming. And yet, on a fundamental level, we seem to be aware somehow that our growing dependence on technology and the convenience it provides separates us from some intangible, yet necessary element that contributes greatly to who we are. Our expectations for growth, and occasional yearning for humanity's long awaited "spiritual awakening," foreshadow an inescapable change that *must* occur in the years to come, and as a species, we seem to be able to sense its arrival.

Meanwhile, doomsday scenarios ranging from fear of comets smashing into the Earth, to ancient prophecies, threat of nuclear war, climate change, and any number of other concerns have led to increased tension. Whatever the future may hold, it comes with an air of hope that still lies hidden away in the mystical nature of our being: and just perhaps, humanity can even find comfort in the notion that the perils we may one day face will not be trials we must face alone.

Through an understanding of the long path through human history that led us to the present day, we learn of the magic, mysticism, and the mysterious molecules, each of which, throughout time, have shown us glimpses of fantastic realities beyond our known world. Through them, we have seen visions of parallel dimensions and worlds afar, along with the denizens of such alien realms. Whether or not their existence is ever proven, the mere idea of intelligences that could exist elsewhere, apart from us, has irrevocably shaped who and what we are, and what we are yet to be in future generations.

With time, we may indeed learn of greater realities that await our discovery today; what we are to learn from those who inhabit such dimensions, whether physical, spiritual, or something else entirely, will forever change us as a civilization.

Upon that eventual moment of discovery, we will finally know the ultimate truth: that despite all of our fear, wandering, and the quest for understanding, *we were never really alone in our search, after all.*

NOTES

Chapter One

1) Partridge, Christopher. *UFO Religions*. Routledge; 1 edition. August 21, 2003.
2) Anonymous. "Dr Dee the Great Conjurer." Bodleian Libraries, University of Oxford. Website. Accessed July 12, 2017.
3) "Dr Dee's Magical Mirror / Dr Dee's Magical Speculum." Museum number 1966, 1001.1. The British Museum.
4) Smith, Charlotte Fell. *John Dee: 1527–1608*. Constable (1909).
5) Ibid.
6) Laycock, Donald. *The Complete Enochian Dictionary: A Dictionary of the Angelic Language As Revealed to Dr. John Dee and Edward Kelley*. Boston: Weiser Books, 2001.
7) Kelley, Edward. *The Stone of the Philosophers*. New Hermetics Press, 2014.
8) Guiley, Rosemary. *The Encyclopedia of Magic and Alchemy*. Facts On File, 2006.
9) Moody, Raymond. *Reunions: Visionary Encounters With Departed Loved Ones*. Ivy Books, 1994.
10) Swedenborg, Emmanuel. *Heaven and its Wonders and Hell From Things Heard and Seen*. 1758.

11) Prabhupada, A. C. Bhaktivedanta. *Easy Journey to Other Planets*. Bhaktivedanta Book Trust, 1972.

12) Hayden, William Benjamin. *On the phenomena of modern spiritualism*. Boston: Otis Clapp, 1855.

13) Simmons, Kurt. "The Madness Hypothesis." The New Philosophy. January-June, 1998.

14) Lewis, James R. (Editor). *The Gods Have Landed: New Religions from Other Worlds*. Suny Press, 1995.

15) Johnson, G., ed. *Kant on Swedenborg: Dreams of a Spirit-Seer and Other Writings*. Swedenborg Foundation, 2002.

16) Blavatsky, Helena P. *The Key to Theosophy*. London: Theosophical Publishing House. 1968 (1889).

17) Saint Germain Foundation. *The History of the "I AM" Activity and Saint Germain Foundation*. Saint Germain Press, 2003.

18) Lewis, James R. (Editor). *The Gods Have Landed: New Religions from Other Worlds*. Suny Press, 1995.

19) Flournoy, Théodore. *From India To The Planet Mars*. University Books, 1963.

20) Partridge, 2003.

21) Boudillion, Daniel V. "Aleister Crowley's Lam & the Little Grey Men: A Striking Resemblance." 15 August 2003.

22) Booth, Martin. *A Magick Life: The Biography of Aleister Crowley*. London: Coronet Books, 2000.

23) Crowley, Aliester. *The Diary of a Drug Fiend*. Weiser Books; 2nd Revised edition edition, 2010.

24) Crowley, Aleister. "Synopsis of six articles on drugs." Spiritual Nature Magazine, 2001.

25) Blavatsky, Helena P. *Voice of the Silence: Centenary Edition*. Quest Books, 1992.

26) Boudillion, 2003.

27) Staley, Michael. "Lam: The Gateway." Starfire (Magazine). Volume One, Number 5. 1994. London, England.

28) Ibid.

29) Ibid.

30) Boudillion, 2003.

31) Ibid.

32) Carter, John. *Sex and Rockets: The Occult World of Jack Parsons*. Feral House, 2005.

33) Nichols, Larry A.; Mather, George; Schmidt, Alvin J. *Encyclopedic Dictionary of Cults, Sects, and World Religions: Revised and Updated Edition*. Zondervan, 2006.

34) Boudillion, 2003.

35) Staley, 1994.

36) Howard, Dana. *Diane: She Came from Venus*. Regency Press, 1956.

37) Lee, Regan. "Marian Apparitions and Esoteric Encounters: Visits with Mary, UFOs, Contactees and the Trickster." Scribd.com (Website). https://www.scribd.com/document/29110733/UFO-Mary-rlee-cwk-WP

38) Pelley, Willam Dudley. *Why I Believe the Dead Are Alive*. Soulcraft Chapels. Noblesville, Indiana, 1954.

39) Ibid.

Chapter Two

1) Ward, Terrence P. "An Interview with Raymond Buckland, American Wicca Pioneer." The Wild Hunt (Magazine), June 1, 2016

2) Interview with Dr. Raymond Moody. Thresholds (Magazine). Vol. 12 No. 4, 1994. http://www.som.org/3library/interviews/moody.html

3) Ibid.

4) Ibid.

5) Ibid.

6) Jones, Gabriel H. "Pythia." Ancient History Encyclopedia (Website). 30 August 2013. Accessed July 21, 2017. http://www.ancient.eu/Pythia/

7) Homer, & Rieu, E. V. (1996). *The Odyssey*. London: Penguin Books.

8) Interview with Dr. Raymond Moody. Thresholds (Magazine). Vol. 12 No. 4, 1994. http://www.som.org/3library/interviews/moody.html

9) Ibid.

10) J. Wiseman, "Rethinking the 'Halls of Hades'." Archaeology. Volume 51, Number 3, 1998.

11) Ibid.

12) Interview with Dr. Raymond Moody. Thresholds (Magazine). Vol. 12 No. 4, 1994. http://www.som.org/3library/interviews/moody.html

13) Collins, Wilkie. *My Miscellanies*. University of Michigan Library, 2009.

14) Alexis, Jonas E. *In the Name of Education: How Weird Ideologies Corrupt our Public Schools, Politics, the Media, Higher Institutions, and History*. Xulon Press; 2nd edition. July 22, 2007.

Chapter Three

1) Stoffel, Mary L. *The Practical Power of Shamanism: Heal Your Life, Loves and Losses*. Innovative Order, 2010.

2) Warren, Joshua P. *Pet Ghosts: Animal Encounters from Beyond the Grave*. New Page Books, 2006.

3) Strassman, Rick. *DMT: The Spirit Molecule. A Doctor's Revolutionary Research into the Biology of Near-Death and Mystical Experiences*. New York: Park Street Press, 2000.

4) Ibid.

5) Ibid.

6) Ibid.

7) Email interview with Rick Strassman, M.D., 2008.

Chapter Four

1) Interview with Ellis Paul. *Take a Stand* (radio). August 15, 2007.
2) Deuteronomy 18:10-11, New International Version.
3) *The Qur'an.* Trans. by Tarif Khalidi. New York: Viking, 2008.
4) Chao, Wei-pang. "The Origin and Growth of the Fu Chi." Nanzan Institute for Religion and Culture: Asian Ethnology Vol. 2. pp. 9–27. 1943.
5) Hunt, Stoker. *Ouija: The Most Dangerous Game.* Barnes and Noble Books, 1985.
6) Ibid.
7) Carroll, R.T., "Ideomotor effect". The Skeptic's Dictionary. 2003.
8) Offut, Jason. *Darkness Walks: The Shadow People Among Us.* Anomalist Books, 2009.
9) Warren, Ed and Lorraine. *Graveyard: True Hauntings from an Old New England.* Graymalkin Media. December 31, 2014.
10) Wickland, Carl A. *Thirty Years Among The Dead.* White Crow Books (New Edition), 2011.
11) Ebon, Martin. *The Satan Trap: Dangers of the Occult.* Doubleday, 1976.
12) Hines, Terrence. Pseudoscience and the Paranormal. New York: Prometheus Books, 2003.
13) Cornelius, J. Edward. *Aleister Crowley and the Ouija Board.* Feral House, 2005.
14) Ibid.
15) Tenuta, Gary Val. *The Secret of Nine: A Synchronistic Puzzle of Metaphoric Proportions.* 2007.

Chapter Five

1) Underhill, Evelyn. *Mysticism: A Study in the Nature and Development of Spiritual Consciousness.* Minneapolis: Dover Publications, 2002.
2) Ibid.
3) Laos, Nicolas K. *Freemasons, World Order, and Mind Wars: The Great Reality of Memphis-Misraim Masonry.* Algora Publishing, New York. 2016.
4) Ibid.
5) Ibid.
6) Smith, William, Sir. *Dictionary of Greek and Roman biography and mythology.* Boston, Little. 1870.
7) Ibid.
8) Sandywell, Barry. Presocratic reflexivity the construction of philosophical discourse c. 600-450 BC. London: Routledge, 1996.
9) Ibid.
10) Shaw, Gregory. *Theurgy and the Soul: The Neoplatonism of Iamblichus.* Penn State Press, 1971.
11) Hollenback, Jess Byron. *Mysticism: Experience, Response, and Empowerment* (University Park PA: The Pennsylvania State University Press, 1996).
12) Ibid.
13) Vetter, Tilmann. *The Ideas and Meditative Practices of Early Buddhism.* Brill, 1988.
14) Violatti, Christian. "Siddhartha Gautama." www.ancient.eu (Website). 9 December 2013. Accessed 26 July, 2017.
15) Vetter, 1988.
16) Bhikku, Thanissaro. "Aggi-Vacchagotta Sutta To Vacchagotta on Fire." 1997. http://www.accesstoinsight.org/tipitaka/mn/mn.072.than.html

17) LeShan, Lawrence L. *How to Meditate: A Guide to Self-Discovery.* Boston: Little, Brown, 1999.

18) Underhill, 2002.

19) Ibid.

20) 2 Corinthians, 12:2-12:9. King James Version.

21) Segal, Alan F. *Paul the Convert: The Apostolate and Apostasy of Saul the Pharisee.* New York: Yale UP, 1992.

22) Ibid.

23) Underhill, 2002.

24) Ibid.

25) Thompson, Richard L. On Interpretation of Vedic Literature. http://www.afn.org/~bvi/literal.html

26) Monier-Williams. Sanskrit-English Dictionary. (Website). http://www.sanskrit-lexicon.uni-koeln.de/cgi-bin/monier/serveimg.pl?file=/scans/MWScan/MWScanjpg/mw0980-vimalaya.jpg

27) Ibid.

28) Shastry, Subbaraya; Josyer, G. R. (1973). *Vymaanika Shaastra - Aeronautics by Maharshi Bharadwaaja.* Mysore: Coronation Press.

29) Mukunda, H.S.; Deshpande, S.M.; Nagendra, H.R.; Prabhu, A.; Govindraju, S.P. "A critical study of the work 'Vyamanika Shastra' " Scientific Opinion: 5–12. 1974.

30) Personal interview with Slawek Wojtowicz, 2009.

31) Ibid.

Chapter Six

1) LeShan, Lawrence L. *How to Meditate: A Guide to Self-Discovery.* Boston: Little, Brown, 1999.

2) Ibid.

3) Personal interview with Slawek Wojtowicz, 2009.

4) Renard, Gary. *The Disappearance of the Universe Straight Talk About Illusions, Past Lives, Religion, Sex, Politics, and the Miracles of Forgiveness*. New York: Hay House, 2004.

5) Wesselman, Hank. *Spiritwalker: Messages from the Future*. New York: Bantam, 1996.

6) Prabhupada, A. C. Bhaktivedanta. *Easy Journey to Other Planets*. Bhaktivedanta Book Trust, 1972.

7) Ibid.

8) Goodman, Felicitas. "Body Posture and Religious Altered State of Consciousness: An Experimental Investigation." Journal of Humanistic Psychology, 26: 81-118. 1986.

9) Ibid.

10) Singleton, Mark; Mallinson, James. *Roots of Yoga*. Penguin Classic, 2016.

11) Sivanda Yoga Center. *The Sivananda Companion to Yoga: A Complete Guide to the Physical Postures, Breathing Exercises, Diet, Relaxation, and Meditation Techniques of Yoga*. Touchstone, 2000.

12) Dharma, Krishna. *Mahabharata: The Greatest Spiritual Epic of All Time*. Torchlight Publishing, 1999.

13) Mckenna, Terence. *Food of the Gods The Search for the Original Tree of Knowledge A Radical History of Plants, Drugs, and Human Evolution*. New York: Bantam, 1993.

Chapter Seven

1) David- Néel, Alexandra. *Magic and Mystery in Tibet*. Dover Publications, 1971.

2) Besant, Annie and C.W. Leadbeater. Thought Forms. 1901

3) Ibid.

4) David- Néel, Alexandra. *Tibetan Journey*. South Asia Books; Facsimile of 1912 edition. 1992.

298

5) Ibid.
6) Jung, Carl. *Flying Saucers: A Modern Myth of Things Seen in the Skies*. (Routledge Classics). New York: Routledge, 2002.
7) Jung, Carl. Letters of C. G. Jung, Volume 2; Volumes 1951-1961. Routledge, 1995.
8) Jung, 2002.
9) Ibid.
10) Ibid.
11) Keel, John. The Mothman Prophecies. New York: Tor Books, 2002.
12) Ibid.
13) Winkler, Gershon. *The Golem of Prague*. Judaica Press, 1980.
14) Rosenburg, R. Yudel. *Niflaos Maharal: HaGolem M'Prague*. Warsaw, 1909.
15) Pelley, William Dudley. *Why I Believe The Dead Are Alive*. Soulcraft Chapels, Noblesville Indiana. 1954.
16) Clark, Jerome and Coleman, Loren. *The Unidentified*. Warner Paperbacks, 1975.
17) Hynek, J. Allen. *The UFO Experience: A Scientific Inquiry*. Ballantine Books, 1977.
18) Singh, Onkar. "It's a man! It's a monkey! It's a..." Rediff.com. (Website). May 18, 2001. http://www.rediff.com/news/2001/may/18mon2.htm
19) Clark, Jerome. *Unexplained!: Strange Sightings, Incredible Occurrences and Puzzling Physical Phenomena*. Detroit: Visible Ink, 1993.

Chapter Eight

1) Proud, Louis. *Dark Intrusions: An Investigation into the Paranormal Nature of Sleep Paralysis Experiences.* San Antonio, New York: Anomalist Books, 2009.

2) Grassie, William. *Advanced Methodologies: In the Scientific Study of Religion and Spirituality.* Metanexus Institute / Xlibris Corporation, 2010.

3) Ibid.

4) Personal Interview with Dr. David Hufford Ph.D. 2009.

5) Ibid.

6) Ibid.

7) Ibid.

8) Ritchey, David. The H.I.S.S. of the A.S.P. Understanding the Anomalously Sensitive Person. New York: Headline Books, 2003.

9) Ibid.

10) Murphy, J.M. Psychiatric labeling in cross-cultural perspective. Science, 191, 1019-1028. 1976.

11) Siegel, Ronald K. Ph.D. Hostage Hallucinations: Visual Imagery Induced by Isolation and Life-Threatening Stress. The Journal of Nervous and Mental Disease, n. 5, Vol. 172, 1984, pp. 264-272.

12) Ibid.

13) Ibid.

14) Ibid.

15) Ibid.

16) Ibid.

17) Ibid.

18) Ibid.

19) Hinton, Devon E., and Byron J. Good, editors. Culture and PTSD: Trauma in Global and Historical Perspective. University of Pennsylvania Press, 2016. JSTOR, www.jstor.org/stable/j.ctt18s318s.

20) Proud, 2009.

21) Ibid.

22) Strassman, Rick, Slawek Wojtowicz, Luis Eduardo Luna, and Ede Frecska. Inner Paths to Outer Space Journeys to Alien Worlds through Psychedelics and Other Spiritual Technologies. New York: Park Street P, 2008.

23) Strassman, Rick. DMT: The Spirit Molecule A Doctor's Revolutionary Research into the Biology of Near-Death and Mystical Experiences. New York: Park Street P, 2000.

Chapter Nine

1) Underhill, Evelyn. *Mysticism: A Study in the Nature and Development of Spiritual Consciousness.* Minneapolis: Dover Publications, 2002.

2) Mckenna, Terence. *Food of the Gods The Search for the Original Tree of Knowledge A Radical History of Plants, Drugs, and Human Evolution.* New York: Bantam, 1993.

3) Ibid.

4) Doniger, Wendy (Translator). *The Rig Veda.* Penguin Classics, 2005.

5) George, Andrew (Translator). *The Epic of Gilgamesh.* Penguin Classics, 2003.

6) McKenna, 1993.

7) Brierley, Daniel I., and Davidson, Colin. "Developments in harmine pharmacology — Implications for ayahuasca use and drug-dependence treatment." Progress in Neuro-Psychopharmacology & Biological Psychiatry, 2012.

8) Metzner, Ralph, Ph.D. (Editor). *Sacred Vine of Spirits: Ayahuasca.* Park Street Press, 2005.

9) Pinchbeck, Daniel. *Breaking Open the Head: A Psychedelic Journey into the Heart of Contemporary Shamanism.* New York: Broadway Books, 2002.

10) Ibid.

11) Narby, Jeremy. *The Cosmic Serpent: DNA and the Origins of Knowledge.* Jeremy P. Tarcher/Putnam; Reprint edition, 1999

12) Ibid.

13) Luna, Luis Eduardo and White, Steven F. *Ayahuasca Reader: Encounters with the Amazon's Sacred Vine.* Synergetic Press, 2000.

14) Tompkins, Peter and Christopher Bird. *The Secret Life of Plants: A Fascinating Account of the Physical, Emotional, and Spiritual Relations Between Plants and Man.* New York: Perennial, 1973.

15) Ibid.

16) "New research on plant intelligence may forever change how you think about plants." PRI.org (Website). January 10, 2014 (accessed July 29, 2017).

Chapter Ten

1) Grimes, William. "Maurice M. Rapport, Who Studied Serotonin, Dies at 91." New York Times, September 2, 2011.

2) Bouchez, Colette. "Serotonin: 9 Questions and Answers." WebMD (Website). Accessed July 29, 2017.

3) Hoffman, Albert. *LSD: My Problem Child.* MAPS, 2005.

4) Ibid.

5) Brierley, Daniel I., and Davidson, Colin. "Developments in harmine pharmacology — Implications for ayahuasca use and drug-dependence treatment." Progress in Neuro-Psychopharmacology & Biological Psychiatry, 2012.

6) Narby, Jeremy. *The Cosmic Serpent: DNA and the Origins of Knowledge.* Jeremy P. Tarcher/Putnam; Reprint edition, 1999

7) Boszormenyi, Z. and Stephen I. Szara, "Dimethyl-tryptamine Experiments with Psychotics," *Journal of Mental Science* 104 (1958): 445-53.

8) Strassman, Rick. DMT: The Spirit Molecule A Doctor's Revolutionary Research into the Biology of Near-Death and Mystical Experiences. New York: Park Street P, 2000.

9) Van Dusen, Wilson. "The Presence Of Spirits In Madness: A Confirmation of Swedenborg in Recent Empirical Findings." Swedenborg Foundation, 1984.

10) Ibid.

Chapter Eleven

1) Corbett L., Christian, S.T., Morin, R.D., Benington, F. & Smythies, J.R. 1978. Hallucinogenic N-methylated indolealkylamines in the cerebrospinal fluid of psychiatric and control populations. British J. Psychiatry 132, 139.

2) Greene, Shaun L. "Tryptamines." Novel Psychoactive Substances, 2013. http://www.sciencedirect.com/topics/neuroscience/tryptamine

3) W.Y. Evans-Wentz (translator and editor), The Tibetan Book of the Dead (Oxford, 3rd ed.; 1957), pp. 90-2, 95-7, 101-4.

4) Strassman, Rick. DMT: The Spirit Molecule A Doctor's Revolutionary Research into the Biology of Near-Death and Mystical Experiences. New York: Park Street P, 2000.

5) Ibid.

6) Ibid.

7) McKenna, Terrence and McKenna, Dennis. *The Invisible Landscape: Mind, Hallucinogens, and the I Ching.* Harper San Francisco, 1994.

8) Strassman, 2000.

9) Stafford, Peter. *Heavenly Highs: Ayahuasca, Kava-Kava, DMT, and Other Plants of the Gods.* Ronin Publishing, 2005.

10) Strassman, 2000.

11) Pinchbeck, Daniel. *Breaking Open the Head: A Psychedelic Journey into the Heart of Contemporary Shamanism.* New York: Broadway Books, 2002.

12) Pickover, Clifford A. *Sex, Drugs, Einstein & Elves Sushi, Psychedelics, Parallel Universes and the Quest for Transcendence.* Minneapolis: Smart Publications, 2005.

13) Pinchbeck, 2002.

14) Lear, John. Written statement (press release), December 29, 1987.

15) Strieber, Whitley. *Communion: A True Story.* Avon, February 25, 1987.

16) Ibid.

17) Strassman, Rick, Slawek Wojtowicz, Luis Eduardo Luna, and Ede Frecska. Inner Paths to Outer Space Journeys to Alien Worlds through Psychedelics and Other Spiritual Technologies. New York: Park Street P, 2008.

18) Ibid.

19) Pinchbeck, 2002.

Chapter Twelve

1) "Is Tesla to Signal the Stars?". Electrical World. April 4, 1896.

2) Corum, K. L., J. F. Corum, and A. H. Aidinejad, "Atmospheric Fields, Tesla's Receivers and Regenerative Detectors". 1994.

3) Joshi, S.T. *I Am Providence: The Life and Times of H.P. Lovecraft.* Hippocampus Press, 2013.

4) Lovecraft, H.P. *The Complete Fiction Works of H.P. Lovecraft.* Chartwell Books, 2016.

5) Hall, Manly P. *The Pineal Gland: The Eye of God.* Martino Fine Books, 2015.
6) Strassman, Rick. DMT: The Spirit Molecule A Doctor's Revolutionary Research into the Biology of Near-Death and Mystical Experiences. New York: Park Street P, 2000.
7) Email interview with Rick Strassman, M.D., 2008.
8) Persinger, Michael A. "Average Diurnal Changes in Melatonin Levels are Associated with Hourly Incidence of Bereavement Apparitions: Support for the Hypothesis of Temporal (Limbic) Lobe Microseizuring." Perceptual and Motor Skills, 1993.

BIBLIOGRAPHY

Alexis, Jonas E. *In the Name of Education: How Weird Ideologies Corrupt our Public Schools, Politics, the Media, Higher Institutions, and History*. Xulon Press; 2nd edition. July 22, 2007.

Ayto, John. Brewer's Dictionary of Phrase and Fable, Seventeenth Edition (Brewer's Dictionary of Phrase and Fable). New York: Collins, 2006.

Blavatsky, Helena P. Voice of the Silence: Centenary Edition. Quest Books, 1992.

Booth, Martin. *A Magick Life: The Biography of Aleister Crowley*. London: Coronet Books, 2000.

Boszormenyi, Z. and Stephen I. Szara, "Dimethyltryptamine Experiments with Psychotics," *Journal of Mental Science* 104 (1958): 445-53.

Besant, Annie and C.W. Leadbeater. *Thought Forms*. 1901.

Bhikku, Thanissaro. *Aggi-Vacchagotta Sutta To Vacchagotta on Fire*. http://www.accesstoinsight.org/tipitaka/ mn/mn.072.than.html (accessed July 25, 2017).
Boszormenyi, Z. and Stephen I. Szara, "Dimethyltryptamine Experiments with Psychotics," *Journal of Mental Science* 104 (1958): 445-53.

Bouchez, Colette. "Serotonin: 9 Questions and Answers." WebMD (Website). Accessed July 29, 2017.

Boudillion, Daniel V. *Aleister Crowley's Lam & the Little Grey Men: A Striking Resemblance*. 2003. http://www. boudillion.com/lam/lam.htm (accessed June 17, 2009).

Brierley, Daniel I., and Davidson, Colin. "Developments in harmine pharmacology — Implications for ayahuasca use and drug-dependence treatment." Progress in Neuro-Psychopharmacology & Biological Psychiatry, 2012.

Carroll, R.T., "Ideomotor effect". The Skeptic's Dictionary. 2003.

Carter, John. *Sex and Rockets: The Occult World of Jack Parsons*. Feral House, 2005.

Chao, Wei-pang. "The Origin and Growth of the Fu Chi." Nanzan Institute for Religion and Culture: Asian Ethnology Vol. 2. pp. 9–27. 1943.

Clark, Jerome and Coleman, Loren. *The Unidentified*. Warner Paperbacks, 1975.

Collins, Wilkie. *My Miscellanies*. University of Michigan Library, 2009.

Corbett L., Christian, S.T., Morin, R.D., Benington, F. & Smythies, J.R. 1978. Hallucinogenic N-methylated indolealkylamines in the cerebrospinal fluid of psychiatric and control populations. British J. Psychiatry 132, 139.

Cornelius, J. Edward. Aleister Crowley And the Ouija Board. New York: Feral House, 2005.

Crowley, Aliester. *The Diary of a Drug Fiend.* Weiser Books; 2nd Revised edition edition, 2010.

Corum, K. L., J. F. Corum, and A. H. Aidinejad, "Atmospheric Fields, Tesla's Receivers and Regenerative Detectors". 1994.

Crowley, Aleister. "Synopsis of six articles on drugs." Spiritual Nature Magazine, 2001.

David- Néel, Alexandra. *Magic and Mystery in Tibet.* Dover Publications, 1971.

David- Néel, Alexandra. *Tibetan Journey.* South Asia Books; Facsimile of 1912 edition. 1992.

Dharma, Krishna. *Mahabharata: The Greatest Spiritual Epic of All Time.* Torchlight Publishing, 1999.

Diagnostic and Statistical Manual of Mental Disorders DSM-IV-TR Fourth Edition. Washington, DC: American Psychiatric Association, 2000.

Doniger, Wendy (Translator). *The Rig Veda.* Penguin Classics, 2005.

Ebon, Martin. *The Satan Trap: Dangers of the Occult.* Doubleday, 1976.

Flournoy, Théodore. *From India To The Planet Mars.* University Books, 1963.

Foster, Barbara M. *Forbidden Journey the life of Alexandra David-Neel*. San Francisco: Harper & Row, 1987.

George, Andrew (Translator). *The Epic of Gilgamesh*. Penguin Classics, 2003.

Goodman, Felicitas. "Body Posture and Religious Altered State of Consciousness: An Experimental Investigation." Journal of Humanistic Psychology, 26: 81-118. 1986.

Grassie, William. *Advanced Methodologies: In the Scientific Study of Religion and Spirituality*. Metanexus Institute / Xlibris Corporation, 2010.

Greene, Shaun L. "Tryptamines." Novel Psychoactive Substances, 2013. http://www.sciencedirect.com/topics/neuroscience/tryptamine (accessed July 28, 2017).

Grimes, William. "Maurice M. Rapport, Who Studied Serotonin, Dies at 91." New York Times, September 2, 2011.

Guiley, Rosemary. *The Encyclopedia of Magic and Alchemy*. New York: Facts On File, Inc; 2006.

Guiley, Rosemary Ellen. *The Encyclopedia of Witches and Witchcraft*. New York: Facts on File, Inc; 1999.

Hall, Manly P. *The Pineal Gland: The Eye of God*. Martino Fine Books, 2015.

Hayden, William Benjamin. *On the phenomena of modern spiritualism*. Boston: Otis Clapp, 1855.

Hines, Terrence. *Pseudoscience and the Paranormal*. New York: Prometheus Books, 2003.

Hinton, Devon E., and Byron J. Good, editors. Culture and PTSD: Trauma in Global and Historical Perspective. University of Pennsylvania Press, 2016. JSTOR, www.jstor.org/stable/j.ctt18s318s.

Hoffman, Albert. *LSD: My Problem Child*. MAPS, 2005.

Hollenback, Jess Byron. *Mysticism: Experience, Response, and Empowerment* (University Park PA: The Pennsylvania State University Press, 1996). 1-2.

Holloway, Paul. *The Hi-Tech Shaman*. Experiencers Ezine, Vol 2, No 1.

Howard, Dana. *My Flight to Venus*. Regency UK, 1954.

Huffman, Carl. "Pythagoras", The Stanford Encyclopedia of Philosophy (Spring 2005 Edition), Edward N. Zalta (ed.)

Hunt, Stoker. *Ouija: The Most Dangerous Game*. Barnes and Noble Books, 1985.

Interview with Ellis Paul. *Take a Stand* (radio). August 15, 2007.

Interview with Raymond Moody. Thresholds (Magazine). Vol. 12 No. 4, 1994. http://www.som.org/3library/interviews/moody.html (accessed August 6, 2009).

Interview with Terence McKenna. http://deoxy.org/ timemind.htm (accessed May 20, 2009).

"Is Tesla to Signal the Stars?" Electrical World. April 4, 1896. pp. 369.

Johnson, G., ed. *Kant on Swedenborg: Dreams of a Spirit-Seer and Other Writings*. Swedenborg Foundation, 2002.

Jones, Gabriel H. "Pythia." Ancient History Encyclopedia (Website). 30 August 2013. http://www.ancient.eu/ Pythia/ (accessed July 21, 2017).

Jung, Carl. Letters of C. G. Jung, Volume 2; Volumes 1951-1961. Routledge, 1995.

Joshi, S.T. *I Am Providence: The Life and Times of H.P. Lovecraft*. Hippocampus Press, 2013.

Jung, C. G. Flying Saucers (Routledge Classics). New York: Routledge, 2002.

Keel, John. *The Mothman Prophecies*. New York: Tor Books, 2002.

Laos, Nicolas K. *Freemasons, World Order, and Mind Wars: The Great Reality of Memphis-Misraim Masonry*. Algora Publishing, New York. 2016.

Lear, John. Written statement (press release), December 29, 1987.

Lee, Regan. "Marian Apparitions and Esoteric Encounters: Visits with Mary, UFOs, Contactees and the Trickster." Scribd.com (accessed July 27, 2017).

LeShan, Lawrence L. *How to meditate a guide to self-discovery.* Boston: Little, Brown, 1999.

Lewis, James R. *The Gods Have Landed: New Religions From Other Worlds.* New York: State University of New York Press, 1995. Pages 1–13.

Lovecraft, H. P. *Dream cycle of H.P. Lovecraft dreams of terror and death.* New York: Ballantine Books, 1995.

Lovecraft, H.P. *The Complete Fiction Works of H.P. Lovecraft.* Chartwell Books, 2016.

Luna, Luis Eduardo and White, Steven F. Ayahuasca Reader: Encounters with the Amazon's Sacred Vine. Synergetic Press, 2000.

Mckenna, Terence. *Food of the Gods The Search for the Original Tree of Knowledge A Radical History of Plants, Drugs, and Human Evolution.* New York: Bantam, 1993.

McKenna, Terrence and McKenna, Dennis. *The Invisible Landscape: Mind, Hallucinogens, and the I Ching.* Harper San Francisco, 1994.

Metzner, Ralph, Ph.D. (Editor). *Sacred Vine of Spirits: Ayahuasca.* Park Street Press, 2005.

Monier-Williams. Sanskrit-English Dictionary. (Website) http://www.sanskrit-lexicon.uni-koeln.de/cgi-bin/ monier/serveimg.pl?file=/scans/MWScan/MWScanjpg/mw0 980-vimalaya.jpg (accessed June 13, 2017).

Moody, Raymond. *Reunions: Visionary Encounters With Departed Loved Ones*. Ivy Books, 1994.

Mukunda, H.S.; Deshpande, S.M.; Nagendra, H.R.; Prabhu, A.; Govindraju, S.P. "A critical study of the work 'Vyamanika Shastra' " Scientific Opinion: 5–12. 1974.

Murphy, J.M. (1976). *Psychiatric labeling in cross-cultural perspective*. Science, 191, 1019-1028.

Narby, Jeremy. *The Cosmic Serpent: DNA and the Origins of Knowledge*. Jeremy P. Tarcher/Putnam; Reprint edition, 1999.

"New research on plant intelligence may forever change how you think about plants." PRI.org (Website). January 10, 2014 (accessed July 29, 2017).

Nichols, Larry A.; Mather, George; Schmidt, Alvin J. *Encyclopedic Dictionary of Cults, Sects, and World Religions: Revised and Updated Edition*. Zondervan, 2006.

Offut, Jason. *Darkness Walks: The Shadow People Among Us*. Anomalist Books, 2009.

Partridge, Christopher. *UFO Religions*. London: Routledge, 2003

Pelley, William D. *Why I Believe the Dead are Alive*. Noblesville: Fellowship Press Inc, 1942.

Persinger, Michael A. "Average Diurnal Changes in Melatonin Levels are Associated with Hourly Incidence of Bereavement Apparitions: Support for the Hypothesis of Temporal (Limbic) Lobe Microseizuring." Perceptual and Motor Skills, 1993.

Personal Interview with Dr. David Hufford Ph.D. 2009.

Pickover, Clifford A. *Sex, Drugs, Einstein & Elves Sushi, Psychedelics, Parallel Universes and the Quest for Transcendence.* Minneapolis: Smart Publications, 2005.

Pinchbeck, Daniel. *Breaking Open the Head: A Psychedelic Journey into the Heart of Contemporary Shamanism.* New York: Broadway Books, 2002.

Prabhupada, A.C. Bhaktivedanta. *Easy Journey to Other Planets.* Los Angeles: Bhaktivedanta Book Trust, 1972.

Proud, Louis. *Dark Intrusions: An Investigation into the Paranormal Nature of Sleep Paralysis Experiences.* San Antonio, New York: Anomalist Books, 2009.

Renard, Gary. *The Disappearance of the Universe Straight Talk About Illusions, Past Lives, Religion, Sex, Politics, and the Miracles of Forgiveness.* New York: Hay House, 2004.

Ritchey, David. *The H.I.S.S. of the A.S.P. Understanding the Anomalously Sensitive Person.* New York: Headline Books, 2003.

Roach, Mary. *Spook: Science Tackles the Afterlife.* New York: W. W. Norton, 2006.

Rosenburg, R. Yudel. *Niflaos Maharal: HaGolem M'Prague.* Warsaw, 1909.

Saint Germain Foundation. *The History of the "I AM" Activity and Saint Germain Foundation.* Saint Germain Press, 2003.

Samorini, Giorgio. *The 'Mushroom-Tree' of Plaincourault.* Eleusis: Journal of Psychoactive Plants and Compounds, n. 8, 1997, pp. 29-37

Samorini, Giorgio. *The 'Mushroom-Trees' in Christian Art.* Eleusis: Journal of Psychoactive Plants and Compounds, n. 1, 1998, pp. 87-108.

Sandywell, Barry. *Presocratic reflexivity the construction of philosophical discourse c. 600-450 BC.* London: Routledge, 1996.

Segal, Alan F. *Paul the Convert The Apostolate and Apostasy of Saul the Pharisee.* New York: Yale UP, 1992.

Shastry, Subbaraya; Josyer, G. R. (1973). *Vymaanika Shaastra - Aeronautics by Maharshi Bharadwaaja.* Mysore: Coronation Press.

Shaw, Gregory. *Theurgy and the Soul: The Neoplatonism of Iamblichus.* Penn State Press, 1971.

Siegel, Ronald K. Ph.D. *Hostage Hallucinations: Visual Imagery Induced by Isolation and Life-Threatening Stress.* The Journal of Nervous and Mental Disease, n. 5, Vol. 172, 1984, pp. 264-272.

Simmons, Kurt. *The Madness Hypothesis.* The New Philosophy Online, 1998.http://thenewphilosophyonline .org/journal /article.php?issue=sanity&page=1001 (accessed August 18, 2009).

Singleton, Mark; Mallinson, James. *Roots of Yoga.* Penguin Classic, 2016.

Sivanda Yoga Center. *The Sivananda Companion to Yoga: A Complete Guide to the Physical Postures, Breathing Exercises, Diet, Relaxation, and Meditation Techniques of Yoga.* Touchstone, 2000.

Smith, William, Sir. *Dictionary of Greek and Roman biography and mythology.* Boston, Little. 1870.

Stafford, Peter. *Heavenly Highs: Ayahuasca, Kava-Kava, DMT, and Other Plants of the Gods.* Ronin Publishing, 2005.

Staley, Michael. "Lam: The Gateway." Starfire (Magazine). Volume One, Number 5. 1994. London, England.

Staley, Michael. *The BabylonWorking.http://user.cyberlink .ch/~koenig/dplanet/staley/staley11.htm* (accessed June 19, 2017).

Strassman, Rick, Slawek Wojtowicz, Luis Eduardo Luna, and Ede Frecska. *Inner Paths to Outer Space Journeys to Alien Worlds through Psychedelics and Other Spiritual Technologies.* New York: Park Street P, 2008.

Strassman, Rick. *DMT: The Spirit Molecule A Doctor's Revolutionary Research into the Biology of Near-Death and Mystical Experiences.* New York: Park Street P, 2000.

Steiger, Brad. *Real Ghosts, Restless Spirits, and Haunted Places.* Detroit: Visible Ink, 2003. 113-15.

Strieber, Whitley. *Communion: A True Story.* Avon, February 25, 1987.

Stoffel, Mary L. *The Practical Power of Shamanism: Heal Your Life, Loves and Losses.* Innovative Order, 2010.

Swedenborg, Emanuel. *Heaven and Hell*. BiblioLife, 2009.

Tenuta, Gary Val. *The Secret of Nine: A Synchronistic Puzzle of Metaphoric Proportions*. 2007.

Thompson, Richard L. *On Interpretation of Vedic Literature*. http://www.afn.org/~bvi/literal.html (accessed August 8, 2009).

Tompkins, Peter and Christopher Bird. *The Secret Life of Plants: A Fascinating Account of the Physical, Emotional, and Spiritual Relations Between Plants and Man*. New York: Perennial, 1973.

Underhill, Evelyn. *Mysticism A Study in the Nature and Development of Spiritual Consciousness*. Minneapolis: Dover Publications, 2002.

Van Dusen, Wilson. "The Presence Of Spirits In Madness: A Confirmation of Swedenborg in Recent Empirical Findings." Swedenborg Foundation, 1984.

Vetter, Tilmann. *The Ideas and Meditative Practices of Early Buddhism*. Brill, 1988.

Violatti, Christian. "Siddhartha Gautama." www. ancient.eu (Website). 9 December 2013. (accessed 26 July, 2017).

Ward, Terrence P. "An Interview with Raymond Buckland, American Wicca Pioneer." The Wild Hunt (Magazine), June 1, 2016.

Warren, Ed and Lorraine. *Graveyard: True Hauntings from an Old New England*. Graymalkin Media. December 31, 2014.

Warren, Joshua P. *Pet Ghosts: Animal Encounters from Beyond the Grave*. New Page Books, 2006.

Wickland, Carl A. *Thirty Years Among The Dead*. White Crow Books (New Edition), 2011.

Winkler, Gershon. *The Golem of Prague: A New Adaptation of the Documented Stories of the Golem of Prague*. New York: Judaica Press, 1980.

Wiseman, James. Insight: Rethinking the "Halls of Hades". Archaeology Magazine, Volume 51 Number 3, May/June1998. http://www.archaeology.org/9805 /abstracts/insight.html (accessed July 26, 2017).

Wesselman, Hank. *Spiritwalker: Messages from the Future*. New York: Bantam, 1996.

W.Y. Evans-Wentz (translator and editor), The Tibetan Book of the Dead (Oxford, 3rd ed.; 1957), pp. 90-2, 95-7, 101-4.

INDEX

324

O

P

331

ABOUT THE AUTHOR

Micah Hanks is a writer, podcaster, and researcher whose interests cover a variety of subjects. His areas of focus include history, science, philosophy, current events, cultural studies, technology, unexplained phenomena, and ways the future of humankind may be influenced by science and innovation in the coming decades.

He is author of several books, including *The Ghost Rockets*, a survey of drone-like technologies of unexplained origin, reported since the Cold War era, and *The UFO Singularity*, which focuses on purported "exotic" aerial phenomena, and how reports of such observations mirror some technological innovations occurring in the present day, along with those expected for tomorrow.

Micah produces The Gralien Report, a science and unexplained mysteries podcast, as well as an "unfiltered" current events podcast, Middle Theory, cohosted with his longtime friend and fellow commentator, Christopher McCollum.

You can follow and learn more about Micah at his websites, www.MicahHanks.com and www.GralienReport.com.

Made in the USA
Las Vegas, NV
17 June 2022

50376044R00193